WITHDRAWN

The U.S. House of Representatives

The U.S. House of Representatives

Reform or Rebuild?

EDITED BY
Joseph F. Zimmerman
AND Wilma Rule

PRAEGER

Westport, Connecticut
London

Library of Congress Cataloging-in-Publication Data

The U.S. House of Representatives : reform or rebuild? edited by Joseph F.
Zimmerman and Wilma Rule.
    p. cm.
    Includes bibliographical references and index.
    ISBN 0–275–96579–1 (hard : alk. paper)—ISBN 0–275–96580–5 (pbk. : alk. paper)
    1. United States. Congress. House. I. Zimmerman, Joseph F. II. Rule, Wilma.
JK1319.U2 2000
328.73'0704—dc21   99–053472

British Library Cataloguing in Publication Data is available.

Library of Congress Catalog Card Number: 99–053472
ISBN: 0–275–96579–1
    0–275–96580–5 (pbk.)

First published in 2000

Praeger Publishers, 88 Post Road West, Westport, CT 06881
An imprint of Greenwood Publishing Group, Inc.
www.praeger.com

Printed in the United States of America

Contents

Preface

The House of Representatives was designed by the Framers of the U.S. Constitution to reflect directly the views of the voters and to be responsive to their wishes. For more than a century, the House generally provided descriptive representation for members of the electorate. After more than 200 years, voter turnout at House elections has dwindled, interest group funding dominates the campaigning of incumbent House members, and 93 percent of the members are reelected. The House no longer responds primarily to citizen concerns, and its legitimacy is seriously questioned. It is in a representation crisis, as its membership of mostly white males does not reflect the people of our nation, particularly minorities and women.

This volume is the outgrowth of a panel, organized by the editors, at the 1997 annual meeting of The American Political Science Association on the subject "How Can the U.S. House Be Made More Representative?" The papers presented at the panel meeting were revised, and the editors of this anthology and editor Robert J-P. Hauck of *PS: Political Science and Politics* recruited additional scholars to contribute to a symposium—"This Old House: Remodel or Rebuild?"—which was published in the March 1998 issue of the journal.

All contributors to the *PS* symposium were invited to include their respective articles as revised in this anthology, and the editors recruited additional authors to expand the coverage and provide additional balance in terms of the views presented. Several authors of chapters in this anthology examine the factors that contribute to the House representational problem and its implications for democratic governance. Other authors present and analyze proposals for institutional, electoral, and campaign finance reforms. Still other authors examine the reform proposals and argue there is no need for fundamental reforms. Two authors suggest only internal reforms are needed to make the House a more effective institution.

The co-editors thank the contributors for their patient and willing revisions to their manuscripts. In a few instances, the co-editors disagree with the contributors' analyses and recommendations but respect them. A special debt of gratitude is owed to Mark E. Rush and Carol M. Swain for preparing chapters on very short notice because illness made it impossible for the originally selected authors to prepare chapters. We also express our gratitude to Robert J-P. Hauck, who was most supportive of our efforts.

We express our appreciation to our universities for assistance, Paula Cotter for research assistance, Carol Lucas for editing the manuscript, and Addie Napolitano for preparing revisions of various chapters and the final manuscript for submission to the publisher.

Part I

The Representation Problem

Chapter 1

A More Representative U.S. House of Representatives?

Wilma Rule and Joseph F. Zimmerman

> In a democratic vision, opportunities to exercise power over government of the state ought to be distributed equally among citizens.
> —Robert A. Dahl, "Equality versus Inequality"

The unrepresentativeness of the U.S. House of Representatives—in terms of ethnicity, gender, race, and socioeconomic status—and its nearly closed system for election have generated questions about the legitimacy and authority of the House as an institution that "represents" citizens and whether the membership of the House should reflect the citizenry at large. This volume offers answers to some of these questions.

A MODEL FOR UNREPRESENTATIVENESS

The following model explains the dynamic, intercorrelated system that perpetuates the unrepresentativeness of the House: high rates of incumbent reelection, large contributions to incumbents' campaigns, noncompetitiveness of political parties in most districts, low voter turnout in elections, and low diversity in representation. In addition, recent U.S. Supreme Court decisions resulting in fewer districts where a "minority" constitutes a majority or supermajority of the population contribute to the perpetuation of unrepresentativeness.[1] The independent variable that drives the model is the majority/plurality election system.

Let us look briefly at each of these factors and the outcomes. First, the high incumbent retention rate (93%) in the period 1978–1996 adversely affects the opportunity for newcomers and limits voters' choice. Turnover in Congress since

Table 1.1
Incumbent Reelection to the U.S. House, 1978–1996

Years	Incumbents Retiring		Challengers Elected		Total New Members		Incumbents Elected	
	N	%	N	%	N	%	N	%
1978	49	11	24	6	73	17	362	94
1980	34	8	37	9	71	16	364	91
1982	40	9	39	10	79	18	356	90
1984	22	5	19	5	41	9	394	95
1986	40	9	9	2	49	11	386	98
1988	23	5	7	2	30	7	405	98
1990	27	6	16	4	43	10	392	96
1992	65	15	43	13	108	25	327	88
1994	48	11	38	9	86	20	349	90
1996	50	12	23	6	73	17	361	94
Mean	40	9	26	7	58	15	365	93

Source: U.S. Bureau of the Census, *Statistical Abstract of the United States* (Washington, DC: U.S. Government Printing Office, 1998), p. 289. This table first appeared in Joseph F. Zimmerman and Wilma Rule, "A More Representative United States House of Representatives?" *PS: Political Science and Politics*, March 1998, p. 7.

1962 has resulted from the voluntary retirement of incumbents.[2] This fact is in stark contrast to the original concept of the House as a body whose composition could change every two years.

Table 1.1 also shows that the number of retirements from the House tends to be lower in presidential years and higher in mid-term elections, when voter turnout is extremely low. This retirement pattern was reversed when retirements increased in a presidential year (1994) and fell in mid-term elections (1996). For the first time in eight elections, the House in 1992 had over 20 percent new members compared to a previous average of only 13 percent.

INCUMBENCY AND LOW DIVERSITY

There were double the typical number of open seats in 1992. Women were elected to one-fourth of the 65 open seats.[3] Other "minorities" and Republicans also increased their share of seats, primarily as a result of redistricting.[4] The proportions of women and minorities, however, remained low—11 percent for women and 13 percent for both blacks and Hispanics, respectively. "Incumbent safety" reappeared as the norm in 1994–1996, and these elections brought no significant increases in the number of women and minority candidates elected (see Table 1.2).

The small proportion of national women legislators (12%) is the most egregious underrepresentation shown in Table 1.2. Their representation/population ratio of .23 indicates their underrepresentation is 77 percent. Among the 51 women members of the House, Latinas and nonminority women have the lowest

Table 1.2
Low Diversity Status Quo: Women and Minority Men Elected to the U.S. House and Representation/Population Ratios, 1996

Group	Women N	Men N	Representation %	Population %	Ratio
African Americans	10	27	8.5	12.6	.67
Latino	4	15	4.4	10.3	.43
Nonminority	37	342	87.1	77.1	1.13**
Percent	11.7*	88.3	100.0	100.0	-

*Representation/Population ratio for women members of the House: 11.7/51% = ratio of .23.

**Four Asian Americans, including one woman, are included in the nonminority figures since Asian population data were unavailable.

Source: Center for the American Woman and Politics, "Women in Elective Office, 1997," a fact sheet issued by the Center, Eagleton Institute of Politics, Rutgers University; U.S. Bureau of the Census, *Statistical Abstract of the United States* (Washington, DC: U.S. Government Printing Office, 1996), p. 279; "Results of the U.S. House, District by District," *New York Times*, November 7, 1996, pp. B8–B9.

ratios. African-American women are higher at about one-third of representation/ population parity. Similar patterns prevail in state legislatures and limit women's recruitment to Congress.[5]

Currently, the United States is nineteenth among 27 long-established democracies that have direct women's representation (see Figure 1.1). Countries with 20 to 43 percent women in parliament utilize the party-list proportional representation (PR) system (see Chapter 15 of this volume), except Australia and Canada. Those at the median and below, such as the United Kingdom, use the plurality/majority electoral system. Most democracies with high proportions of women in their elected legislative bodies have the political will to nominate and elect additional women representatives in order to make their legislatures more representative.

ONE-SIDED CAMPAIGN CONTRIBUTIONS

Closely related to incumbent retention is the practice of political action committees (PACs) giving double the funds to incumbents than to challengers (see Table 1.3). In addition, incumbents receive over four times as much money as do candidates for scarce, open House seats.[6] "Soft money"—given to the two political parties or other groups for campaigning, voter registration drives, and so on—is not included in Table 1.3, but its use and impact are analyzed in Chapter 6 of this volume.

The campaign finance system places an almost insurmountable hurdle in front of most challengers of an incumbent House member seeking reelection. In fact, only 7 percent of the challengers are victorious on average (see Table 1.1). The need for an incumbent to raise a large amount of money for campaigns generates reliance upon interest groups for funds. The Republican victory of 1994 resulted

Figure 1.1
Percentage of Women in 27 Single or Lower Houses of National Legislatures in Long-Established Democracies, 1999

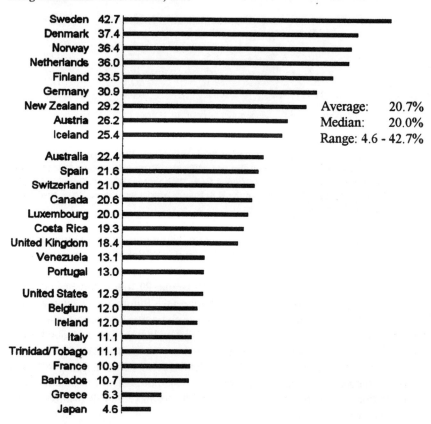

Sweden 42.7
Denmark 37.4
Norway 36.4
Netherlands 36.0
Finland 33.5
Germany 30.9
New Zealand 29.2   Average: 20.7%
Austria 26.2   Median: 20.0%
Iceland 25.4   Range: 4.6 - 42.7%

Australia 22.4
Spain 21.6
Switzerland 21.0
Canada 20.6
Luxembourg 20.0
Costa Rica 19.3
United Kingdom 18.4
Venezuela 13.1
Portugal 13.0

United States 12.9
Belgium 12.0
Ireland 12.0
Italy 11.1
Trinidad/Tobago 11.1
France 10.9
Barbados 10.7
Greece 6.3
Japan 4.6

Source: Inter-Parliamentary Union, ''Women in National Parliaments'' (1999) (http://www.ipu.org/ wmn-e/classif.htm) and Inter-Parliamentary Union, *Democracies Still in the Making* (Geneva: Inter-Parliamentary Union, 1997); also Center for the American Woman in Politics, ''Women Elected to Congress, 1999,'' a fact sheet issued by the Center, Eagleton Institute of Politics, Rutgers University, January 1999.

in a switch in business PACs' support from the incumbent Democrats to incumbent Republicans, leaving the Democrats increasingly dependent on organized labor for campaign finance in 1996.[7] Although these groups may receive no special favors, the appearance of favoritism contributes to public cynicism and apathy regarding the House and its representativeness.

Whether Democrat or Republican, a ''safe incumbent'' in the House with all or most political resources—newsletter, name recognition, media attention, and hundreds of thousands of dollars to spend—usually swamps his or her challenger.[8] Voters have minimal choice, and those who vote for the loser may have

Table 1.3

Political Action Committee (PAC) Contributions to U.S. House Campaigns, 1991–1996 (in millions of dollars)

	1995-96	1993-94	1991-92
Incumbents	$281.7 (59%)	$224.1 (53%)	$203.5 (51%)
Challengers	121.6 (26%)	100.6 (24%)	91.3 (23%)
Open Seats	72.2 (15%)	96.6 (23%)	101.1 (26%)
Total	$475.5 (100%)	$421.3 (100%)	$395.9 (100%)

Source: U.S. Bureau of the Census, *Statistical Abstract of the United States* (Washington, DC: U.S. Government Printing Office, 1996), p. 302.

a sense of futility. Strengthening the enforcement powers and increasing the staffing of the Federal Election Commission (FEC) could help, to a degree, to even the financing of campaigns of candidates by ensuring that campaign finance statutes are enforced vigorously.

PUBLIC OPINION AND VOTER BOYCOTT

Polls reveal the public has little hope Congress will enact major campaign finance or other reform.[9] Furthermore, 41 percent of the public reported having little confidence in Congress, and the same percentage had only some confidence, according to a 1994 Gallup poll.[10] This evidence supports the argument the boycott of House elections reflects some voter dissatisfaction over the perceived inefficacy of an individual's vote, resulting in an attitude of "It won't make any difference, so why vote?"

By 1998 disaffection with the House had grown to greater proportions when 62 percent of the public disagreed with the House's impeachment of President William ("Bill") Clinton.[11] After House members voted 228–206, a slim 52.5 percent, to charge the president with perjury concerning his relationship with a White House intern, 65 percent of the public stated it was better for the country that he finish his term. Moreover, 72 percent of the public polled approved of the way Clinton was handling his job.[12]

The preceding sentiment accords with a study of 29 democracies that links voters' belief in the inefficacy and lack of salience of their votes to low election turnout in countries using the single-member district electoral system. By contrast, most countries with PR have turnouts of approximately 80 percent of voters, since every vote counts toward a party's representation in parliament.[13]

A majority of the registered voters in the United States do not participate in House elections, and in presidential elections at least 40 percent do not vote.[14] The average turnout in House mid-term elections among the voting age population was 37 percent from 1982 to 1994, and in presidential elections it was 48 percent.[15]

Table 1.4
Voting by 18–24-Year-Olds in U.S. House and Presidential Elections, 1980–1996
(in percentages of registered voters)

	U.S. House Elections				Presidential Elections			
	1982	1986	1990	1994	1980	1988	1992	1996
18 - 20 yrs.	20	19	18	16	36	33	38	31
21 - 24 yrs.	28	24	22	22	43	38	46	33
All voters	48	46	45	45	59	57	61	54

Source: U.S. Bureau of the Census, *Statistical Abstract of the United States* (Washington, DC: U.S. Government Printing Office, 1998), p. 296.

Among 18–24-year-olds—whose actions, plans, and dreams are apt to affect considerably the United States' future in the 21st century—low and declining rates of voting are even more alarming.[16] In the 1994 House elections only 19 percent voted among those aged 18–24 registered to vote. Among 18-, 19-, and 20-year-olds (those ages gaining suffrage in 1971), 84 percent of those registered did not participate in the U.S. House elections (see Table 1.4). The presidential election of 1996 saw a larger, but still very low, turnout of 32 percent of young people aged 18–24.[17] Moreover, Table 1.4 shows this voting level was 10 percent lower than in 1980 compared to the overall turnout decline of 5 percent at that time.

Research on the reasons for nonvoting among the youth indicates that young people follow their alienated nonvoting parents in attitudes and behavior.[18] The underlying causes of this downward cyclic trend, as far as the House of Representatives is concerned, include the inability to displace incumbents and achieve preferred policies and cynicism regarding political leaders.[19]

REFORM POSSIBILITIES

Since the single-member district (SMD) system is the major causal factor of the lack of diversity and unrepresentativeness of the House, proposals for reform must begin with some consideration of other electoral arrangements. To produce a more representative House, the electoral system should ensure the effectiveness of ballots cast by any group of voters—be they women, ethnic, or socioeconomically disadvantaged—is not diluted or canceled, rendering the group powerless to elect others or to have its members elected. It should maximize participation at the polls, promote the representation of competing interests in the House, facilitate citizen access to House members, provide equity in representation for various groups, and help legitimate the authority of the House.[20]

Several proportional and semi-proportional representation electoral systems meet the preceding criteria and presently are operating successfully in other democratic nations and in local governments in the United States.[21] No constitutional amendment is necessary for changing the system by which representatives are chosen for the House. A simple act of Congress allowing states to choose their representatives by a form of *proportional or semi-proportional representation* in multi-member districts is all that is needed. Representative Cynthia McKinney (D-GA) introduced such a bill in 1997—"The Voter's Choice Act" (H.R. 3068)—that, in addition to PR, would allow use of the cumulative or limited vote systems for selecting House members.

Another electoral system possibility is the *mixed member proportional representative system*, sometimes termed the "additional member system." Voters may have one representative directly "accountable" to them who serves with other representatives chosen to allow proportional representation of each party in the legislature. In this system one-half of the legislators typically are elected from single-member districts, and one-half from a slate of political party candidates. Legislative seats based on party votes are awarded in proportion to a party's percentage of the total party votes. For example, if an environmental party won nine SMD seats and ten percent of the national PR vote, it would be awarded ten representatives (9 + 1 from the party's PR slate) in a 100-member legislature. A mixed PR system was adopted recently by New Zealand and produced greater minority and gender representation and party choices.[22]

Another PR advantage is the incentive for nominating diverse candidates. Adding a "minority" group member or woman candidate enhances a party's ticket and increases the party's chances of gaining additional votes. But in single-member districts in the United States, there is a disincentive for elites to field candidates of diverse backgrounds, especially when few open seats make stakes high. Nevertheless, U.S. political parties can initiate steps to *encourage the nomination of more underrepresented group members*, as the Labour and Liberal parties have done successfully in the United Kingdom (see Chapter 13 in this volume). In developing democracies where a substantial women's presence is desired, *a proportion of seats has been set aside solely for women's election.*[23]

Term limits also could help ensure the election of a more representative House by increasing the prospect a member of a different group will replace the incumbent. But this change would require a constitutional amendment. Moreover, term limits for SMDs probably would leave intact some one-party districts and would not allow the multiparty choices that PR offers. Other disadvantages include the loss of politically experienced legislators who become "termed out" or resign early.[24]

There is a widespread consensus the campaign finance system needs major reform. Public funding of elections, instant disclosure of contributors, banning of unlimited "soft money," and increasing appropriations for the Federal Election Commission to enable it to enforce current laws more effectively are among the campaign reforms being considered. But the division among reform organizations lessens the probability of any substantial change.[25]

Other proposed reforms include *expanding the size of the House* from the current 435 members, established in 1910, which would not require a constitutional amendment and could be a step toward a more representative House. Moreover, holding House elections in conjunction with presidential elections most probably would increase voter turnout. But this change, in common with term limits, would require a constitutional amendment and would leave the SMD election system intact with all of its negative consequences for the House.

CONCLUSIONS

The evidence presented in this volume highlights the critical need for campaign finance and electoral system reforms if the House is to be converted into a truly representative body. The SMD system produces representational distortions because of its "winner take all" nature, and the greatest distortion is produced by the plurality rule when three or more candidates split the votes and allow a candidate with a minority of the votes to be elected. Furthermore, SMD limits the ability of many underrepresented groups to win a seat unless their members constitute a majority of the voters in a district whose lines must be redrawn decennially. Widespread gerrymandering also contributes to the unrepresentativeness of the House because incumbents often are protected by state legislatures, which redraw district lines.[26] This practice suggests that some type of multi-member PR system would be preferable in states with more than one representative.

James Madison's *Federalist Number 10* might well be the future guideline for elections to the House. As Robert A. Dahl pointed out, Madison's genius was discerning that the smaller the polity, the greater the possibility of dominance by one faction or party.[27] Expand the territory, and men (and women) can govern the nation better. In these days, when many of our representatives are defenders or supporters of a special interest, Madison provides the best argument for large, multi-member House districts and some form of PR. A manufacturing interest, an agricultural one, and others in the same district, for example, all could be represented if more than one representative served the district.

With this reform, we are convinced more people will vote, more incumbents will be dislodged, and women and minorities will have a fair chance for electing their respective candidates since the parties will nominate them in order to gain a higher proportion of the votes. But the campaign finance problem would remain. Any electoral reform must be coupled with reform of campaign finance. Similarly, campaign finance reform without electoral reform will leave us with the present and growing crisis of underrepresentation in the House.

AN OVERVIEW

In Part I, "The Representation Problem," Wilma Rule and Joseph F. Zimmerman present a model explaining the unrepresentativeness of the House and data on reelection of incumbents and underrepresentation of women and certain minority groups and outline reform possibilities that are explained and analyzed in detail in subsequent chapters.

In Part II, "The Ideal and the Historical Reality," Gayle Binion authoritatively presents the suffrage ideals for the House of Representatives and traces the voting exclusions and inclusions. Barbara Burrell and Carol M. Swain expertly present women's and minorities' representation in the House. Mark E. Rush's critique of electoral proposals follows with some cautions regarding hidden costs and unintended consequences.

Clyde Wilcox and Wesley Joe's chapter on campaign finances, legitimacy of the House, and suggested changes launches Part III, "Causes and Consequences of Unrepresentativeness." Ronald Gaddie and Lesli E. McCollum unscramble the complex relationship between the size of campaign finance expenditures and various House incumbents. Mark Franklin and Diana Evans focus their analysis on the reasons voter turnout for House elections is lower than voter turnout for presidential elections and suggest reforms to increase voter participation in elections. Mark E. Rush's examination of "minority majority" districts and key court decisions follows. Wilma Rule's comparative chapter contrasts U.S. and European election systems and representation. John R. Hibbing and Elizabeth Theiss-Morse end Part III with their reasons for ignoring public dissatisfaction with U.S. political institutions.

Part IV, "Reform Possibilities," opens with Arend Lijphart's "Reforming the House: Three Moderately Radical Proposals" and is followed by three chapters describing and evaluating new approaches that could be adopted to facilitate the election of a more representative House. Lijphart, in examining reforms, supplies comparative data, and Alice Brown highlights women's role in developing plans for the new mixed-proportional representation system for Scotland's parliament. Stanley M. Caress' chapter focuses on the effects of term limits on California politics. In "Eliminating Disproportionate Representation in the House," Joseph F. Zimmerman evaluates various electoral systems and practices for reforming the House. C. Lawrence Evans and Walter J. Oleszek conclude major reforms are not needed and suggest minor reforms for improving administration of the House. The final chapter in Part IV is by Daniel H. Lowenstein who critically examines several articles in the *PS* symposium.

Part V, "Prospects for Reform," has but one concluding chapter, "The Outlook for Reform," by co-authors Zimmerman and Rule.

NOTES

1. *Bush v. Vera*, 116 S.Ct. 1941 (1997).

2. Ronald K. Gaddie, "Research Note: Congressional Seat Swings: Revisiting Exposure in House Elections," *Political Research Quarterly*, September 1997, pp. 699–710.

3. Debra L. Dobson, "Whatever Happened to the Year of the Woman?" *Public Perspective*, vol. 7, no. 5, 1996, pp. 5–7, 32–33.

4. Charles S. Bullock III, "Winners and Losers in the Latest Round of Redistricting," *Emory Law Journal*, vol. 44, no. 3, 1995, pp. 943–77.

5. Wilma Rule, "Women's Underrepresentation and Electoral Systems," *PS: Political Science and Politics*, December 1994, pp. 689–92.

6. U.S. Bureau of the Census, *Statistical Abstract of the United States* (Washington, DC: U.S. Government Printing Office, 1996), p. 291.

7. Jill Abramson and Steven Greenhouse, "Labor's Victory on 'Fast Track' Shows Power," *New York Times*, November 12, 1997, p. 1.

8. *Monopoly Politics* (Washington, DC: Center for Voting and Democracy, 1997).

9. "Most Doubt a Resolve to Change Campaign Financing, Poll Finds," *New York Times*, April 8, 1997, pp. A1, A10.

10. U.S. Bureau of the Census, *Statistical Abstract of the United States*, p. 285.

11. Adam Nagourney with Michael R. Kagan, "Public Support for the President, and for Closure, Emerges Unshaken," *New York Times*, December 21, 1998, p. 1.

12. Ibid.

13. U.S. Bureau of the Census, *Statistical Abstract of the United States*, p. 218.

14. Ibid., p. 297.

15. Ibid.

16. See *New Millennium Project on Youth, Politics, and Voting* (Lexington, KY: National Association of Secretaries of State, 1999).

17. U.S. Bureau of the Census, *Statistical Abstract of the United States*, p. 296.

18. "Why Citizens Shun the Polling Booth," *Public Perspective*, February/March 1997, pp. 42–44.

19. James D. Hunter and Daniel C. Johnson, "A State of Disunion?" *Public Perspective*, February/March 1997, pp. 35–38.

20. Joseph F. Zimmerman, "Fair Representation for Minorities and Women," in Wilma Rule and Joseph F. Zimmerman, eds., *United States Electoral Systems: Their Impact on Women and Minorities* (Westport, CT: Greenwood Press, 1992), pp. 9–11.

21. Andrew Reynolds et al., *The International IDEA Handbook of Electoral Systems Design*, 2nd ed. (Stockholm: International Institute for Democracy and Electoral Assistance, 1997); Edward Still, "Cumulative Voting and Limited Voting in Alabama," in Rule and Zimmerman, eds., *United States Electoral Systems*, pp. 183–96.

22. Jack Nagel, "Constitutional Reform and Social Difference in New Zealand," *Cardozo Journal of International and Comparative Law*, vol. 4, no. 2, 1996, pp. 373–94.

23. Inter-Parliamentary Union, *Democracy Still in the Making* (Geneva: Inter-Parliamentary Union, 1997).

24. Stanley M. Caress, "The Impact of Term Limits on Legislative Behavior: An Examination of a Transitional Legislature," *PS: Political Science and Politics*, December 1996, pp. 671–76.

25. Michelle Cottle, "Where Are the Good Guys When We Need Them?" *The Washington Monthly*, September 1997, pp. 20–25.

26. Gordon E. Baker, "Whatever Happened to the Reapportionment Revolution in the United States?" in Bernard Grofman and Arend Lijphart, eds., *Electoral Laws and Their Political Consequences* (New York: Agathon Press, 1986), pp. 257–76.

27. Robert A. Dahl, *Democracy and Its Critics* (New Haven, CT: Yale University Press, 1989).

Part II

The Ideal and the
Historical Reality

Chapter 2

The First Two Centuries

Gayle Binion

Who are the electors of the federal representatives? Not the rich, more than the poor; not the learned, more than the ignorant; not the haughty heirs of distinguished names, more than the humble sons of obscurity and unpropitious fortune. The electors are to be the great body of the people of the United States. . . . No qualification of wealth, of birth, of religious faith, or of civil profession is permitted to fetter the judgment or disappoint the inclination of the people.

—James Madison, 1788[1]

The House of Representatives, as the preceding quotation suggests, was envisioned as the "popular" or "people's" side of the U.S. Congress. This intent is clear not only from the arguments in *The Federalist Papers* but as well from the debates at the constitutional convention. In contrast with the mandated, indirect methods for selecting U.S. senators and the president, the electorate for the House of Representatives is required by Article 1, § 2 to be the same as that for the "most numerous branch" of each state's own legislature.[2] Thereby created was a national "rule" for defining the federal franchise while simultaneously deferring to each state's judgment as to "who" may be entrusted with the right to vote. Reflecting the pattern of compromise that emerged from the Philadelphia convention, this clause struck a balance between those favoring universal white, male, adult suffrage and those supporting, in addition, property qualifications to vote.[3]

With respect to the qualifications for *holding* this office, the Constitution in Article 1, § 2, prescribed a uniform set of requirements for the House: one must be at least 25 years of age, a citizen, and an inhabitant of the state represented.

Court decisions as late as the mid-1990s have continued to view these membership requirements as exhaustive, not subject to expansion by either the states or the House.[4] The oddity, thus, of the electoral rules of the early decades of the Republic was that they allowed for a broader spectrum of persons to serve in the House than to vote for the office. In practice, however, the House of Representatives consistently has been composed of a narrower range of demographic diversity than the electorate at any given time.[5]

In contrast to constitutionally fixed requirements for service in the House, the "most numerous branch" provision for the suffrage in House elections left the states relatively free to determine voter eligibility prior to the ratification of the 13th, 14th, and 15th Amendments to the U.S. Constitution after the Civil War.[6] While the power conferred by the Constitution led to a modicum of variation among the states with respect to their policies concerning race, wealth, residency, and age, there nevertheless was a common pattern.[7] The franchise through the early 19th century was almost exclusively a right of adult, white, male owners of real property. These common statutory limitations created a potential electorate of only 6 to 20 percent of the population.[8] To the 20th-century way of thinking about democracy, this concept of representation would be viewed as a very limited one, but in a world characterized largely by monarchic power, the principle of electoral accountability to even this small a stratum of the governed was rather radical.[9] *Federalist Paper Number 57* suggests this very minimal electorate was by conscious design. Therein it is noted that each of the original 65 congressional districts would have between 5,000 and 6,000 voters. Given that the population at the time was approximately 3 million people, the expectation was that only one in ten persons would be eligible to vote, a figure close to that reported by numerous historians.[10] Thus, the constitutional structure designed to allow mass voices to be heard in the House and the reflective and rarefied ones in the Senate was erected within a very limited framework of popular government, a framework that has undergone continual expansion during the 19th and 20th centuries. By the end of the first two centuries of the Republic, states remained free to disfranchise noncitizens, convicted felons, those under 18 years of age, and those deemed mentally incompetent, but, as demonstrated in the balance of this chapter, other formal bars to suffrage—based on gender, age, residency, property ownership, and race—have been either abolished or rendered minimal. Constitutional amendments, changes in federal and state statutory law, and litigation in the federal courts all have contributed to the dramatically enlarged political community entitled to select members of the House.[11]

ELIMINATING THE PROPERTY REQUIREMENT

> [U]njustified discrimination in determining who may participate in political affairs or in the selection of public officials undermines the legitimacy of representative government.
>
> —*Kramer v. Union Free District*, 1969[12]

While the systems varied as to the size or value of the real property taxed that met the condition of being "propertied," there was uniform agreement in the original thirteen states that holding taxable land gave one a stake in the society sufficient to justify the vote.[13] Various sociopolitical analyses of colonial America also suggest that those holding real property very much feared the potential political power of those without, including the powers of taxation and confiscation. Despite the commonality of these policies, property requirements became less common almost immediately after the formation of the union and all but disappeared by the mid-19th century. Vermont and Kentucky—which entered the union in 1791 and 1792, respectively—were the first states to recognize universal white adult male suffrage, and no state entering the union after 1817 premised the franchise on property ownership.[14]

The significant political change in this regard was due to several factors. Jacksonian democracy and the evolving political culture of the time stressed the equality of all citizens across social classes, thereby empowering have-nots to demand the vote, and a widening circle of political candidates viewed large masses of (generally propertyless) immigrants as a good source of electoral support. But the change from a landholding electorate to a broadened suffrage was due as well to the changing nature of the economy and modes of production. From an agrarian, land-based society, the nation was evolving into one characterized by manufacturing and commerce in which wealth and status were not strictly tied to ownership of the land.[15]

ADDRESSING RACIAL BARRIERS

No debate in American history has been more fundamental or contentious than that surrounding racial equality. Movement from a union founded on the protection of slavery, to one officially committed to civil rights has been a long and bloody experience. Not only were most African Americans unable to vote at the time of the adoption of the Constitution, but those held in bondage were counted as only three-fifths of freemen in the census determinative of states' seats in the House. The very slow process of incorporation into the political community of African Americans required Court decisions, constitutional amendments, federal statutory law and, most especially, administrative enforcement of the Voting Rights Act of 1965 against recalcitrant states and local governments.[16] It is, therefore, a fact of American history that the House, designed to represent and be populated by members of the white race, only slowly and incompletely has come to include racial minorities within its constitutencies and membership.[17]

In the early years of the Republic, free black men were enfranchised in most northern states, whereas the southern states treated them as little more than "slaves without masters."[18] Because northern blacks were especially unlikely to own real property, the absence of a racial test for voting did not result in their enfranchisement. Therefore, when property qualifications for voting began to disappear through the admission of new states into the Union that did not have these policies and the repeal of property qualifications in the existing states, a more formal method of exclusion of African Americans from the franchise became common in the states.[19] The largely white-only electorate of the House remained constitutionally legitimated until the passage of the 14th and 15th Amendments and remained a practical reality, especially in the South, until the second half of the 20th century.

The critical foundations for *federal* protections of voting rights for blacks are found in the 13th, 14th, and 15th Amendments because they not only specifically protect the franchise but also fundamentally redefine U.S. citizenship. The 13th Amendment outlawed slavery, and the 14th Amendment made the federal government the source of U.S. citizenship and required the states to respect the "privileges and immunities" of this citizenship.[20] Also relevant to voting rights in the 14th Amendment are the Equal Protection and Representation Clauses. Under the latter (never enforced) clause, states denying the vote on the basis of race were to have their seats in the House reduced proportionally. Under the Equal Protection Clause, as interpreted by the judiciary, states are prohibited from discriminating on the basis of race in the granting of the franchise. The 15th Amendment, ratified in 1870, specifically protects the voting rights of U.S. citizens from discrimination on the basis of "race, color, or previous condition of servitude."

Because states no longer legally could prohibit blacks from voting after the ratification of the 14th and 15th Amendments, other mechanisms of disfranchisement developed quickly. While physical, social, and economic intimidation was effective means of preventing African Americans from voting, states nevertheless developed more formalized methods of ensuring their "legal" disfranchisement. Prominent among these were the white primary, the literacy test, and the poll tax.

With respect to the white primary, a practice without subtlety in its discriminatory design, the Court acted on its own independent authority to interpret and apply the 14th and 15th Amendments.[21] In the case of literacy tests and poll taxes, although the Supreme Court issued some very important decisions, it basically awaited the lead of the executive and legislative branches or deferred to their authority. Literacy tests, although not uncommon in other parts of the country, were unknown in the southern states until 1890, when the states with the largest black populations began to institute them. While a modicum of literacy may be valued in a voter because it is suggestive of a more intelligent use of the franchise, the adoption of literacy and "interpretation" tests by the southern states, only well after the ratification of the 15th Amendment, quite clearly had the purpose and effect of denying the vote to African-American citizens. Several features of literacy tests were especially pernicious in their racial purposes and consequences: "grandfather" clauses, exceptions for property holders and those of "good moral character," and entirely discretionary administration by local voter registrars.

The "grandfather clause" exempted from literacy tests all persons whose grandfathers had voted (generally) before blacks were legally entitled to do so. This exemption from literacy tests, available to white registrants, was unavailable to blacks whose grandfathers had been denied the right to vote. The clause also was not related even remotely to the states' interest in a literate electorate. The Supreme Court declared this practice unconstitutional in 1915.[22] But the literacy test *per se* and other questionable exemptions from it remained intact in many states until the mid-1960s.

As recently as 1959 the Supreme Court rejected a "frontal attack" on literacy tests. In a unanimous opinion written by Justice William O. Douglas, the Court held there was no evidence presented of unequal application of the test on a racial basis.[23] But such evidence was soon to be gathered, and such practices were to be documented with aggregate statistics, by the U.S. Department of Justice and Congress. On the basis of such evidence, the Department of Justice brought suit against Louisiana and Mississippi under the 14th and 15th Amendments and federal enforcement legislation. In two related decisions in 1965, the Supreme Court upheld both the authority of the federal government to bring suit and a finding of excessive and racially discriminatory discretion in the administration of the challenged literacy tests.[24] The Court, however, still declined to hold literacy tests were *per se* unconstitutional. Spurred by the civil rights movement, Congress already had begun to act against literacy tests as well as other roadblocks to the effective enfranchisement of blacks. The 1964 Civil Rights Act, although it dealt largely with open accommodations and employment discrimination, contained an important voting provision. For the purpose of federal elections, citizens with six years of formal education were presumed to be literate, and states were restricted further to administering only literacy tests conducted entirely in writing.[25] These were important steps, with significance for defining the electorate of the House, but they governed only federal elections and were not self-enforcing through federal administrative activity. Far more consequential has been the 1965 Voting Rights Act, employing federal administrative machinery for enforcing voting rights in any state or county in which voter registration or electoral turnout falls below 50 percent.[26]

INCORPORATING WOMEN

> Being unanimously of the opinion that the Constitution of the United States does not confer the right of suffrage upon any one, and that the constitutions and laws of the several States which commit that important trust to men alone are not necessarily void, we affirm the judgment.
>
> —*Minor v. Happersett*, 1975[27]

The restriction of the franchise to only adult males left women outside the political community as defined by the unamended Constitution. Aside from the enfranchisement of propertied widows at some of the New England town meetings, the only state of the original thirteen to allow women to vote was New Jersey. It is not clear if this situation was due to an accidental reference to "inhabitants of this Colony of full age" in its colonial constitution or was a result of the Quakers' egalitarian influence.[28] In either case, women voters very nearly defeated John Condit, a powerful legislator, who in turn was influential in the repeal of women's suffrage in the state's 1807 constitution. The vote thereafter was exercised by 19th-century women in only a few locations and for generally limited purposes. Women were empowered to vote in school elections in Kansas, Kentucky, and Michigan on the assumption they were knowledgeable about and interested in the education of children. The general franchise was available to women in the territories of Utah, Wyoming, and Colorado, where women's suffrage was effected as a bulwark against what the pioneer settlers viewed as undesirable male drifters who took up residence in these communities.

Although the movement for women's suffrage took form in the 1830s and was formalized at the Seneca Falls, New York, convention in 1848, it took nearly a century of political work for this right to be protected nationally by the 19th Amendment to the U.S. Constitution. When women attempted to secure the franchise through litigation under the 14th Amendment's clause protecting the "privileges and immunities of citizens of the United States" from abridgment by the states, the Supreme Court, as per the earlier quotation from *Minor v. Happersett*, developed the theory citizenship *per se* did not guarantee the right to vote.[29] The suffrage movement thereby was forced to wage a state-by-state campaign to convince states' legislatures and governors, their courts, or their voting publics in referenda to support the electoral rights of women within the states' own laws.

While a parallel movement simultaneously was focused on Congress, clearly a constitutional amendment would be nearly impossible to get out of the two houses, and even if successful, the advocates still would need the support of three-fourths of the state legislatures in order to effect ratification. By the time of the ratification of the 19th Amendment (1920), more than 30 states had enfranchised women, most within the previous ten years. The 19th Amendment was nevertheless important as a statement of national values and as a means to ensure the vote for women in the one-third of the states where the internal political processes were not supportive of women's vote.[30]

WELCOMING THE NEWCOMER

> Durational residence law . . . divide[s] residents into two classes, old residents and new residents, and discriminate[s] against the latter to the extent of totally denying them the opportunity to vote. The constitutional question presented is whether the Equal Protection Clause of the Fourteenth Amendment permits a State to discriminate in this way among its citizens.
>
> —*Dunn v. Blumstein*, 1972[31]

Like property qualifications for the franchise, durational residency requirements long were justified by the states with the argument a person needs to live
in a jurisdiction for a period of time in order to have a stake in the community
and to be a knowledgeable voter. Until residency requirements came under constitutional attack, about one-half of the states had minimum residency requirements of one year, and most of the rest applied a standard of six months. A
majority of states also disfranchised those who, despite meeting the state's residency requirement, moved to a new county or precinct within one to six months
before an election. In addition to the minimum time periods to establish residency in a state or precinct, some states declared particular classes of persons
(primarily members of the U.S. military stationed within their borders) to be
forever transients.

The legitimacy of these residency requirements was called into question during the 1960s in the wake of three developments. The first was a recognition
that because modern mass communications made information on public issues
readily available to new voters, they could learn about the issues in a relatively
short time. Second, it became apparent state record-keeping systems were, or
could be, modernized to minimize the time necessary to update them and to
prevent electoral fraud. Finally, census and research data demonstrated that more
than 5 million otherwise eligible voters were disfranchised by durational residency requirements.

Congress took note of these factors and included a section in its 1970 Voting
Rights Act amendments protecting the right to vote in *presidential* and *vice
presidential* elections for those who move just prior to an election.[32] While other
residency requirements, including those governing House elections, were left
legally intact, soon thereafter they were to be restricted by Court decisions under
the Equal Protection Clause of the 14th Amendment.[33] Several trial and appellate
courts had disagreed about the constitutionality of the residency requirements,
and it fell to the Supreme Court to resolve inconsistencies among the subordinate
courts' rulings.

The Court in *Dunn v. Blumstein* in 1972, held the state could not demonstrate
that laws requiring residency of one year in the state and 30 days in the county
were necessary to meet a "compelling governmental interest."[34] The Court's
decision rested not only on the unequal denial of the right to vote but also on
the law's punitive effects on the right of interstate travel and migration, rights
protected under the Privileges and Immunities Clause of the 14th Amendment.
By judicial mandate, therefore, *Dunn* applied to all other elections the limitations
on state power to enforce residency laws that Congress through statutory law
had applied to only presidential elections. While not setting a maximum 30-day
pre-election cutoff for registration, the Court did suggest this time period would
be a reasonable one to allow the state to meet legitimate needs, including the
prevention of fraud. The Court set no firm rule, however, and in subsequent
cases it has upheld registration closure as great as 50 days before an election.[35]

In addition to durational residency requirements for all voters, states also traditionally defined certain categories of persons as ineligible for electoral residency. Members of the armed forces and residents of other federal enclaves, as well as college students living away from their parents, were in many states unable to register to vote in their places of domicile. These states operated on the "irrebuttable presumption" such people were inherently transient. Like the durational residency requirement, these restrictions on the granting of the franchise were minimized by congressional and judicial action during the 1960s and 1970s.[36]

WEIGHING VOTES EQUALLY

No review of the development of the constituency of the House would be complete without some attention to the debate over its district boundaries. The U.S. Constitution apportions House seats to the states after each decennial census, and the state legislatures thereafter are expected to alter district boundaries as necessary. There is a complementary common requirement in state constitutions that legislative boundaries be reviewed after each decennial census to ensure a fair apportionment of legislative seats.

Population migrations, largely from rural to urban areas, and the failure of state and local legislatures to redraw their district boundaries left some districts in the 1960s with 50 or 100 times as many people as a neighboring district. After numerous unsuccessful attempts to have the Equal Protection Clause interpreted to require equal populations among legislative districts, the Supreme Court in 1962, in *Baker v. Carr*, rendered the issue justiciable, and in 1964 in *Reynolds v. Sims*, the Court determined that such population equality is constitutionally required for state senate districts.[37]

The House was not exempt from the doctrine of "one person-one vote." In *Wesberry v. Sanders*, decided just prior to *Reynolds*, and by a margin of only five to four, the Court reasoned the constitutional stricture that the House be elected "by the people" required that each representative represent "as nearly as practicable" the same number of people.[38] Aside from the population inequalities resulting from a guarantee each state has at least one member of the House and the difficulty associated with *absolute* numerical equality, little room thereafter was left for any substantial population variation among each state's house districts. Indeed, the district boundaries for the House have been held to an even higher standard of population equality than have those for state and local governmental units. In the case of state legislatures, a maximum 10 percent population deviation has been acceptable to the Supreme Court, whereas for the congressional districts *all* population variances must be proven to be justified.[39]

ENFRANCHISING THE YOUNG

The grant of the franchise to 18-year-olds by Congress is in my view valid across the board.

—William O. Douglas, 1970[40]

Young voters are the only demographic group for whom requirements for House service are more restrictive than the qualifications to be an elector. Historically, nearly all states set the minimum age for voting at 21, while one must be at least 25 years of age to serve in the House.[41] In practice, however, few people have been elected to this office under the age of 30. There also has been a turnout pattern in the United States in which young voters, especially those under 30, are the least likely to cast a ballot. In sum, young people exercise the least electoral voice and occupy the fewest House positions.

A desire to give effective voice to the young generated a movement in Congress to lower the voting age to 18, in part because that was the age of military conscription. While initial attempts to accomplish this goal through a constitutional amendment began in the early 1940s, in 1970 Congress enacted §302 of the Voting Rights Act, which, *inter alia*, prohibited the states from denying the vote to any citizen over the age of 18. The law applied to *all* elections, federal and state, and its constitutionality immediately was challenged by Oregon and Arizona. The states argued Congress had exceeded its authority, which extends only to setting rules for the "time, place, and manner" of federal elections. In a rare instance of original jurisdiction in which the Supreme Court conducted the trial on the merits, it reached a very splintered conclusion. Four justices believed that the Congress had this power under section 5 of the 14th Amendment, while four others believed that aside from specific constitutional restrictions on states' power over voting, determining who shall vote is a matter left entirely to the states. Only Justice Black distinguished between federal and state elections, upholding Congress' power to protect the 18-year-old vote in federal elections but denying that it has this power over state elections. Consequently, the Court's 1970 decision was split, with Justice Black forming the majority of five on each point in the decision.[42]

The outcome of the litigation on the 18-year-old vote was but a Pyrrhic victory for the states. Left with the prospect of conducting elections with different ballots for those 18 through 20 years old, states had no real option but to defer to the federal initiative. A constitutional amendment (the 26th) ensuring for those 18 or older the right to vote in all elections was ratified in a record time of only four months.

CONCLUSION

At the end of its first two centuries, the House of Representatives was changed remarkably with respect to its electoral constituencies. Through constitutional amendments, federal and state statutory law, and judicial decisions, racial minorities, women, people without real property, newly arrived residents, and those between the ages of 18 and 21 have all become part of the formal political community responsible for the selection of the lower house of the Congress. While theories of democratic representation may require far more than formal universal suffrage, such suffrage is arguably the *sine qua non* of democracy.

Issues involving *equal* representation also have been the subject of significant attention during the latter years of these first two centuries. The judicial caveats concerning the malapportionment of the House have recognized that equality, at minimum, requires that House districts be of approximately equal population within a state so as to ensure each vote is of substantially equal value. But other issues of equality remain subject to debate, including the demographics of House members *vis-à-vis* the general public (the "mirror" principle), the selection of boundaries for House districts to reflect racial or ethnic residential patterns (the "affirmative action" principle), and the consequences of campaign financing systems for the openness of the political process (the "undue influence principle").

NOTES

1. James Madison, *Federalist Number 57, The Federalist Papers* (New York: New American Library, 1961), p. 351.

2. In addition to *Federalist Number 57*, justification for the "popular" nature of the House is found in, *inter alia, Federalist Papers Numbers 53, 58–61*. Uniqueness of the House in this respect is apparent when compared with the methods for selection of U.S. senators and members of the Electoral College. For an excellent overview of the debates at the constitutional convention on these matters, see Catherine Drinker Bowen, *Miracle at Philadelphia* (Boston: Little, Brown, 1966).

3. A. Whitney Griswold quoted Jefferson as taking the most radical position on universal suffrage, while Hamilton and the other conservative Federalists, believers in the "stake in society" theory of democracy, thought it critical that voters be holders of real property. See his "Jefferson's Republic: The Rediscovery of Democratic Philosophy," in John P. Roche, ed., *American Political Thought* (New York: Harper & Row, 1967), pp. 25–26. Bowen reported the initial vote on the question of constitutionally mandating the "popular" election of the House was two in favor and eight opposed. See Bowen, *Miracle at Philadelphia*, p. 77.

4. Justice John Paul Stevens, writing for the majority of the Supreme Court in *U.S. Term Limits, Incorporated v. Thornton* (514 U.S. 779), concluded in 1995 the "Framers intend[ed] that the States have no role in the setting of qualifications" for the House (p. 806). In dissent, Justice Clarence Thomas noted that shortly after the ratification of the Constitution, five states supplemented the constitutional qualifications for membership in their House delegations, commonly requiring property ownership and residency in the House districts created by the states' legislatures. See Ibid., p. 866. See also *Powell v. McCormack*, 395 U.S. 486 (1969), holding that Article 1, § 2, prohibits the House from refusing to seat a duly elected member. The Court distinguished between qualifications to be seated and the power, subsequently, of the House to expel a member. The majority view in both *Term Limits* and *Powell* echoes the argument put forth by Hamilton in *Federalist Number 60* that "the qualifications of the persons who may choose or be chosen, . . . are defined and fixed in the Constitution."

5. Roger H. Davidson and Walter J. Oleszek document the socioeconomic backgrounds of House members over two centuries have been consistently well above the norm in society. See their *Congress and Its Members* (Washington, DC: CQ Press, 1998),

pp. 120–25. With the gradual opening of the franchise to minorities, women, and those without real property, the demographics of the House have broadened considerably but do not come close to the diversity of the population. The 105th House, elected in 1996, had but 11 percent women, 7 percent African Americans, and 5 percent Latinos, whereas women are more than half of the general population, African Americans are 12 percent, and Latinos are 7 percent. Statistical underrepresentation of minorities may be a consequence of the selection of the boundaries for House districts (on this latter point, see the Persons and Rule chapters). The cost associated with waging a competitive congressional campaign may explain the underrepresentation of those with limited means. Davidson and Oleszek documented the need to raise more than $.5 million to wage a competitive campaign (ibid., p. 88). The power of incumbency and political careerism in recent years also have been cited as barriers to electoral opportunity, but significant evidence suggests that this phenomenon is not a new one. Nearly every member (97%) in the first House (1789–1791) had prior political experience, the highest to date. See Roger H. Davidson, *The Role of the Congressman* (New York: Pegasus, 1969), p. 52. Charlene Bangs Bickford and Kenneth R. Bowling examine the backgrounds of the members of the first House. See their *Birth of the Nation* (Madison, WI: Madison House, 1989), p. 12. For a more general discussion of careerism, see Davidson and Oleszek, *Congress and Its Members*, pp. 33–34.

6. The 13th Amendment outlawed slavery, and the 14th and 15th Amendments instituted restrictions on state governments with respect to their treatment of their own citizens and residents. The significance of these amendments for the franchise is examined later.

7. For some of the rather minor, but interesting, variations in the earliest state laws on suffrage, see Donald C. Bacon, Roger H. Davidson, and Morton Keller, *The Encyclopedia of the United States Congress* (New York: Simon & Schuster, 1995), pp. 2070–72.

8. See Andrew Sinclair, *The Emancipation of the American Woman* (New York: Harper & Row, 1965), p. 31; Bacon et al., *The Encyclopedia of the United States Congress*, p. 2071. They are using figures of eligibility among *free* persons, thus citing numbers as high as 25 percent. Michael Parenti examined the desire of the Framers to limit the franchise. See his *Democracy for the Few*, 2nd ed. (New York: St. Martin's Press, 1977), pp. 50–58.

9. It should also be noted the philosophical tome that most influenced the American Revolution, *Second Treatise on Civil Government* by John Locke, also premised representative government on the enfranchisement of adult, propertied males.

10. While we do not have reliable turnout figures for the earliest days of the republic, Bacon et al. cite the finding that only 9 percent *of adults* voted in the 1824 presidential election, the earliest for which data are available. See Bacon et al., *The Encyclopedia of the United States Congress*, p. 2070.

11. While formal bars to voting for the House have become minimal, turnout in federal elections remains low, typically hovering below 50 percent of voting-age population. See Norman J. Ornstein, Thomas E. Mann, and Michael Malbin, eds., *Vital Statistics on Congress 1997–1998* (Washington, DC: CQ Press, 1998), p. 51. Structural disincentives to exercising the franchise, affecting these data, include voter registration requirements, elections held on workdays, and the common state practice of linking voter registration to jury pools.

12. *Kramer v. Union Free School District*, 395 U.S. 621, at 626 (1969).

13. Bacon et al., *The Encyclopedia of the United States Congress*, p. 2071.

14. Ibid., p. 2072.

15. It should be noted that property qualifications are still permissible for voting in some more limited electoral arenas, such as narrowly empowered "special districts." See Gayle Binion, "The Franchise," in Robert J. Janosik, ed., *The Encyclopedia of the American Judicial System* (New York: Charles Scribner's Sons, 1987), pp. 1107–8.

16. *Voting Rights Act of 1965*, 69 Stat. 437, 42 U.S.C. § 3531.

17. See note 5 documenting the statistical underrepresentation of racial minorities within House membership.

18. Donald G. Nieman, *Promises to Keep: African-Americans and the Constitutional Order, 1776 to the Present* (New York: Oxford University Press, 1991), p. 28.

19. Ibid.

20. As examined later, however, the Supreme Court in a woman's rights case rejected the argument that a "citizen" is necessarily entitled to the right to vote.

21. See, for example, *Smith v. Allwright*, 321 U.S. 649 (1944) and *Terry v. Adams*, 345 U.S. 461 (1953).

22. *Guinn v. U.S.*, 238 U.S. 347 (1915).

23. *Lassiter v. Northhampton County Board of Elections*, 360 U.S. 45 (1959).

24. *Louisiana v. U.S.*, 380 145 (1965) and *U.S. v. Mississippi*, 380 U.S. 128 (1965), respectively.

25. *Civil Rights Act of 1964*, 78 Stat. 268, 2 U.S.C. § 206.

26. Low voter involvement is presumed to reflect a pattern of discrimination in the jurisdiction. In practice, this trigger figure has allowed the federal government to oversee the electoral policies in the southern states, Arizona, and some northeastern and western counties. Its most controversial application, highly contested during the 1990s, has been with respect to the selection of district boundaries to enhance the opportunity of African Americans to be elected to the House.

27. *Minor v. Happersett*, 88 U.S. 162 at 178 (1975).

28. On this point see Bacon et al., *Encyclopedia of the United States Congress*, p. 2071.

29. *Minor v. Happersett*, 88 U.S. 162 (1875). The Court was able to reach this conclusion in part, because of the 15th Amendment, which protects adult males from being denied the franchise on the basis of race. The Court reasoned that if the general language of the 14th Amendment, prohibiting the states from denying citizens the "privileges and immunities" of that citizenship, included the right to vote, the 15th Amendment would have been unnecessary.

30. Women's suffrage guaranteed by the 19th Amendment has not been accompanied by substantial representation of women *within* the House of Representatives. Jeannette Rankin, the first woman seated in the House (1917), had been an instrumental leader of the suffrage movement in Montana, a state that granted women the right to vote in 1914. The coalition she had built around the suffrage issue became the core of her political support. See Barbara Sinclair Deckard, *The Women's Movement: Political, Socioeconomic and Psychological Issues* (New York: Harper & Row, 1975), pp. 292–93. Thereafter, not until 1945 did ten women simultaneously serve in the House, and not until 1983 that 20 served. A dramatic acceleration in women's numbers in the House occurred in 1993, when women increased from 28 to 48 members. Women were 50 voting members out of 435 in the 105th Congress (1997). See Ornstein et al., *Vital Statistics on Congress 1997–1998*, p. 40.

31. *Dunn v. Blumstein*, 405 U.S. 330 at 334–35 (1972).

32. *Voting Rights Act Amendments of 1970*, 84 Stat. 314, 42 U.S.C. § 1973. Voters relocating more than 30 days prior to a presidential election must be permitted to register at their new residence. Those who move within 30 days of a presidential election must be permitted to vote by absentee ballot at their previous address. The Supreme Court upheld Congress' power over durational residency requirements affecting federal elections. See *Oregon v. Mitchell*, 400 U.S. 112 (1970).

33. It should be noted the 1970 amendments already had created a significant incentive for the states to bring their electoral rules for other offices into line with those applicable to the presidential election. To do otherwise, at least with respect to the quadrennial election when a president is chosen, was exceptionally expensive, as separate ballots would be required for newly arrived residents.

34. *Dunn v. Blumstein*, 405 U.S. 330 (1972).

35. See *Burns v. Fortson*, 410 U.S. 686 (1973) and *Marston v. Lewis*, 410 U.S. 679 (1973), in which the Court concluded Georgia and Arizona, respectively, had demonstrated their need for 50 days of administrative lead time. The Court in *Burns* cautioned, however, that "the 50-day registration period approaches the outer constitutional limits in this area."

36. See, for example, *Carrington v. Rash*, 380 U.S. 89 (1965), requiring states to provide to members of the military the opportunity to demonstrate their residency and intention to remain in the community to which the military had sent them. Three years after *Carrington*, Congress changed relevant federal legislation from presuming that members of the military continued to reside in their states of origin, to facilitating their acquiring residency in the states in which they are stationed. See also *Evans v. Cornman*, 398 U.S. 419 (1970), applying the same principle to the disfranchisement of residents of the National Institutes of Health. Finally, states slow to acknowledge the right of college students to vote at their campus addresses were forced to do so under *Symm v. U.S.*, 439 U.S. 1105 (1979). The Supreme Court summarily upheld an injunction against this discriminatory practice, and states slowly have complied with the mandate of the 26th Amendment.

37. *Baker v. Carr*, 369 U.S. 186 (1962); *Reynolds v. Sims*, 377 U.S. 533 (1964).

38. *Wesberry v. Sanders*, 376 U.S. 1 (1964). House members have been elected predominantly on a district basis. For a discussion of the debate over the legitimacy of anything other than district-based elections, see Kenneth C. Martis, *The Historical Atlas of United States Congressional Districts 1789–1983* (New York: The Free Press, 1982), pp. 2–5.

39. See, for example, *Mahan v. Howell*, 410 U.S. 315 (1973).

40. Justice William O. Douglas, concurring in part, dissenting in part, in *Oregon v. Mitchell*, 400 U.S. 112 at 135 (1970).

41. In 1943, Georgia lowered the voting age to 18, and Kentucky did the same in 1955. When admitted to the Union in 1959, Alaska set the age at 19, and Hawaii at 20. See Bacon et al., *The Encyclopedia of the United States Congress*, p. 2079.

42. *Oregon v. Mitchell*, 400 U.S. 112 (1970).

Chapter 3

Women and Representation in the 1990s: Old Barriers and New Resources?

Barbara Burrell

While writing this chapter in the summer of 1998, I walked in parades, distributing candy and stickers to children (and sometimes adults), scrambled eggs at a county farm breakfast, stuffed envelopes, cleaned computer files, and distributed literature in an attempt to elect the first woman from Wisconsin to the national legislature. "Making history" was one of the campaign themes of the 2nd congressional district primary election. Both the Democratic and Republican Parties nominated a woman for the seat, thereby guaranteeing history. The issue of the numerical representation of women in the Congress, thus, continues to be a major factor in American elections and lawmaking.

At the close of the 1990s, the House of Representatives and the Senate continue to be highly unrepresentative regarding the numerical presence of women. As we know from other chapters in this volume, the structure of the American electoral system limits the ability of an "out-group" to rapidly achieve parity in the numbers of its members elected to national office. This chapter explores the extent to which women have made gains in getting elected to the House of Representatives since the "Year of the Woman" in 1992, further considers the structural barriers to women's gaining numerical equality with men in the U.S. House, and asks whether the resources available to women candidates have increased.

Twenty-eight (4.6%) of the 435 House members in the 102nd Congress (1991–1992) were women. In the "Year of the Woman," that number increased to 47 (10.8%). After nearly doubling their numbers and more than doubling their percentage in 1992, women made no gains in the 104th Congress (1995–1996) and only some incremental gains during the 105th Congress (1997–1998). In the 1996 election, 51 women were elected to the House. Four other women (including two House widows) won special elections bringing the total to 55 (12.6%) in 1998.

The average reelection rate for all incumbents was 92 percent (1990 through the 1996 election). The backlash of 1994—the so-called year of the angry white male—had a rather debilitating effect on a positive trend in the numbers of women in the national legislature. Eight of the 44 female representatives (18%) running for reelection were defeated. Had female incumbents been reelected at the national average of 92 percent, 40 of them would have been victorious instead of 36.

OLD BARRIERS—INCUMBENCY

Incumbency remains the major barrier to more equal representation of women in the House of Representatives in the 1990s (see Table 3.1). The vast majority of incumbents are men who tend to run for reelection and usually win. Little incentive exists to run against an incumbent. Few women have mounted such challenges, and when they have done so, they have been no more or less successful than male challengers. Those of us who have studied women's candidacies have stressed this feature of the electoral system as the biggest factor in limiting women's abilities to increase their membership in the House.[1] The limited gains women have made in being elected to the House since the 1992 "Year of the Woman" attest to that fact.

NEW RESOURCES

To win election to the U.S. House, women candidates must mobilize resources—money, turnout of women at the polls, and favorable media coverage.

Money

It may seem strange to list money as a possible new resource for women candidates. Money or the ability to raise large amounts to finance a campaign for Congress has been one of the major obstacles to more competitive races. Candidates in the 1996 House races raised $505.4 million. Democratic incumbents running in the general election raised a median amount of $523,000, while Republican incumbents raised a median $700,220. These figures compare with a median of $112,694 for challengers to the Democratic incumbents and a median of $80,754 for challengers to the Republican incumbents.[2]

Perceptions are important. For years, the general perception was that women could not raise the same amounts of money as men. It was believed they did not know how to ask for large amounts from potential donors, voters were less likely to support female candidates, and party organizations were less likely to back their candidacies in winnable seats for the party. If those perceptions were

Table 3.1
Incumbency in the U.S. House of Representatives, 1990–1996

Year	Number running for re-election	Number unopposed*	Number obtaining more than 55% of the vote	Number winning
1990				
All	407	82	384	391
Men	383	82	362	367
Women	24	0	22	24
1992				
All	383	30	286	324
Men	355	30	267	299
Women	28	0	19	25
1994				
All	382	47	312	347
Men	338	42	279	311
Women	44	5	33	36
1996				
All	379	20	315	357
Men	337	18	281	317
Women	42	2	14	40

*Unopposed means no major party opposition.
Source: ''Election Summaries,'' *Congressional Quarterly Weekly Reports.*

accurate reflections of reality in the past, empirical research shows them no longer to be true.

In 1978, 16 women served in the House of Representatives, less than 4 percent of the House membership. In that year's elections 46 women were major party nominees for Congress. They raised an average of $88,000 compared with $115,000 for the 754 male candidates. The inability of women to raise the same amounts of money as men to finance their campaigns long has been thought to be a major factor in accounting for so few women running and being elected to public office, particularly national offices.

As part of the second feminist movement, women began to organize to train potential women candidates in campaign techniques to address that seeming disparity and to increase the number of women running for and winning public office. They also began to raise money for women candidates, primarily from other women since women did not have access to some of the traditional, usually male-dominated sources of campaign financial support.

Women had not been major campaign contributors in the past. But by mobilizing women as donors, groups such as the Women's Campaign Fund, EMILY's List, and the WISH List, have expanded greatly the participation of women in the political process. Women increasingly are contributing to political campaigns. The pool of financial contributors has expanded to women's advantage. In 1988 for the first time, women major party nominees as a group raised on average more money than their male counterparts for the House of Representatives. Women nominees have continued to equal or surpass male nominees in raising funds for their campaigns. In the 1996 election cycle, EMILY's List with 66,000 members was the number one political action committee (PAC) in disbursements, disbursing $12,494,230. The Women's Campaign Fund was nineteenth, disbursing $2,450,019. Women candidates receive similar amounts of money as male candidates from PACs, parties, and large contributors in the 1990s.

Somewhat ironically, this newfound ability of women to raise substantial amounts of money to fund their candidacies has generated complaints from their challengers. For example, her primary opponent accused Lois Pines, a 1998 Massachusetts attorney general candidate, of being too "aggressive and threatening" in her fund-raising techniques. According to a *Boston Globe* report, "It [was] no accident that [he] chose the day when a woman for the first time in Massachusetts history reached the $1 million mark in campaign contributions to propose a spending cap. She's getting too far ahead of him."[3] A similar phenomenon of "crying foul" occurred in the 1998 Wisconsin 2nd congressional district primary, when Democratic hopeful Tammy Baldwin out-fund-raised all opponents due to her strong backing from EMILY'S List. One of her primary opponents attempted to make this fact an issue against her.

If women are now able to compete more equally in the money game, to what extent is campaign finance reform a "women's issue, or more precisely, a women's candidacy issue?" Groups seeking reform have examined it from that perspective and have run into problems articulating a message centered on equality for women. The problem is that those women who have been successful under the current system with the help of PACs such as EMILY'S List have argued against limiting the influence of such PACs, which in general benefit incumbents more than challengers. Reforms have to give challengers greater access to monetary resources, however, if they are to help increase the number of women mounting viable campaigns for the national legislature and, therefore, make the House (and Senate) more representative. Reforms that will benefit the group have to take precedence over the advantage to the few in the current system.

Citizens' Voting Calculus

Survey research and voter turnout figures suggest women candidates tend to be advantaged in the minds of the voters. Recent research has shown women are more likely to vote for women candidates, while men are more likely to vote against them. Dolan found that in 1992 "[w]omen voters are more likely to support women House candidates than are men and are also more likely to use gender-related issue positions in determining their vote choice when there is a woman candidate."[4] In their review of exit polls for statewide races from 1990 through 1994, Seltzer, Newman, and Leighton concluded: "The sex of the candidate did affect the gender gap. On average, women have been slightly more likely than men to vote for women candidates. The average gender gap (the tendency for women to vote more Democratic than men) was several points greater when the Democratic candidate was a woman and several points smaller when the Republican candidate was a woman than when both candidates were men. Relative to men voters, women voters have given a several-point advantage to women candidates in statewide races over the past several election cycles."[5]

This gender gap is to women's advantage because there are more women in the population, and since 1980 women have been turning out in larger proportions than men. In fact, the differential turnout rate in presidential elections has grown with each presidential election, to the advantage of women. In 1996, 55.5 percent of the eligible female population reported voting, compared with 52.8 percent of the male population. According to the U.S. Bureau of the Census survey, 56,108,000 women turned out in 1996 compared with 48,909,000 men. Thus, the gender gap in voting behavior that has emerged in races with women candidates rebounds to women's favor because women tend to be the majority of voters. The message from EMILY's List, we should note, has changed from a focus on the underfinancing of women's campaigns for public office to an emphasis on turning out women voters. Chairwoman of EMILY's List Ellen Malcolm's call is, "We've got to get out there and get women to vote."[6] However, this advantage is at the margin. Elizabeth Cook explained that "although sex of the candidates is a factor, incumbency, partisanship, and ideology drive most vote decisions."[7] But we know how things have changed when a woman running for Congress has many voters identify with her experiences as a divorced single mother of three as happened in the 1998 election.[8]

Media Coverage of Women's Candidacies

We rely very heavily on the news media for our information about political campaigns, and media coverage is important to electoral success. Regarding women's candidacies, empirical questions concern how the news media report on women candidates and how the sex of candidates affects the coverage of political campaigns. Are women candidates treated differently than male candidates? Kim Kahn's research on the campaigns of women running for statewide offices in the 1980s found women candidates for the Senate consistently received less campaign coverage than their male counterparts, and the coverage they received was more likely to be negative, emphasizing they were unlikely to win. Reporters tended to emphasize the same issues that male candidates did while largely ignoring alternative issues female candidates emphasized.[9] That disparity appears to have diminished in the 1990s.

Kevin Smith, replicating Kahn's study for 1994 races for governor and U.S. senator, found much smaller coverage differences, and gender-based patterns of coverage were not always to the disadvantage of female candidates.[10] Of course, candidates for the House, especially challengers, would probably be grateful for any press attention at all.

CAVEATS

If women are going to win, they first have to run. Thirty-two seats were open in the primaries in the 1998 elections for the House. In three of these contests, both parties nominated women (four incumbent female representatives were retiring from the House). Women won 14 (22%) of the 64 nominations for these seats. Thirty-one women sought their party's nomination. However, women ran in less than one-half of the Republican primaries, and there were no women in nearly 40 percent of the Democratic primaries. Women ran in 19 of the 32 Democratic primaries and in 9 of the 32 Republican primaries. Women constituted 17 percent of all of the Democratic Party primary candidates and 10 percent of the Republican Party primary candidates. These figures show a limited opportunity structure for voters to select women to represent them in Congress. The rate at which women are running and winning nominations to the House guarantees, at best, an incremental climb toward parity.

The 1998 election results with respect to women candidates' success continued trends emphasized in this chapter. None of the female incumbents running for reelection lost. Six women were newly elected to the House—all ran for open seats. Their election brings the number of female representatives to 56— 12.9 percent of the House membership.

Much more research needs to be conducted into the process by which individuals come to seek these all-important nominations. The major parties have made a public relations effort suggesting they are recruiting good women candidates. But when a seat opens up, who immediately gets mentioned as a possible successor? Note, for example, the situation Grace Napolitano faced in the 1998 campaign when she announced her candidacy to replace the retiring Esteban Edward Torres. She apparently angered him and other Democrats because he had endorsed his son-in-law and aide. Ms. Napolitano had served as mayor of Norwalk, California, a city in the district. She won the primary.[11] We need to know to what extent and under what circumstances the situation Fowler and McClure describe in *Political Ambition* occurs. They tell that according to Betsy Toole, the New York Democratic party's vice chairwoman in 1984, when the

30th congressional district seat became open, she thought, "Women—that's what went through my mind when I first heard Conable's seat was vacant. The right woman could win in this district, you know."[12]

The recruitment process needs a serious, systematic analysis from the perspective of gender. For example, how does the rhetoric of promotion of female candidacies play against the conflicting idea that the parties stay out of primary campaigns?

What little research that has been conducted on the recruitment stage of the process suggests barriers at that stage to women's candidacies. In a recent study of women holding local office in four states, 64 percent reported party leaders had discouraged potential women candidates from running for office because of their sex. That study also found that party chairs consistently preferred candidates like themselves, and since the vast majority of party chairs were men, this fact was a problem for the recruitment of women candidates.[13]

Celinda Lake's study conducted in 1994 for the National Women's Political Caucus found that among a poll of likely candidates, women were less than one-half as likely as men to have considered running for office. The women were also more concerned with a number of factors—such as the impact on their families of running and the amount of time necessary to mount a successful campaign—than was the potential male candidate pool. The women also were less confident about their chances for election than were men.[14]

This summary of barriers and opportunities for women's candidacies and election to the House presumes the maintenance of our current system of majority/plurality elections and our current financing system of campaigns and no limit on the number of terms members can serve. It assumes the political parties will not adopt any form of a quota system regarding the nomination of women. Thus, although women who ran in the 1990s appear to have had access to the same resources or more resources than men in comparable races, the opportunities to mount viable races have been few, and the incentives to initiate a campaign have been lacking. The end result is a House sorely unrepresentative for over one-half of the population. Politically, women have come a long way, but until the electoral system changes to become more women-friendly, women will continue to have a long way to go to gain parity in their presence among national lawmakers.

NOTES

1. Georgia Duerst-Lahti, "The Bottleneck: Women Becoming Candidates," in Sue Thomas and Clyde Wilcox, eds., *Women and Elective Office: Past, Present, & Future* (New York: Oxford University Press, 1998), pp. 15–25; Robert Darcy, Susan Welch, and Janet Clark, *Women, Elections, and Representation*, 2nd ed. (Lincoln: University of Nebraska Press, 1994); Barbara Burrell, *A Woman's Place Is in the House: Campaigning for Congress in the Feminist Era* (Ann Arbor: University of Michigan Press, 1994); Susan J. Carroll, *Women as Candidates in American Politics*, 2nd ed. (Bloomington: Indiana University Press, 1994).

2. These figures are from a Federal Election Commission April 14, 1997, press release.

3. Eileen McNamara, "A Glass Ceiling for Fund-Raising?" *Boston Globe*, May 30, 1998, p. B1.

4. Kathleen Dolan, "Voting for Women in the 'Year of the Woman,' " *American Journal of Political Science*, January 1998, pp. 272–93.

5. Richard A. Seltzer, Jody Newman, and Melissa Voorhees Leighton, *Sex as a Political Variable* (Boulder, CO: Lynne Rienner, 1997).

6. Scott MacKay, "York Sees the Dough Rise When EMILY Pays a Visit," *Providence Journal-Bulletin*, August 31, 1998, p. 1B.

7. Elizabeth Adell Cook, "Voter Reaction to Women Candidates," in Thomas and Wilcox, *Women and Elective Office*, pp. 217–36.

8. Terry Neal, "As More Women Run, Gains in Congress Predicted," *Washington Post*, October 1, 1998, p. A16.

9. Kim Fridkin Kahn, "The Distorted Mirror: Press Coverage of Women Candidates for Statewide Office," *Journal of Politics*, February 1994, pp. 154–73.

10. Kevin B. Smith, "When All's Fair: Signs of Parity in Media Coverage of Female Candidates," *Political Communication*, January–March 1997, pp. 71–82.

11. Neal, "As More Women Run, Gains in Congress Predicted," p. A16.

12. Linda L. Fowler and Robert D. McClure, *Political Ambition: Who Decides to Run for Congress* (New Haven, CT: Yale University Press, 1989), p. 102.

13. David Niven, "Party Elites and Women Candidates: The Shape of Bias," *Women & Politics*, vol. 19, no. 2, 1998, pp. 57–79.

14. As reported in Georgia Duerst-Lahti, "The Bottleneck: Women Becoming Candidates," in Thomas and Wilcox, *Women and Elective Office*.

Chapter 4

Minorities in the House: What Can We Expect in the Next Century?

Carol M. Swain

By the year 2050 racial and ethnic minorities are expected to constitute 47 percent of the U.S. population. The nation will have more diversity than ever before. African Americans and Hispanic Americans will experience the most population growth, with Hispanics expected to surpass blacks by the year 2010. Together the two groups will compose about one-fourth of the national population.[1] Will the House of Representatives reflect the diversity of the changing national population, or will the institution remain as it has been for more than 200 years, a body dominated by wealthy white males with mostly legal backgrounds? In 1999, there were 37 (8.5%) blacks in Congress, down from 39 in 1993 and 38 in 1995 and 1998 and up from 13 in 1970. Hispanics, the fastest growing minority in the country, had seen their numbers rise from 5 in 1970 to 21 (4.8%) in 1999. The House had three Asian representatives (less than 1%) and no Native Americans in 1999. Political minorities add to the diversity of the House. Between 1990 and 1999 the number of women representatives in the House jumped from 29 to 56 (12.9%). Adding to this diversity were the three openly gay members of the 106th Congress.

By comparison, a House whose membership was proportional to the U.S. population in 1999 would be 13 percent African-American, 51 percent women, 12 percent Hispanic, 4 percent Asian, and about 1 percent Native American.[2]

Greater percentages of the preceding groups automatically would create a more descriptively representative institution and might increase substantially the influence these groups exert over policy outcomes. Moreover, the presence of more minorities in Congress could mean increased occupational diversity and greater levels of political experience among freshmen if previous patterns hold.[3]

What is the growth potential of minorities in the House as we enter the 21st century? Will the number of minorities experience significant increases, or will some groups have difficulty retaining their existing gains? In this chapter I argue the growth potential of minorities in the House of Representatives will vary greatly by whether the group is a political or racial minority. As nonthreatening political minorities, white women could see their numbers grow at a much faster rate than for African Americans and Hispanic Americans. For reasons described later, the latter groups face far more uncertainty in the political environment. While white women have seen steady growth since 1971, when they totaled eleven, racial minorities, with a slight retrenchment for African Americans, have remained constant since the big boost created by race-conscious districting that followed the 1990s census (see Table 4.1).

UNDERSTANDING THE LEGAL ISSUES

Current debates about minority representation in Congress have been shaped by a series of U.S. Supreme Court decisions that started with *Shaw v. Reno* (113 S.Ct. 2816, 1993), included *Miller v. Johnson* (115 S.Ct. 2475, 1995), and ended with *Bush v. Vera* (116 S.Ct. 1941, 1996), *Shaw v. Hunt* (116 S.Ct. 1894, 1996), and *Hunt v. Cromartie* (119 S.Ct. 1545, 1999). In these cases, the Court repeatedly ruled race-conscious districting can be a violation of the 14th Amendment rights of white voters, and racial classifications of any kind will be subjected to strict scrutiny, its highest form of judicial review. In the first *Shaw* case the Court used a challenge by white voters in North Carolina's 12th district to call into question the race-conscious districting plans that followed the 1990 census. Reacting to the creation of a serpentine district that ran roughly 160 miles along Interstate 85, connecting African-American populations in disparate parts of the state, Justice Sandra D. O'Connor, writing for the majority, proclaimed: "[R]acial classifications of any sort pose the risk of lasting harm to our society. They reinforce the belief, held by too many for too much of our history, that individuals should be judged by the color of their skin. Racial classifications with respect to voting carry particular dangers. Racial gerrymandering, even for remedial purposes, may balkanize us into competing factions; [and] it threatens to carry us further from the goal of a political system in which race no longer matters."[4]

In *Miller v. Johnson* (1995) the Court ruled race-conscious districting would be subject to strict scrutiny. Therefore, any state engaging in race-conscious districting must demonstrate a compelling state interest for the plan to withstand heightened judicial scrutiny. In *Bush v. Vera* (1996), *Hays v. Louisiana* (115 S.Ct. 2431, 1995), and *Shaw v. Hunt* (1996), the Court upheld the Voting Rights Act but rejected arguments race-conscious districting is necessary for states to comply with the act's key provisions.

In *Hunt v. Cromartie* (1999) the Court allowed a political gerrymander to stand in which black voters in North Carolina's 12th district constituted 47 percent of the population. The Court refused to grant summary judgment to the plaintiffs after the facts of the case were found to be in dispute. Summary

Table 4.1
Black Representatives by Year and Congress, 1901–1999

Year	Congress	Number of Voting Black Representatives
1901-1929	57th-70th	0
1929-1935	71st-73rd	1
1935-1945	74th-77th	1
1943-1945	78th	1
1945-1955	79th-83rd	2
1955-1957	84th	3
1957-1963	85th-87th	4
1963-1965	88th	5
1965-1967	89th	6
1967-1969	90th	6
1969-1971	91st	10
1971-1973	92nd	13
1973-1975	93rd	16
1975-1977	94th	17
1977-1979	95th	17
1979-1981	96th	16
1981-1983	97th	18
1983-1985	98th	20
1985-1987	99th	20
1987-1989	100th	22
1989-1991	101st	23
1991-1993	102nd	25
1993-1995	103rd	39
1995-1997	104th	38
1997-1999	105th	38
1999-2001	106th	37

Sources: "African-Americans in Congress," *Congressional Quarterly Weekly,* November 7, 1998; David A. Bositis, *The Black Vote in '98* (Washington, DC: Joint Center for Political and Economic Studies, November 1998).

judgment allows a court to render a decision when both sides can agree on the facts. In this case, the facts were ambiguous enough that the plaintiffs were unable to convince the Court the General Assembly had used the race of constituents, rather than partisanship or incumbency protection, as the primary districting criterion. According to James Blumstein, in order to "trigger strict scrutiny under the equal protection clause, a race discrimination claimant must establish that the government acted deliberately on account of race. But, in situations where race is not obviously the basis of action, a plaintiff bears a considerable evidentiary burden in isolating race as a controlling factor."[5]

Not all majority-minority districts are unconstitutional. Minority districts that occur because minority populations are compact and cohesive enough to meet the three-prong test delineated in *Thornburg v. Gingles* (106 S.Ct. 2732, 1986) are presumably constitutional. According to *Gingles*, a minority district is constitutional when a geographical area includes a large, politically cohesive minority population (of sufficient size to constitute a majority in a single-member district) whose choices of political candidates regularly have been defeated at the polls by blocs of white voters. Districts that meet the *Gingles* standards include John Lewis' Georgia district, Earl Hillard's Alabama district, and William Jefferson's Louisiana district. In each of these districts and similar majority black districts scattered throughout the country, there are compact minority populations of sufficient size to meet the one-person, one-vote standard articulated in *Wesberry v. Sanders* (376 U.S. 1 1964).

Since 1995 minority districts not meeting these criteria have been invalidated in Florida, Georgia, Louisiana, North Carolina, and Texas. Despite dire predictions Congress would be bleached, and the number of blacks in Congress after the 1996 elections would be small enough to fit into the back of a taxicab, all black incumbents who stood for reelection easily won in 1996 and 1998, as I argued they would be in articles I wrote for the *American Prospect* (1995) and the *Chronicle of Higher Education* (1996).[6] Although the resources and experiences that come as part of the incumbency advantage helped ensure these victories, civil rights activists predicted defeat for the black candidates. The incumbency advantage, which I described as relevant in 1995, was embraced after the 1996 elections as part of what seemed to be a face-saving effort to dismiss the reelections of the threatened black incumbents as not being so significant after all.

WHERE WE STAND TODAY

Although black representatives from invalidated black-majority districts in the South were reelected easily in newly drawn white-majority districts, some retrenchments are likely to occur in the future as incumbents resign or retire. There is no reason to expect a white-majority district with a black incumbent (e.g., the Georgia districts that reelected Cynthia McKinney and Sanford Bishop) to automatically elect another black once the seat becomes open. To cite examples from the past, the Kansas City, Missouri, district that elected Alan Wheat six times replaced him with a white woman after he gave up his seat. The same pattern occurred in Atlanta, Georgia during the 1970s, when Andrew Young resigned from his white-majority district and was replaced by a white candidate, Wyche Fowler. Consequently, no one should be unduly surprised if something similar happens when Julia Carson (D-IN) leaves her 70 percent white-majority district. Open congressional seats are unlikely to be reserved for blacks since these seats are too desirable not to be hotly contested. In open-seat elections, financial resources and celebrity status can be crucial factors in determining the strength of a given candidate.

In the future, therefore, African Americans and Hispanics may see declines in their overall percentages in the House of Representatives. White women are in a very different situation since their numbers have not been boosted by race-conscious districting, and any declines for women in the House could come from reductions in the number of minority women, which accounts for a non-trivial portion of their growth.[7] Twelve of the 56 women in the 106th Congress are African Americans. All but 3 represent districts that are less than 50 percent black. Six of the 12 represent districts where the combined black and Hispanic population exceeds 50 percent. Because the circumstances that have led the number of blacks and Hispanics in Congress to leap from 25 to 39, and 11 to 17, respectively, have been altered by Court decisions, it is reasonable to think these numbers over time could revert in the direction of their pre-1990s redistricting levels. The loss of racial and ethnic minorities could have a negative impact on the number of women in Congress.

Relevant to this analysis is the Court's interpretation of its no-retrogression standard articulated in *Beer v. United States* (425 U.S. 130, 1976), which stipulated a redistricting or an electoral change cannot leave minority voters worse off. It is not clear how the Court will interpret this standard if efforts are made after the 2000 census to increase the minority populations of white-majority districts with black incumbents. We will have to wait and see if the Court will allow changes that substantially alter the minority percentage of the population.

Unless the composition of the Court changes drastically, any significant positive changes in the number of minorities in Congress will have to come from (1) population growth and segregated living patterns, (2) drastic changes to the electoral system, or (3) the increased elections of black candidates from white-majority districts. Over the long run, the impact on minority representation will depend on the Court's definition of representation and how expansive that definition is. In Chapter 9 of *Black Faces, Black Interests* I described the limitations of relying solely on minority-majority districts as the dominant source of increased African-American representation, and I examined alternative sources of additional black representation.[8] Broader definitions of representation and strategies for maximizing this societal good take on increasing urgency. It is useful to explore the nature of representation and current issues surrounding minority representation.

UNDERSTANDING THE COMPLEXITY OF REPRESENTATION

Concerns about the racial, ethnic, and political composition of institutional bodies frequently focus on numbers and percentages as legitimate gauges for measuring the degree of representation that a given group has achieved. Along with concepts like democracy, freedom, and interests, representation lends itself to heated debates about what it is and how it ought to function in a democratic society.[9] Hannah Pitkin's work is the starting point for all recent discussions of representation, but new theorists with their own interpretations of the concept have added a richness to the debate about how women and racial minorities are affected by current electoral arrangements and institutional makeups.[10] Among these, Anne Phillips, Will Kymlicka, Iris Young, and Charles Taylor have produced studies that are cited widely and are particularly relevant for discussions of multiculturalism and gender representation.[11] For purposes of this chapter, however, I focus primarily on the traditional debate over the value of maximizing descriptive versus substantive representation of racial minorities.

Descriptive representation refers to the statistical correspondence of particular demographic characteristics in the population—for example, race, gender, religion, occupation, or age—with those of the representative. For example, women's representing women is a form of descriptive representation as is blacks' representing blacks and Latinos', Latinos.[12] Anne Phillips referred to this type of representation as the "politics of presence," which she deeply values along with the importance of the "politics of ideas," which is akin to substantive representation of tangible interests.[13] David Canon referred to these concepts as the "politics of difference" versus the "politics of commonality." The "politics of difference" occurs when a legislator who is descriptively representative of a given group seeks primarily to represent the needs of the racial, ethnic, or gender group of which he or she is a member. The "politics of commonality" focuses on the representation of identifiable interests that do not require shared descriptive attributes since they are not unique, and someone outside the group cannot identify them and provide adequate representation. Canon attempted to carve out a middle ground between these two by arguing that, at least among white and black representatives, neither concept accurately describes the nature of the representation that most legislators give their constituents. Our knowledge from a variety of scholarly sources, including Richard Fenno, Swain, and other congressional scholars, suggests Canon is correct.[14] The activities of legislators are far too varied for the average member to practice one form of representation to the exclusion of others. Most issues found on a given legislative agenda are not specific to race or gender.

I refer to the "politics of ideas" or the "politics of commonality" simply as substantive representation of tangible articulated interests. This representation can be measured by the extent to which the politician identifies with and pursues the policy interests of constituents. As shown in *Black Faces, Black Interests*, substantive representation does not depend on shared race or gender between the representative and his or her constituency. Its presence can be determined by examining the responsiveness of the representative to the electorate, using several different indicators, including committee service, quality of casework, racial and ethnic makeup of the staff, languages spoken in district offices, and how and where the representative spends time. Bernard Grofman argued: "Being typical may be roughly synonymous with being representative, but it is neither a sufficient nor necessary condition for effective representation."[15] On this point, Grofman and I agree wholeheartedly. Descriptive representation often brings with it substantive representation, but it can also create a false appearance that gives a representative cover for inaction. Moreover, the election or appointment of minorities who do not share the concerns and values of a majority of

their racial and ethnic groups easily can fill demands for descriptive representation. For example, Republican J. C. Watts (OK) and Justice Clarence Thomas
provide African Americans with a degree of descriptive representation that many
blacks feel that the group could do without.

New studies demonstrate black representatives represent black interests better
than white legislators. Kenny Whitby, for example, argued the policy interests
of most African Americans are better reflected in the legislative activities of
black lawmakers.[16] However, much of Whitby's data support my conclusions
in *Black Faces, Black Interests* about the nature and the quality of representation
that white Democrats provide their black constituents.[17] Paul Frymer has argued
the Democratic and Republican Parties (although for different reasons) have
marginalized black voters, and the congressional Black Caucus and its activities
have been the primary means of keeping minority issues on the legislative
agenda.[18] Arguing in favor of the continued creation of black-minority districts,
David Canon found these districts do not violate the interests of white constituents since black incumbents tend to be very responsive to white voters.[19]

Although David Lublin has found increases in the number of blacks in Congress through race-conscious districting have made the institution less responsive
to their policy interests, he nevertheless argued in favor of race-conscious districting as a means of increasing black representation.[20] Lublin takes special
exception to the work of Charles Cameron, David Epstein, and Sharyn
O'Halloran, who demonstrated minorities can be elected in districts that are less
than 50 percent African-American.[21] Both Lublin and Canon defend the types
of racial gerrymanders the U.S. Supreme Court invalidated in 1995.[22] In its 1999
decision in *Hunt v. Cromartie* the Court upheld a district similar to the optimal
percentages Cameron et al. (1996) have supported. I believe Lublin's and
Canon's energies could best be expended on a search for alternative remedies
to enhance the substantive and descriptive representation of racial and ethnic
minorities. Both scholars spend a portion of their time attempting to dismiss the
growing number of elections in which white-majority constituencies have
elected black candidates.

The number of white-majority-white districts that have elected black candidates is sensitive to whether the scholar chooses to examine the voting-age
population of the district or the district's overall population. I am puzzled as to
why most scholars use overall population percentages rather than voting-age
percentages when assessing the likelihood of a legislative district's electing a
black candidate. The latter figures would seem more appropriate for assessing
the frequency in which white-majority districts have elected minority candidates.
For even more precision, scholars should calculate voter turnout by race in
districts that elect black candidates. Such data would show an increase in the
number of white-majority districts that have elected black candidates, which
would include Bill Clay's St. Louis, Missouri. Although Clay's district is 52.6
percent black in overall population, its voting-age population has been around

48.0 percent for the past two decades.[23] Nevertheless, Clay a liberal Democrat, has been easily elected despite opposition from well-financed white opponents.

THE REAL TRADE-OFF FOR RACIAL MINORITIES

Race-conscious redistricting of the 1990s significantly increased the descriptive representation of African Americans but left the group worse off. In terms of power and influence African Americans are worse off with 37 members of Congress than they were in 1990, when they numbered 25. When the Democrats lost control of Congress to the Republicans, it profoundly changed the career paths of many high-seniority Democrats who floundered in the unfamiliar turf of being members of the minority party after having spent 42 years in power. Since the ascendance of the Republicans in 1994, high-seniority Democrats have left the institution at a fairly steady pace. The retirements of thirteen senior black representatives since 1993 have meant a loss of more than 100 years of accumulated seniority.[24] Table 4.2 presents demographic data on the black members of the 106th Congress. Of the 37 blacks in Congress, only 7 have more than ten years of seniority. Like the black representatives who started the congressional Black Caucus in the early 1970s, these younger legislators dislike the seniority rule because they see many heads above them. If the Democrats reclaim the House in the next election, African-American representatives will not be positioned to claim many committee chairs. Nor will they have the support of experienced Democratic legislators such as Patricia Schroeder (D-CO), who left Congress in 1996 after having served for more than 21 years, and Louis Stokes (D-OH), who left after having served 30 years. It will take decades for African Americans to reach the influence they had prior to race-conscious districting and the ascendance of the Republicans.

Consequently, the real trade-offs of maximizing one form of representation at the expense of another are nontrivial costs that will have a lasting impact. Although I have argued that aggressively pursuing descriptive representation at the expense of substantive representation can be harmful to the needs and preferences of racial minorities, others seemed prepared to make that trade-off. Phillips believes that the "politics of ideas"—that is, substantive representation by representatives outside one's group—is inadequate to ensure effective representation of members of politically excluded groups. Expressing the views of many activists, she argued: "Contemporary demands for political presence have often risen out of the politics of new social movements. . . . Women do not want to change their sex, or black people the colour of their skin, as a condition for equal citizenship; nor do they want their differences discounted."[25] Answering the question of whether blacks should be represented by blacks and women by women, Jane Mansbridge gave a qualified "yes."[26] While fully recognizing the complexity of minority representation, Mansbridge argued there are some situations involving disadvantaged groups in which constituents may want to be represented by individuals whose backgrounds and experiences mirror those of

Table 4.2
Black Members of the 106th Congress

Member	District	Year Elected	Campaign Expenditure[1] (most recent)	BVAP[2] (%)	HVAP[3] (%)
Sanford D. Bishop	D-GA-2	1992	$774,474	35.1	1.6‡
Corrine Brown	D-FL-3	1992	$330,201	42.3	
Julia M. Carson	D-IN-10	1996	$572,617	27.2	1.0
William L. Clay	D-MO-1	1968	$366,550	48.0	0.9
Eva Clayton	D-NC-1	1992	$300,049	46.5	0.7‡
James E. Clyburn	D-SC-6	1992	$196,440	58.3	0.5‡
John Conyers, Jr.	D-MI-14	1964	$267,039	65.3	1.0
Elijah E. Cummings	D-MD-7	1996	$691,787	67.8	0.9
Danny K. Davis	D-IL-7	1996	$410,662	59.8	4.1
Julian C. Dixon	D-CA-32	1978	$97,495	39.9	26.4
Chaka Fattah	D-PA-2	1994	$412,478	58.4	1.5‡
Harold E. Ford, Jr.	D-TN-9	1996	$679,843	54.1	0.7
Alcee L. Hastings	D-FL-23	1992	$276,708	45.7	9.1‡
Earl F. Hilliard	D-AL-7	1992	$223,582	63.5	0.3
Jesse Jackson, Jr.	D-IL-2	1995	$729,699	66.0	5.9
William J. Jefferson	D-LA-2	1990	$301,082	60.7	3.8
Eddie Bernice Johnson	D-TX-30	1992	$416.694	42.4	15.1‡
Stephanie Tubbs Jones	D-OH-11	1998		54.8	1.0
Carolyn C. Kilpatrick	D-MI-15	1996	$174,457	68.2	3.7
Barbara Lee	D-CA-9	1998		29.2	10.7
Sheila Jackson Lee	D-TX-18	1994	$477,866	43.5	13.7‡
John Lewis	D-GA-5	1986	$207,661	57.2	1.8‡
Cynthia McKinney	D-GA-4	1992	$1,015,197	32.8	3.3‡
Carrie Meek	D-FL-17	1992	$257,039	54.0	24.1
Greg Meeks	D-NY-6	1998		54.5	16.0
Juanita Millender-McDonald	D-CA-37	1996	$327,257	34.2	40.8
Major R. Owens	D-NY-11	1982	$129,983	72.4	11.1
Donald M. Payne	D-NJ-10	1988	$404,017	57.3	11.5
Charles R. Rangel	D-NY-15	1970	$1,086,065	46.7	43.6
Bobby L. Rush	D-IL-1	1992	$156,219	67.8	3.1
Robert Scott	D-VA-3	1992	$176,104	61.2	1.2
Bennie G. Thompson	D-MS-2	1993	$361,452	58.1	0.5‡
Edolphus Towns	D-NY-10	1982	$533,824	59.4	18.5
Maxine Waters	D-CA-35	1990	$235,851	44.0	38.5
Melvin L. Watt	D-NC-12	1992	$148,001	32.6	0.8‡
Albert R. Wynn	D-MD-4	1992	$343,875	55.8	6.1
J.C. Watts	R-OK-4	1994	$1,363,291	6.5	3.3

[1]Data from *1998 Almanac of American Politics*.

[2]Data from David A. Bositis, *The Black Vote in '98* (Washington, DC: Joint Center for Political and Economic Studies, November 1998).

[3]Data from *Congressional Districts in the 1990's: A Portrait of America* (Washington, DC: Congressional Quarterly, 1993).

‡Percentages do not reflect redistricting that occurred after the 1990 census.

group members.[27] This desire is particularly true, she argues, in contexts of "group mistrust, uncrystalized interests, a history suggesting inability to rule, and low *de facto* legitimacy."

Mansbridge and Phillips raise legitimate concerns especially relevant for enhancing our understanding of the complexity of representation and the values that lead to moral disagreement among scholars supportive of more diversity in institutional settings but critical of demands for descriptive representation that seem to come at the expense of greater substantive representation.

For the House to become more representative of the American public, the strategies of activists may have to change. One issue receiving detailed discussion among scholars and activists is proportional representation (PR), which conceivably could increase both the descriptive and substantive representation of political and racial minorities. PR also runs the risk of bringing with it unintended consequences that could undermine original goals and lead to changes in institutional rules that could work against minorities. In the absence of alternative electoral systems, examined later, the strategies I advanced in 1993 remain the best hope for substantially increasing the overall representation of racial minorities.

DO WE NEED TO CHANGE THE ELECTORAL SYSTEM?

Some scholars have argued the lack of proportionality of minorities in legislative bodies is a reflection of an unfair electoral system that works against minorities by combining single-member plurality districts with winner-take-all rules. While a growing number of Western democracies have debated the feasibility of changing their electoral systems, and many have taken steps to do so, the United States has lagged far behind.[28] In fact, the subject of proportional representation for federal elections is barely on the radar screen despite the efforts of activists who attribute low voter turnout, wasted votes, issueless campaigns, and discrimination against women and racial minorities to the existing electoral system.[29]

Cumulative voting is among the methods most frequently mentioned as offering minority voters the best opportunity to elect candidates of choice.[30] This system allows voters to have as many votes as seats to be filled. For example, a state like North Carolina with twelve representatives might opt for four multi-member districts with three seats. African Americans and other minorities would have the option of spreading their votes across candidates or concentrating them on a single candidate. If a single African-American candidate competed against several white candidates in each of the four multi-member districts, black voters could possibly elect four black representatives if they voted cohesively for a single candidate, while the white voters split their votes across the other candidates.[31] Blacks have had some success in getting elected in the few places where cumulative voting has been tried as a court-ordered remedy for past discrimination.[32]

Some proposals to change the electoral system have reached Congress in recent years. The representatives who have pushed most vigorously for repeal of a law Congress enacted in 1967 mandating single-member districts for House elections are African Americans whose districts were invalidated in 1995. Georgia's Cynthia McKinney introduced the first of several bills in 1996 that would allow states some flexibility on how they filled their congressional seats. More recently, in the 106th Congress, Mel Watts (D-NC) has sponsored a similar bill that would give states the option of electing their representatives in multi-member districts. So far Watts has eleven co-sponsors. Ironically, many voting rights activists once considered multi-member districts as racially discriminatory devices designed to thwart the intentions of the Voting Rights Act (VRA). After aggressively using it to strike down multi-member districts, activists now believe this electoral arrangement can benefit minorities by softening the impact of the loss of black-majority districts.[33]

In the past, women and minorities were in conflict over issues of fairness and the desirability of pursuing single-member districts versus multi-member districts. In many areas of the South, women lost the battle. The single-member districts that helped elect blacks often disadvantaged them, sometimes by causing their numbers to plummet after such an electoral change. Wilma Rule and Pippa Norris demonstrated multi-member districts increase the likelihood women will enter and win legislative races. Furthermore, they show the countries with multi-member districts and some form of proportional representation tend to elect more women officeholders.[34] The system works so that "political parties have an *incentive* to place women on their respective lists to broaden their appeal. But in single-member districts where only one person is elected, political elites have a *disincentive* to risk backing a woman candidate," Rule argues.[35] Similarly, Richard Matland and Deborah Brown wrote slating women in multi-member districts avoids the zero-sum politics of single-member districts, appeases women activists, and avoids the probability that a woman candidate will compete against an ambitious male candidate one-on-one.[36]

Although changing circumstances have brought advocates for women and blacks closer together on the subject of multi-member districts, it will take substantial coalition building to approach the votes needed to enact a congressional bill repealing the 1967 law. Minorities will need the support of allies from both political parties who would have to be convinced the current system is unfair and electoral reform would work to everyone's advantage. It is not clear how many incumbents would jump on the bandwagon since their own elections occurred in single-member districts. African-American legislators have not been successful in getting unanimous black support in the Congress for initiatives to change the electoral system. For the Watts bill to stand a chance of passage, it will be necessary to convince a majority of legislators the same electoral system that got everyone elected is hopelessly flawed and is in need of serious reform. A groundswell of support is not likely to emerge anytime soon. As of June 1999 none of the white women in Congress, none of the Republicans, and only a minority of congressional Black Caucus members were listed among the bill's co-sponsors.

Some legislators may be deterred by fear the proposed changes to the electoral system could lead to negative, unanticipated consequences that could be harder to resolve than current problems. The same electoral changes that could make it easier for women, blacks, gays, and lesbians to win office might do the same for representatives of extremist groups such as the Klu Klux Klan and the Citizens Council—a David Duke, for example, might be assured a seat in the House under a PR system. Moreover, mixed electoral systems that combine a PR system with cumulative voting are not flawless. They assume polarized voting and a single minority candidate whom voters can elect by engaging in strategic voting. Electing a minority candidate, however, becomes far more uncertain if more than one minority candidate competes against several white candidates. The minority vote can be split so that no minority candidate is elected. Moreover, nothing in the system would prevent white Americans from voting strategically to ensure the elections of white candidates. Even when the system worked as anticipated, numerical minorities would still be a minority when they reached the legislature and would still risk being tyrannized by the majority in the manner that Lani Guinier examined in her many writings on the subject.

CONCLUSIONS

I started this chapter by looking at the growth potential of minority members in Congress during the next century. White women, I argue, are far more likely to see sustained growth than either blacks or Hispanics. In fact, the latter groups may see numerical declines when minority representatives of white-majority districts resign or retire and risk replacement by white representatives. Currently, seven blacks in Congress represent white-majority legislative districts (see Table 4.2). When these incumbents retire, such districts may opt for white candidates, or they may once again elect minority candidates. Racially polarized voting patterns cannot be taken for granted. Electorates sometimes behave in unpredictable ways. Examples of this unpredictability have occurred in some black-majority cities where white mayors have replaced blacks. What some advocates view as a loss of black power has caused voting rights activists to look more favorably at runoff primaries in which a second election is held between the top two vote getters if none of the candidates have meet a certain threshold, usually 50.1 percent. In common with multi-member districts, such primaries once were viewed as racially discriminatory devices, but changing times and changing circumstances have brought about new thinking and new strategies.[37] Building on what we know from the scholarly literature about campaigns, elections, and race, I believe strategies can be designed to enhance minority representation without drastically altering the electoral system. Moreover, I do not believe adoption of semi-proportional representational systems is something that we can reasonably expect to occur in the United States in the near future. Given occasional discord and instability in countries like Israel and Italy where List-PR systems reign supreme, this failure to adopt PR may be a blessing in disguise (see Chapter 15 in this volume). In Israel extremist religious groups have been able to play key roles, often undesirable, in the formation of coalition governments. In addition, limited accountability and frequent instability have led Italy to abandon a pure form of proportional representation in favor of a mixed system. The United States can follow the examples of other Western democracies by experimenting with different electoral systems, or party leaders can exert greater efforts at removing financial and other barriers that impede the election of minority candidates. The House of Representatives can look more like the American people, reflecting their racial, ethnic, and political diversity, which can only grow during the next century.

NOTES

I thank James Blumstein, David Hillman, and Bruce I. Oppenheimer for their helpful comments and suggestions.

1. David Bositis, ed., *Redistricting and Minority Representation* (Washington, DC: Joint Center for Political and Economic Studies, 1998), p. 5.

2. U.S. Bureau of the Census, Internet Release, December 12, 1998.

3. Carol M. Swain, "Women and Blacks in Congress: 1870–1996," in Lawrence C. Dodd and Bruce I. Oppenheimer, eds., *Congress Reconsidered*, 6th ed. (Washington, DC: Congressional Quarterly Press, 1997), pp. 81–99.

4. Carol M. Swain, *Black Faces, Black Interests: The Representation of African-Americans in Congress* (Cambridge, MA: Harvard University Press, 1995), p. viii.

5. James B. Blumstein, "Racial Gerrymandering and Vote Dilution: *Shaw v. Reno* in Doctrinal Context," *Rutgers Law Journal*, Spring 1995, pp. 579–80.

6. Carol M. Swain, "The Future of Black Representation," *American Prospect*, Fall 1995, pp. 78–83; Carol M. Swain, "Supreme Court's Decisions on Minority Districts Could Benefit Minority Voters," *The Chronicle of Higher Education*, September 27, 1996, pp. B3–B4. See also Carol M. Swain, "An Optimist's View of Minority Representation," in Bositis, *Redistricting and Minority Representation*, pp. 195–99; and Carol M. Swain, "Not Wrongful by Any Means: The Court's Decision in Redistricting Cases," *Houston Law Review*, Summer 1997, pp. 315–21.

7. Wilma Rule, "Why Women Should Be Included in the Voting Rights Act," *National Civic Review*, Fall–Winter 1995, pp. 355–66.

8. Carol M. Swain, "Strategies of Increasing Black Representation of Blacks," in Swain, *Black Faces, Black Interests*, pp. 193–206.

9. W. B. Gallie, "Essentially Contested Concepts," in Max Black, ed., *The Importance of Language* (Englewood Cliffs, NJ: Prentice-Hall, 1962); William E. Connolly, *The Terms of Political Discourse*, 2nd ed. (Princeton, NJ: Princeton University Press, 1983).

10. Hannah F. Pitkin, *The Concept of Representation* (Berkeley: University of California Press, 1967).

11. Will Kymlicka, *Multicultural Citizenship: A Liberal Theory of Minority Rights* (New York: Oxford University Press, 1995); Anne Phillips, *The Politics of Presence*

(New York: Oxford University Press, 1995); Iris M. Young, *Justice and the Politics of Difference* (Princeton, NJ: Princeton University Press, 1990); Charles Taylor, *Multiculturalism and the Politics of "Recognition"* (Princeton, NJ: Princeton University Press, 1992).

12. Swain, *Black Faces, Black Interests*, p. 5.

13. Phillips, *Politics of Presence*.

14. Richard F. Fenno, *Home Style: House Members in Their Districts* (Glenview, IL: Scott, Foresman, 1978); Swain, *Black Faces, Black Interests*.

15. Bernard Grofman, "Should Representatives Be Typical to Their Constituents?" in Bernard Grofman, Arend Lijphart, Robert McKay, and Howard Serrow, eds., *Representation and Redistricting Issues* (Lexington, MA: Lexington Books, 1982), p. 99.

16. Kenny Whitby, *The Color of Representation* (Ann Arbor: University of Michigan Press, 1999).

17. For more information see Charles Bullock III's review of *The Color of Representation* in *The American Political Science Review*, June 1999, pp. 462–63.

18. Paul Frymer, *Uneasy Alliances: Race and Party Competition in America* (Princeton, NJ: Princeton University Press, 1999).

19. David T. Canon, *Race, Redistricting, and Representation* (Chicago: University of Chicago Press, 1999).

20. David Lublin, *The Paradox of Representation* (Princeton, NJ: Princeton University Press, 1997).

21. Charles Cameron, David Epstein, and Sharyn O'Halloran, "Do Majority-Minority Districts Maximize Substantive Black Representation in Congress?" *The American Political Science Review*, December 1996, pp. 784–812.

22. David Lublin, "Racial Redistricting and African-American Representation: A Critique of Do Majority-Minority Districts Maximize Substantive Black Representation in Congress," *The American Political Science Review*, March 1999, pp. 183–86; David Epstein and Sharyn O'Halloran, "A Social Science Approach to Race, Redistricting, and Representation," *The American Political Science Review*, March 1999, pp. 187–91.

23. *Congressional Districts in the 1990s: A Portrait of America* (Washington, DC: Congressional Quarterly Press, 1993), p. 425.

24. David A. Bositis, *The Black Vote in '98* (Washington, DC: Joint Center for Political and Economic Studies, November 1998).

25. Phillips, *Politics of Presence*, p. 8.

26. Jane Mansbridge, "Should Blacks Represent Blacks and Women Represent Women? A Contingent 'Yes,' " *Journal of Politics*, August 1999, pp. 628–57.

27. Ibid.

28. Andrew Reynolds and Ben Reilly, eds., *The International IDEA Handbook of Electoral System Design*, 2nd ed. (Stockholm: Institute for Democracy and Electoral Assistance, 1997).

29. Douglas J. Amy, *Real Choices, New Voices: The Case for Proportional Representation in the United States* (New York: Columbia University Press, 1993).

30. Other systems include limited voting and preference voting. With limited voting the number of votes is less than the number of seats being filled, while preference voting allows voters to rank their preferences for candidates. See Robert Brischetto, "Latino Voters and Redistricting in the New Millennium," in Bositis, *Redistricting and Minority Representation*, pp. 43–90; Lani Guinier, *Tyranny of the Majority* (New York: Free Press, 1994).

31. The Center for Voting and Democracy has developed a number of such plans to demonstrate to different states how multi-member districts could be used to elect members of Congress. For more information, please consult the Center's *Electing the People's House* (Washington, DC: Center for Voting and Democracy, 1998).

32. Guinier, *Tyranny of the Majority*.

33. Bernard Grofman, Lisa Handley, and Richard G. Niemi, *Minority Representation and the Quest for Voting Equality* (New York: Cambridge University Press, 1992).

34. Wilma Rule and Pippa Norris, "Anglo and Minority Women's Underrepresentation in the Congress: Is the Electoral System the Culprit?" in Wilma Rule and Joseph F. Zimmerman, eds., *United States Electoral Systems: Their Impact on Women and Minorities* (Westport, CT: Greenwood Press, 1992), pp. 41–54.

35. Wilma Rule, "Women, Representation, and Political Rights," in Mark E. Rush, ed., *Voting Rights and Redistricting in the United States* (Westport, CT: Greenwood Press, 1998), pp. 177–93.

36. Richard Matland and Deborah D. Brown, "District Magnitude's Effect on Female Representation in U.S. State Legislatures," *Legislative Studies Quarterly*, November 1992, pp. 469–92.

37. Charles S. Bullock and Loch K. Johnson, *Runoff Elections in the United States* (Chapel Hill: University of North Carolina Press, 1992).

Chapter 5

Making the House More Representative: Hidden Costs and Unintended Consequences

Mark E. Rush

Even a brief survey of contemporary political literature in print and on the Internet indicates that criticism of American political institutions is alive and well. Regarding the House of Representatives, critics cite several flaws that indicate just how *un*representative the political process and the House are. These criticisms include "high rates of incumbent reelection, large contributions to incumbents' campaigns, noncompetitiveness of political parties in most districts, low voter turnout in elections and low diversity in representation."[1] In response, calls abound for reforms such as term limits, increased use of initiatives and referenda, proportional representation, and campaign spending restrictions.

It is important to remember that "reform" is frequently just another way of saying "change." "Reform," of course, implies *improvement*. But advocates of reform proposals do not always explain how they will differ from mere *change*. As well, it is not necessarily clear reformers have identified bona fide ailments in the American political system. In many cases, the objects of contemporary reform proposals are nothing more than the smooth workings of the constitutional system. Advocates of direct democracy, for example, are unhappy with the clearly *representative* nature of the political system contemplated by the Framers of the U.S. Constitution. Those who would restrict campaign spending must contend with prevailing interpretations of the 1st Amendment equating political spending with political speech. On the other hand, the entrenchment of incumbents, low voter turnout, low representative diversity, and the noncompetitiveness of elections are products of the single-member plurality electoral system. Thus, attempts to remedy these problems do not necessarily run afoul of the Constitution.

In this chapter, I offer a guarded, skeptical response to general calls for reform to the American political system and specific proposals to enhance the representativeness of the House. To reformers whose desires conflict with the values underlying the constitutional system, I suggest that they need to do more than simply argue this or that reform proposal will improve the operation of the political system. They need to address the extent to which their calls for reform of the *political* system may require changes in the *constitutional* structure—and explain why the structure is in need of repair. To those with more modest goals, such as increasing the competitiveness of elections and diversity of congressional representation, I suggest that their reform proposals are insufficient to achieve their desired ends. I therefore ask whether they are willing to pay the high price necessary to create the political process they desire.

CONSTITUTIONAL ISSUES

The constitutional ramifications of calls for political reform are manifested clearly by recent U.S. Supreme Court decisions. In several recent cases, the Court either struck down attempts to reform some element of the electoral process or upheld laws that reformers regard as problematic. In response to the Court's restricting the extent to which the Voting Rights Act can be used to draw "majority-minority" districts, Representative Cynthia McKinney (D-GA) introduced the Voters' Choice Act, which would permit states to elect their congressional delegations by proportional representation (PR).[2] In *Colorado Republican Federal Campaign Finance Committee v. Federal Election Commission* (FEC) the Court limited the FEC's ability to restrict campaign spending.[3] In *U.S. Term Limits v. Thornton* the Court struck down an attempt by the Arkansas legislature to place term limits on that state's congressional representatives.[4] Finally, in *Timmons et al. v. Twin Cities Area New Party*, the Court upheld a Minnesota ban on fusion candidacies that, critics contended, discriminated unfairly against minor parties.[5]

Each of these decisions thwarted reforms or legislation that would have diversified electoral competition. The Court's racial gerrymandering decisions stymied attempts by states to enhance minority representation. Restricting FEC's ability to control campaign spending and striking down term-limits legislation enhanced the ability of incumbents to remain in office. Finally, the decision to allow bans on fusion candidacies certainly will make it more difficult for minor parties to challenge the dominance of the Democrats and Republicans.

While reformers lament such decisions, it is important to bear in mind that the Court was upholding values and visions of the political process enshrined in the Constitution. In *Shaw v. Reno, Bush v. Vera,* and *Miller v. Johnson*, the Court found that the unfettered creation of majority-minority districts ran afoul of the 14th Amendment's equal protection of the laws clause. While there was nothing inherently unconstitutional about term limits, the Court ruled a state's imposition of them on candidates for election to Congress upsets the constitutional balance between the state and federal governments. Finally, in *Colorado Republican*, the Court reaffirmed its assertion in *Buckley v. Valeo* that "restrict[ing] the speech of some elements of society in order to enhance the relative voice of others is wholly foreign to the First Amendment.''[6]

Constitutional concerns notwithstanding, there are also serious practical short-comings to many reform proposals. For example, advocates of spending restrictions and public financing of elections are convinced such actions would encourage more candidates to run for office.[7] By lowering the cost of campaigning, spending limits would remove the advantages of wealth and therefore lower the economic barrier to entry deterring potential candidates who are unsure of their financial backing. With the proliferation of candidates, voters would have a more meaningful choice on Election Day.

Yet, public financing could also limit the voters' ability to support their preferred candidates or work against the election of others. Public financing would take the voters' money—in the form of tax dollars—and funnel it into the coffers of any candidate who qualifies under the public financing provisions. As a result, voters could find their tax dollars being distributed among candidates whom they do not support. One can only wonder what voter responses would be if the local Nazi or Klansman qualified for public financing.

Term limits also bear a substantial practical cost (see Chapters 14 and 15 in this volume). While they provide a sure-fire method of ejecting candidates from office, they are a blunt instrument that most certainly will remove good, effective legislators along with the bad ones. Term-limits advocates may be willing to pay this price, but why pay such a price when high turnover among congressional incumbents in the elections of 1992 and 1994 indicated term limits are unnecessary?

MAKING CONGRESS MORE REPRESENTATIVE: AT WHAT PRICE?

The numerous proposals for reforming the House can be broken down into two broad categories: those making the House more *responsive* and those making it more *representative*. Calls for enlarging the House and term limits are examples of the former (see Chapters 12 and 15 in this volume).

Proponents of enlarging the House argue the large population of each congressional district makes it virtually impossible for any member of Congress to have much sense of the interests of his or her voters. As Kromkowski and Kromkowski noted, the average constituency size has increased steadily throughout American history.[8] Currently, congressional constituencies are at least twice the size of those in most other nations. Only the European parliament has districts that compare in size to those of the U.S. House of Representatives.[9]

Enlarging the House—by shrinking the population size of congressional districts—would bring the representatives closer to their constituents, but it would not necessarily enhance congressional diversity. So long as House members are elected by single-member districts (SMDs), women and minorities will remain at an electoral disadvantage. Accordingly, scholars such as Arend Lijphart propose that the House be elected by PR as well as enlarged.[10] SMDs, coupled with formidable ballot access hurdles and bans on fusion candidacies, work to the advantage of the Democratic and Republican Parties and discriminate against women, third parties, and minorities.[11]

Theoretically, PR should produce a more diverse legislature than one whose members are elected in single-member districts. But, practically, PR *alone* does not ensure this result. In PR countries, more women and minorities are elected to office. But, in many cases, this result is because parties are required to nominate quotas of women, or the legislatures have special provisions for minority seats.[12] Furthermore, PR may mathematically raise the threshold of exclusion and therefore make it more difficult for minority groups to elect candidates than it would be under a single-member system.[13]

While PR might make the House more *descriptively* representative of the divisions within the polity, it would not necessarily make it any more *responsive* to the people. Douglas Amy noted, for example, the single-member system produces virtually meaningless choices among "tweedle-dee and tweedle-dum" candidates nominated by parties committed to avoiding any substantive discussions of important political issues.[14] But, with the exception of independents, candidates are nominated by political parties. As a result, Amy's criticism has more to do with the structure and function of political parties than with the ideological commitments of individual candidates.

While more parties might win seats in the House under PR, this change would not necessarily make the quality of legislation or political debate any better—unless we were to change the nature of parties as well. For diversification of the legislature to be more than just a cosmetic change, it would need to be accompanied by a strengthening of party organizations in order to spare us the travails of "tweedle-dee and tweedle-dum" candidates and enable the newly represented parties to present and pursue their agendas effectively.

To ensure such cohesion, political parties would require greater control over their membership and nomination processes. Yet, as a result of previous reform initiatives, such as the direct primary, party elites can do little to construct cohesive platforms or control who seeks their nomination.[15] Such reforms gave voters much more control over party nominations and thereby allowed "outsiders" to challenge the influence of party insiders.[16] As a result, virtually anyone can seek a party's nomination, and we can hardly hold party officials accountable for ensuring all nominees adhere to a coherent party line.

Thus, while strengthening the parties would clearly address reformers' concerns about making electoral choices more meaningful, it would also make the nomination process less accessible to the average citizen. It would thereby reverse the democratizing emphasis of electoral reforms that began in 1968.

THE PRICE OF REFORM

My goal in this chapter has been to note that reforms bear very real costs and entail choices that are inevitably zero-sum. Reformers justify their calls for change by relying on the successful implementation of alternative electoral systems in other countries or in state and local governments in the United States. But what works in other countries and state and local governments may not meet with the same success in a nation that is as ethnically, racially, and religiously heterogeneous as the United States. Furthermore, it is important to note that such arrangements do not always work as well as advocates suggest.

Increasing the size of the House and dispensing with the single-member electoral system probably would put an end to the two-party system. But while a multiparty system might result in a more diverse legislature, the system also would put an end to the simplicity with which the two-party House is organized. Since a multiparty system is less likely to create an outright legislative majority, the legislature would have to form a coalition—after an election was over. As a result, the coalition could be as unrepresentative of the voters' will as any government formed under the single-member system.[17]

The transition to the list type of PR in New Zealand provides an instructive example of the unforeseen shortcomings of PR (see Chapters 12 and 15 in this volume). While the conversion to PR was hailed by many scholars, New Zealand voters have become frustrated with the process of forming government coalitions after the elections.[18] As well, Italy, long a user of List-PR, recently incorporated single-member districts into its electoral system to help fight corruption, instability, and a perceived lack of accountability that characterized its political system under PR.[19]

In Britain, the recently released Report of the Independent Commission on the Voting System also advocated a conversion to PR—but not without significant and thoughtful challenges.[20] Michael Pinto-Duschinsky, for example, pointed out that while PR may produce legislatures that are more diverse in partisan terms, PR does not necessarily enhance the ability of the voters to change governments.[21] He noted that in the 50 years after World War II, the main governing party in Germany, Italy, Japan, and Switzerland (nations that use List-PR) never was ousted from office. In Westminster countries (Britain, Canada, India, and New Zealand), sitting governments were ousted in 25 of 58 elections.

As well, partisan diversity does not necessarily ensure diversity of legislative composition. In Cambridge, Massachusetts, for example, the single-transferable vote (STV) type of PR has been used in nonpartisan elections for City Council since 1941. STV-PR is regarded as an especially attractive electoral system because it gives voters the greatest flexibility in choosing candidates.[22] Despite such high praise, the average reelection rate of City Council incumbents in Cambridge has been 85.14 percent.[23]

CONCLUSION

Those who seek to reform the American political system draw upon relatively recent experiments with alternative electoral arrangements in other countries. While such experimentation is certainly commendable, American reformers overlook the obvious: for all its warts, the American political system has endured for over 200 years. Clearly, something must be working right.

We therefore must consider whether Congress and the system by which its members are elected are really in need of repair and whether the proposed remedies might not be worse than the maladies they are designed to cure. Regardless of the method of elections, the constitutional system remains firmly grounded in Madison's republican solution to the problem of factions. The federal organization of the country, coupled with a system of separated powers, ensures that compromise is necessary to enact legislation and therefore militates against discrete interests. Using PR to multiply the number of discrete partisan labels borne by members of Congress simply will reinforce the extent to which such compromise will be necessary to form a governing majority while moving the process of government formation farther away from the voters. While there is nothing inherently wrong with such a system, it is not clear it would be any improvement over the existing system.

NOTES

This chapter is the revised version of an article that appeared in *PS: Political Science and Politics*, vol. 31, no. 1, March 1998, pp. 21–24.

1. Joseph F. Zimmerman and Wilma Rule, "A More Representative United States House of Representatives?" *PS: Political Science and Politics*, March 1998, pp. 5–10. See also Douglas Amy, *Real Choices, New Voices* (New York: Columbia University Press, 1993).

2. See *Shaw v. Reno*, 509 U.S. 630 (1993), *Bush v. Vera*, 116 S.Ct. 1941 (1996), *Miller v. Johnson*, 515 U.S. 900 (1995), H.R. 3068 (1997).

3. *Colorado Republican Federal Campaign Finance Committee v. Federal Election Commission*, 116 S.Ct. 2309 (1996).

4. *U.S. Term Limits v. Thornton*, 514 U.S. 779 (1995).

5. *Timmons et al. v. Twin Cities Area New Party*, 117. S.Ct. 1364 (1997).

6. *Buckley v. Valeo*, 424 U.S. 1 at 49 (1976).

7. See, for example, David Donnelly, Janice Fine, and Ellen S. Miller, "Going Public," *The Boston Review*, April/May 1997. (Available: www.polisci.mit.edu/bostonreview/br22.2).

8. Charles A. Kromkowski and John A. Kromkowski, "Why 435? A Question of Political Arithmetic," *Polity*, Fall 1991, pp. 136–37.

9. Francis Jacobs, Richard Corbett, and Michael Shackleton, *The European Parliament*, 3rd ed. (London: Catermill International, 1995), p. 15.

10. Arend Lijphart, "Reforming the House: Three Moderately Radical Proposals," *PS: Political Science and Politics*, March 1998, pp. 10–13.

11. See Amy, *Real Choices, New Voices*; Wilma Rule and Pippa Norris, "Anglo and Minority Women's Underrepresentation in Congress: Is the Electoral System the Culprit?" in Wilma Rule and Joseph Zimmerman, eds., *United States Electoral Systems and Their Impact on Women and Minorities* (Westport, CT: Greenwood Press, 1992), pp. 41–54.

12. See, for example, Wilma Rule, "Women, Representation and Political Rights,"

in Mark E. Rush, ed., *Voting Rights and Redistricting in the United States* (Westport, CT: Greenwood Press, 1998), pp. 180–83.

13. See Mark E. Rush, "Postscript: The Promise of Electoral Systems and the Perils of Electoral Reform," in Rush, ed., *Voting Rights and Redistricting in the United States*, pp. 261–70. See also James Campbell, *Cheap Seats: The Democratic Party's Advantage in U.S. House Elections* (Columbus: Ohio State University Press, 1996).

14. Amy, *Real Choices, New Voices*, p. 5.

15. See James W. Ceasar, *Reforming the Reforms: A Critical Analysis of the Presidential Selection Process* (Cambridge, MA: Ballinger, 1982); Nelson W. Polsby, *The Consequences of Party Reform* (New York: Oxford University Press, 1983); Richard S. Katz and Robin Kolodny, "Party Organization as an Empty Vessel: Parties in American Politics," in Richard S. Katz and Peter Mair, eds., *How Parties Organize* (London: Sage, 1994), pp. 23–50.

16. See Samuel Kernell, *Going Public: New Strategies of Presidential Leadership* (Washington, DC: Congressional Quarterly, 1997), pp. 38–46.

17. For additional discussion on the complications that would arise from an enlarged or proportionally elected legislature, see, for example, C. Lawrence Evans and Walter Oleszek, "If It Ain't Broke Bad, Don't Fix It a Lot," *PS: Political Science and Politics*, March 1998, pp. 24–28.

18. See, for example, Arend Lijphart, "The Demise of the Last Westminster System? Comments on the Report of New Zealand's Royal Commission on the Electoral System," *Electoral Studies*, August 1987, pp. 97–103.

19. Richard S. Katz, *Democracy and Elections* (New York: Oxford University Press, 1998).

20. Available: www.official-documents.co.uk/document/cm40/4090/4090.htm (1998).

21. Michael Pinto-Duschinsky, "Send the Rascals Packing," *Times Literary Supplement*, September 25, 1998, pp. 10–14.

22. See Andrew Reynolds and Ben Reilly, eds., *The International IDEA Handbook of Electoral Systems Design*, 2nd ed. (Stockholm: International Institute for Democracy and Electoral Assistance, 1997), pp. 83–88.

23. This percentage refers to the reelection rate of incumbents who stood for reelection. Overall, in any given year, the reelection rate of the City Council was 76.98 percent.

Part III

Causes and Consequences of Unrepresentativeness

Chapter 6

Delegitimation on the Installment Plan: The Demise of Congressional Campaign Finance Law

Clyde Wilcox and Wesley Joe

> I think it is clear, Mr. President, that the few remaining pillars holding up our crumbling election system finally collapsed.
> —Senator Russell Feingold, addressing the U.S. Senate[1]

> The campaign finance system in America . . . in 1996 . . . went from the political equivalent of a low-grade fever to Code Blue—from a chronic problem needing attention sooner or later to a crisis, with a system clearly out of control.
> —Norman J. Ornstein, Thomas E. Mann, Paul Taylor, Michael J. Malbin, and Anthony Corrado, Jr.[2]

In 1997 scholars and journalists who study campaign finance, professionals who raise or regulate campaign money, policymakers, and other thoughtful observers of American elections increasingly used phrases like "broken" and "out of control" to describe the way we finance House (and Senate) elections. More than 70 campaign finance bills were introduced in the 105th Congress, with a bewildering array of proposals. The GOP leadership, which had come to power promising fundamental reforms, made it clear it was opposed to any legislation that might erode the Republicans' substantial fund-raising advantage. Eventually, the House passed a campaign finance bill over the objections of the leadership, although many members cast a "free vote" for the bill because they knew it would die in the Senate.

Campaign finance regulations needed reform before the 1996 election, but the 1996 campaigns made the need for reform more urgent. In 1996 party officials raised record amounts of "soft money" and directed that money into specific federal campaigns. Coalitions of interest groups spent tens of millions of dollars attacking or defending candidates in "issue advocacy" campaigns and did not disclose their spending or the sources of their funds to the Federal Election Commission (FEC). Groups like the Christian Coalition distributed tens of millions of "nonpartisan" voter guides with thinly disguised endorsements of candidates, again without disclosing their activity. Taken together, these changes may signal a change from candidate-centered campaigns toward campaigns in which coalitions of interest groups and party committees play the central role.

In addition to the particular problems of our electoral finance system, a general issue is the damage inflicted on both the perception and the reality of congressional representativeness. The system's dependence on private money effectively auctions political voice with real policy consequences. Although much research suggests that campaign contributions exert little influence on roll call votes, money can influence the work of the House in other important ways. Hall and Wayman found political action committee (PAC) gifts bias House members' crucial committee work.[3] With legislation increasingly bundled into omnibus bills assembled in long bargaining sessions outside committees, it is increasingly easy for party leaders to reward generous interests, as a large tobacco windfall in the initial 1997 budget demonstrated. Moreover, the "Keating Five" scandal shows money can affect "constituency" service agendas. Beyond the reality, the inevitable press exposés of such "mutual aid society" escapades breed public cynicism about the influence of money on government business.

The growing circumvention of disclosure requirements also threatens to eat away at public confidence in congressional representativeness. Public trust in the procedural fairness of government depends on the belief that citizens can readily obtain information about the activities of those who rule.[4] If the public becomes convinced the true financing of elections is largely secret, this belief is likely to exacerbate the already pervasive suspicion "special interests" have hijacked the legislative process. Absent effective disclosure, the public would know only that much is hidden and infer the worst from whatever explodes in the occasional lurid press anecdote. Overall, the current system of financing campaigns is slowly eroding the legitimacy of the House.

THE SYSTEM CRUMBLES

The Federal Election Campaign Act (FECA) amendments of 1974 established a system of private financing of congressional campaigns (a provision for public financing was dropped in conference), with limits on the amounts that parties, interest groups through PACs, individuals, and candidates could contribute to or spend on behalf of campaigns. This regulatory regime never was put into practice, for almost immediately the U.S. Supreme Court struck down portions of FECA in *Buckley v. Valeo* and allowed private citizens and interest groups to spend unlimited amounts of money to independently advocate the election or defeat of candidates.[5] In 1979 Congress allowed individuals and groups to give unlimited amounts to the parties to help build infrastructure, mobilize voters, and elect state and local candidates. Recent Supreme Court decisions have allowed party committees to spend unlimited amounts independently to advocate election of specific candidates and allowed interest groups to spend unlimited amounts to promote issue positions in advertisements that mention candidates by name. By 1996 the regulatory regime for House campaigns bore little resemblance to the system designed by Congress 22 years earlier.

The critiques of the financing of House and Senate campaigns are many and varied. This chapter focuses on three problems that are sometimes linked in the debate to issues of representativeness: the rising costs of campaigns, the growing number of routes around contribution limits, and the increasingly porous nature of the disclosure system.

When politicians and reform groups indict the campaign finance system, they regularly focus on the costs of campaigns. There is little doubt that the costs of House campaigns are increasing more rapidly than inflation. In 1996 House general election candidates spent nearly $420 million, a figure dramatically higher than the $230 million spent in 1988. In 1996 the costs of beating an incumbent appear to have risen sharply. In 1992 the median spending by a victorious House challenger was somewhat less than $400,000, while in 1996 the figure approached $1 million. Incumbents who won close races and open-seat candidate winners spent on average more than $700,000 in 1996.

Although many reformers cite the high costs of election as a problem *per se*, most of these expenditures involve communicating with voters through television, radio, and direct mail. Electoral competition must entail a vigorous debate, and the costs of communicating the arguments of congressional candidates in 1996 were, in fact, less than the costs of explaining to consumers the differences among various brands of beer. We do not believe that House elections are necessarily too expensive, but we think it probable the high costs of mounting a successful campaign constitute a barrier to entry for many prospective candidates, especially those with fewer personal resources and those who may lack ties to wealthy interest groups. Facing an incumbent with a substantial war chest and the ability to raise money rapidly and easily, some prospective candidates may choose to forgo a challenge.

Early money is very important to nonincumbent candidates, for it gives them access to consultants, polls, and early advertising to gain name recognition—all of which helps them raise more money later in the campaign.[6] This "seed money" comes from many sources—party committees, interest groups, and the candidate's own bank account.[7] Seed money is available for certain kinds of candidates—those backed by labor unions or women's groups, for example, or those with ties to party leaders—but without access to these pools of cash nonincumbents must rely on their own resources to launch their campaigns, occasionally taking out second mortgages on their own homes.[8] If the costs of campaigns deter candidates who lack personal resources or ties to wealthy groups, the diversity of positions represented in congressional elections will be diminished, and the representativeness of the House will be limited.

A second critique is that the current system allows special interests to dominate the financing of campaigns at the expense of ordinary citizens. Although the goal of the original FECA amendments was to limit the influence of any single group, today there are many ways that groups can influence a specific election. A PAC can give $10,000 to any candidate who runs in a primary and general election and can collect individual contributions from the members of the group and pass them along to the candidate in a bundle. Large companies often can contribute sizable sums to candidates. The nonpartisan Center for Responsive Politics reports in 1996 Amway bundled more than $144,000 to Sue Myrick (R-NC), and groups bundled far larger sums in Senate races. In theory bundling is reported to the FEC, although in practice much corporate bundling goes unreported.

PACs also can spend unlimited amounts to advocate the election or defeat of a candidate in *independent expenditures*. Historically, most independent expenditures have been focused on presidential and Senate contests, but in a few House races independent expenditures have been substantial. In 1986 the American Medical Association (AMA) spent more than $250,000 to advocate the election of David Williams, who challenged Pete Stark. Williams raised only slightly more than $60,000; AMA thus had more to say on behalf of Williams than the candidate was able to say himself. In 1996 PACs spent nearly $3.0 million on behalf of, and more than $1.6 million against, House candidates.

Groups also can give unlimited amounts of money to parties as "soft money," which in theory is to go to building the parties and electing state and local candidates but not federal candidates, but in practice both parties have found ways to channel soft money into specific House races.[9] In 1996 party soft money receipts skyrocketed—in 1992 the parties raised less than $90 million, but in 1996 the total was substantially more than $250 million, and in 1998 the parties raised far more than they had in the 1994 elections. The parties used this money for many purposes, including "issue advertising" that clearly was intended to promote specific federal candidates. Major soft money donors in the past, such as Gallo Wines and Archer-Daniels Midland Corporation, have received particularistic benefits from Congress. In 1996 the leading soft money contributors were Phillip Morris, Seagrams, RJR Nabisco, and the Walt Disney Company. Phillip Morris gave more than $3 million, mostly to the GOP. Soft money from tobacco companies may have influenced a 1997 budget bill that provided the industry with an almost $85 billion subsidy, although that provision was withdrawn after it was exposed by the *Washington Post*. In 1998 a U.S. district judge ruled bans on foreign contributions do not apply to soft money, opening the door for parties to seek large contributions from overseas interests.

Bundling, independent expenditures, and soft money are disclosed to the Federal Election Commission, but interest groups have other ways to help candidates and parties that are not disclosed. In 1996 coalitions of interest groups spent tens of millions of dollars in "issue advocacy campaigns" that often featured pictures of federal candidates but did not use any of the "magic words" (e.g., "vote for," "support," "defeat") that the Supreme Court has ruled constitute direct electoral advocacy. In theory issue advocacy allows groups to voice their concerns on the issues of the day without endorsing candidates, but in practice advertisements in 1996 clearly were aimed at electing or defeating candidates. The American Federation of Labor and Congress of Industrial Organizations (AFL–CIO) claims to have spent $35 million in specially targeted House races, often in collaboration with the Sierra Club and National Abortion and Reproductive Rights Action League (NARAL). The National Federation of Independent Businesses (NFIB) led a coalition of groups that countered such advertisements. In many House races, the totals spent in issue advocacy campaigns dwarfed the money spent by the candidates, and the candidates themselves often complained that their campaigns were no longer under their control.[10] Issue advocacy was less salient in the 1998 campaigns, and it is too early to tell if the 1996 or 1998 elections will be more typical of the role of such communications.

Other organizations specialized in "nonpartisan" voter mobilization efforts, although the nature of the communications and their targeting suggest a clear partisan intent. The Christian Coalition distributed tens of million of voters' guides in conservative churches across the country that provided pictures of the candidates, summarized their positions, and encouraged conservative Christians to vote. These guides made it clear which candidates the coalition favored, both with unflattering portraits of Democratic candidates and with misrepresentation of their issue positions; FEC is suing the coalition for illegal corporate contributions. Such efforts are so clearly partisan that party committees often make contributions directly to these organizations to aid the efforts. The Republican Senatorial Campaign Committee (RSCC) gave $175,000 to the National Right to Life Committee in 1994, for example. Because many of these groups have a quasi-party function, contributions to them by other interest groups (not disclosed to the FEC) constitute yet another way for organized interests to give to parties.

Parties and party leaders also have formed a dazzling variety of policy institutes, foundations, and think tanks, each of which can raise money from private interests and aid the party and party candidates in a variety of ways. GOPAC raised millions of dollars that were spent to help build a Republican majority, and its contributors, whose identities have not been disclosed, were promised in fund-raising letters to be able to work with Newt Gingrich directly. In July 1997 the Senate hearings into campaign finance issues disclosed that the GOP National Policy Forum, which developed issue positions for Republican candidates and kept GOP consultants and activists on its payroll, sponsored conferences on issues that ran simultaneously with House and Senate markups, at which committee chairs and industry representatives could exchange views. Corporations that sent representatives to these conferences were asked to make large, sometimes six-figure contributions.

By the end of the 1996 election cycle there existed myriad ways for organized groups to channel resources to parties and candidates, and there were no practical limits on this support. These gifts ensure groups at least access to policymakers, making it likely that the communications that members receive from citizens are increasingly unrepresentative of constituency opinion. The rapidly multiplying channels for big donations also increase citizen cynicism about the political process. Because many of the new paths for group resources do not depend on donations PACs raise from their members but instead come primarily from group treasuries, there is less citizen input to the process.

There are two other troubling implications of many of these latter routes for group access. First, increasing amounts of campaign resources are being channeled "off the books" in activity that is not disclosed to the Federal Election Commission. When corporations form PACs and raise money from executives and stockholders to give to candidates, it is possible for journalists and political scientists to "follow the money." When corporations give to GOPAC, the National Policy Forum, or the Christian Coalition, or when they spend money to buy advertising that implicitly endorses candidates, it is impossible to trace it all. These developments threaten to undermine the greatest success of FECA— the disclosure system and its resulting transparency.

Moreover, as groups and parties mount campaigns on behalf of candidates, select issues and themes for their advertisements, and make public claims, accountability is diminished. If a candidate makes a false claim about her or his opponent, voters may hold that candidate accountable. When a coalition of interest groups makes the same misleading claim, there is little to constrain them. The issue advocacy campaigns of 1996 are likely to be a precursor of heavily concentrated efforts by coalitions of groups to influence elections, with millions of dollars spent speaking for candidates who in turn have less money to make their own case to the voters.

Indeed, in the 1996 campaign a variety of groups were formed, solely to spend issue advocacy money in campaigns. Some of these "issues" were narrowly confined to particular races, including one ad that accused a candidate of beating his wife. The groups spent millions of dollars, but voters in the district had no way of knowing who was giving this money or what their true agenda was. A Washington, D.C.,-based company, TRIAD Corporation, created several such groups and channeled money from wealthy conservatives to groups that would spend it in close races. The company is under investigation for coordinating its activities with campaigns and for allowing contributors to bypass the contribution limits.

A THOUSAND REFORMS BLOOM

More than 70 campaign finance reform bills were introduced in the 105th Congress, and these bills contained a vast diversity of proposals. Some advocated public financing, while others unleashed parties to collect and spend private money; some would have imposed strict spending limits; and one would have eliminated all limits; some encouraged small individual donations, others encouraged gifts from within the district, and others increased the limit on all individual gifts.

Despite the best (or, rather, worst) efforts of the Republican leadership in both chambers, congressional supporters of campaign finance reform managed to force roll call floor votes and win majorities in the second session of the 105th Congress. A bipartisan coalition mounted a discharge petition, forcing the Speaker to agree to a vote on reform. Remarkably, the House passed the Shays-Meehan bill, which would have banned all party soft money at the national and subnational levels. It would have made it easier to raise hard money by doubling the individual overall contribution limit and indexing contribution limits to candidates and committees to inflation. The bill also would have changed the definition of express advocacy to bring issue advocacy advertisements under FECA regulation and required candidates to file their reports electronically. The House decisively rejected the only seriously competing proposal, advanced by a bipartisan group of freshmen. The weaker bill, which garnered only 147 votes, would have allowed state and local party organizations to raise soft money, prohibited only national party organizations from raising and spending soft money, and not required disclosure of issue ads. The victory was all the more surprising given the procedural barricades built by reform opponents. In the House, reform proposals had to win under a set of exotic rules dubbed "Queen of the Hill," in which only the reform proposal that passed with the most votes would be forwarded to the Senate. The House leadership further stacked the deck against Shays-Meehan by allowing consideration of 258 amendments.

Nevertheless, the Shays-Meehan bill passed by a 252–179 majority. Editorial pages throughout the nation hailed the passage of the bill. The *New York Times* praised reform leaders for demonstrating that "standing up for principles can mobilize public opinion and change the accepted rules of the game."[11] But the victory proved short-lived. Senate Majority Leader Trent Lott (R-MI) and Senator Mitch McConnell (R-KY) engineered an ultimately successful filibuster against the Senate's Shays-Meehan counterpart, sponsored by Senators John McCain (R-AZ) and Russell Feingold (D-WI). Although 52 senators voted for cloture, Senator McCain surrendered to the minority and withdrew his measure, thus ending prospects for reform in the 105th Congress.

In some ways it is surprising a truly bipartisan reform coalition in the House was able to pass such a bill over the objections of the GOP leadership. Yet the ultimate failure of reform in an election year marked by heightened attention to fund-raising irregularities is sobering. The House Republicans, once the proponents of truly radical reform, now benefit from the system, and although the class of 1994 continues to agitate for reform, their cries become increasingly muted as they scramble to build campaign war chests. Democrats, desperate to recapture control before the GOP majority becomes firmly entrenched, decry soft money as they increasingly rely on it to counter the growing Republican advantage in PAC contributions. With campaign finance dead in the 105th Congress, however, attention has already turned to the future. With the GOP retaining control of the House and Senate in the 1998 elections, reform may be even less likely in the 106th Congress. There is little consensus among politicians or scholars about what should or will happen in the 106th House.

Teams of political scientists have proposed significant reforms, but there has been no clear consensus about the nature of the problems or the solutions. A task force assembled by Herbert Alexander issued a thoughtful and provocative report and set of recommendations (http://www.usc.edu/dept/CRF/DATA/ne-wrnewt.htm), but the nine leading scholars generated three separate dissents on such serious topics as spending limits, limits on party contributions, and constitutional issues. Despite some overlapping personnel, the proposals differ somewhat from the proposals issued by the Brookings Working Group (http://www.brookings.edu/GS/NEWCFR/reform.htm).

Although campaign reform did not pass the 105th Congress, reform is clearly on the public agenda. Major national newspapers have focused serious attention on the issue, scholars who study campaign finance reform are issuing proposals, philanthropic foundations are funding studies, and polls show that the public is deeply dissatisfied with the status quo. One poll funded by the Pew Charitable Trust indicated that a majority of Americans believe that money "gives one group more influence by keeping another from having its fair say." The pretest of a survey of congressional contributors funded by the Joyce Foundation revealed that even a majority of House contributors favored fundamental campaign finance reform.

What kinds of reforms would lead to a more representative House? If the high costs of campaigns deter some candidates, we might increase the diversity of voices in elections by lowering the costs of launching a campaign. Partial public funding for general and perhaps primary election candidates could provide seed money that would let candidates communicate their messages. Subsidies or free media time might also encourage candidates to run; the Brookings Working Group has proposed a broadcast bank that would provide free time to candidates and parties in general election campaigns. The task force suggested a higher limit for the first contributions received by a campaign to make it easier to raise seed money. Reforms like these would allow challengers to make their case and see if the public responds and perhaps encourage a more representative pool of candidates.

The problems of unlimited contributions and spending by groups cannot be fully solved under current U.S. Supreme Court rulings, and although we might prefer a more nuanced reading of the 1st Amendment, electoral campaigns are clearly at the core of protected speech. Banning or strictly limiting soft money while increasing the contribution limits for hard money to the parties seems a necessary first step. Indeed, a survey of small and large contributors conducted by one of us shows that more than three-quarters of all contributors would favor eliminating soft money, including a sizable majority of those who make such contributions. Several proposals would limit issue advocacy by attempting to define much of it as campaign activity or by banning the use of corporate and labor treasury funds. Incentives for small contributions might help candidates find alternative sources of funding. If there is partial public funding, it would be possible to structure the system to discourage issue advocacy campaigns by providing offsetting funds to those candidates who face substantial independent expenditures or issue advocacy advertising.

Strengthening the disclosure system is essential to restoring public trust. By requiring the disclosure of the sources and spending of money for issue advocacy and of the funding of partisan think tanks, foundations, and other quasi-party groups, it would be possible to maintain at least a rudimentary understanding of where the money comes from and where it goes. The task force further recommended that no committee be able to spend a contribution of more than $200 unless it is able to provide full information about the donor—name, address, and principal place of business. To encourage accountability, reforms might channel money through candidates and parties by raising the contribution limits to both. Indeed, even PACs, once the scourge of campaign finance reformers, are significantly more accountable than coalitions of groups buying issue advocacy ads, so limits to PACs might be raised as well.

DELEGITIMATION ON THE INSTALLMENT PLAN?

The alternative to reform, and the most likely short-term prospect, is continuation with what might be termed ''delegitimation on the installment plan.'' Absent reform, soft money, issue advocacy, and activity outside the disclosure laws probably will dominate future congressional elections. Thus, the current trends will yet again advance toward the point where they begin to endanger the legitimacy of the political system. Legitimacy depends on perceptions of procedural fairness.[12] The public already believes that the current election finance system privileges affluent organized interests. Indeed, a recent Pew Center poll reported that ''the power of special interest groups in politics'' ranked statistically even with ''international terrorism'' as the most frequently named threat to the nation's future.[13] Contrary to popular wisdom, a *New York Times/* CBS News poll found that the relative absence of public action owes not to apathy but to demoralization over the conclusion that neither party will enact reform.[14] In the aftermath of the Oklahoma City bombing, however, the system needs proactive, effective reform to spare the Republic from the kinds of reform movements that might eventually come roaring out of deeper public cynicism and despair.

NOTES

This chapter is a revised version of an article—''Dead Law: The Federal Election Finance Regulations, 1974–1996''—that appeared in *PS: Political Science and Politics*, vol. 31, no. 1, March 1998, pp. 14–17.

1. Russell Feingold, *Congressional Record*, January 21, 1997, p. S385.

2. Norman J. Ornstein, Thomas E. Mann, Paul Taylor, Michael J. Malbin, and Anthony Corrado, Jr., *New Campaign Finance Reform Proposals for the 105th Congress* (Washington, DC: Brookings Institution, 1996).

3. Richard L. Hall and Frank W. Wayman, "Buying Time: The Moneyed Interests and the Mobilization of Bias in Congressional Committees," *The American Political Science Review*, September 1990, pp. 797–820.

4. Mark E. Warren, "Democracy and Trust," paper presented at the annual meeting of the American Political Science Association, San Francisco, August 1996.

5. *Buckley v. Valeo*, 424 U.S. 1 (1976).

6. Robert Biersack, Paul S. Herrnson, and Clyde Wilcox, "Seeds for Success: Early Money in Congressional Elections," *Legislative Studies Quarterly*, vol. 18, November 1994, pp. 535–52.

7. Clyde Wilcox, "I Owe It All to Me: Candidates' Investments in Their Own Campaign," *American Politics Quarterly*, September 1988, pp. 266–79.

8. Paul Herrnson, *Honest Graft: Campaign Finance Reform and Political Parties* (Los Angeles: Citizen's Research Foundation, 1997).

9. Ibid.

10. Guy Gugliotta and Ira Chinoy, "Outsiders Made Erie Ballot a National Battle," *Washington Post*, February 10, 1997, p. A1.

11. "A Victory for Shays-Meehan," *New York Times*, August 7, 1998, p. A20.

12. E. Allan Lind and Tom R. Tyler, *The Social Psychology of Procedural Justice* (New York: Plenum Press, 1988); Tom R. Tyler, *Why People Obey the Law* (New Haven, CT: Yale University Press, 1990).

13. Francis X. Clines, "Most Doubt a Resolve to Change Campaign Financing, Poll Finds," *New York Times*, April 8, 1997, p. 1.

14. Ibid.

Chapter 7

Money and the Incumbency Advantage in U.S. House Elections

Ronald Keith Gaddie and Lesli E. McCollum

The lack of competition in House elections has been an area of concern for congressional scholars since the mid-1970s. It has been attributed to the benefits enjoyed by incumbents, who are able to increase their electoral success through connections with their constituencies, which result in the decline in the number of closely contested races. In the last three election years, during which there has been a change in majority party and a substantial increase in descriptive representation of women, Latinos, and blacks, incumbents nonetheless were re-elected at rates of 89.9 percent (1992), 91.4 percent (1994), and 94.6 percent (1996). Of the 273 new legislators elected in regularly scheduled elections between 1992 and 1996, 183 (67%) were elected via open seats, while only 83 (30%) defeated incumbents.

Scholars argue that stellar rates of retention in congressional elections undermine the representativeness of the electoral system since opportunities for challengers are limited, and incumbents become insulated from the public. David Mayhew, in bringing attention to the demise of competitive incumbent elections, concluded that entrenched and unchallenged incumbents isolated government from the public, thereby stagnating the institution by limiting turnover to what at the time were increasingly rare open seats,[1] Sandy Maisel subsequently argued that "[o]nly through elections can the citizens hold the government accountable; and only through competition can elections be effective agents of democracy"; therefore, secure incumbents divorced government from accessibility and accountability.[2] Because the very electoral system that is supposed to ensure representativeness now is being accused of perpetuating the opposite, the reasons for low competition in House elections should be explored.

This chapter examines the nature of the incumbency advantage, with a particular focus on the 1996 elections. Specifically, we assess the extent to which incumbents are effectively using their positions to attract more money and therefore secure electoral success. We explore the relationship between money and incumbent security from three dimensions: (1) we highlight the financial advantages of incumbents over their challengers through time; (2) we describe the institutional structure of relationships between incumbent legislators and special interests that contribute to the financial advantages that incumbents enjoy over challengers; and (3) we test the relationship between the size of the incumbency advantage and levels of spending by incumbents and challengers. In the end, we offer suggestions for making congressional elections more competitive.

FINANCIAL ADVANTAGES OF INCUMBENTS OVER CHALLENGERS

The root causes of the incumbency advantage in congressional elections, the extent of the advantage, and the consequences of an entrenched incumbency for representative democracy have been the subject of extensive research.[3] One of the most common explanations for the incumbency advantage is money: incumbents, by virtue of their political positions, are able to attract and spend more money in their campaigns than challengers.[4] Incumbents' use of political office to attract valuable political assets has been characterized as "rent-seeking" behavior.[5] Because they perceive the need for ample money to secure reelection, incumbents in competitive situations will discount their price for providing legislation and thereby attract rents in the form of campaign finance. There is ample empirical evidence to support the rent-seeking model, including sophisticated, multivariate studies of corporate, labor, and trade political action committees (PACs).[6] The challengers who emerge to contest incumbents are often underfunded, either due to their own poor connections or because of the unwillingness of political contributors to finance their campaigns.[7]

The tremendous advantage possessed by incumbents, when accessing sources of campaign finance, contributes to the magnitude of incumbent spending advantage and has been pointed to as a principal component of incumbent safety (see Chapter 6 in this volume). Jacobson observed the spending habits of incumbents have become less reactive and more preemptive.[8] In a series of bivariate regression analyses of the relationship between challenger and incumbent spending, Jacobson observed the changes in incumbent spending as related to changes in challenger spending have been relatively stable since the 1970s. The slope of the increase in incumbent spending, as it relates to challenger spending, varied between $.49 and $.82 spent by an incumbent for every additional $1.00 spent by challengers (constant 1994 dollars). However, in general, incumbents dramatically have increased spending. In Figure 7.1 we graph the intercepts, from year to year, of these regressions. The intercept, which reflects the amount of money spent by an incumbent assuming no challenger spending, increased from $116,000 in 1972, to over $450,000 in 1996 (constant 1994 dollars). In-

Figure 7.1
Estimated Incumbent Spending, Assuming No Challenger Expenditures, 1972–1996

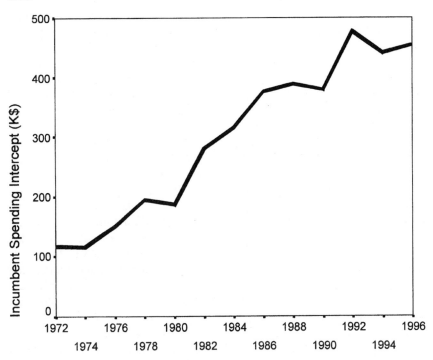

cumbents are investing more money in campaigns even without a serious financial challenge.

Even when challengers spend money, they are at a disadvantage. Incumbents have outspent their general election challengers by approximately 3:1 since 1982. In the most recent election at the time of this writing, 1996, the ratio of incumbent to challenger spending was down slightly to 2.5:1. The average amount of money spent by an incumbent in 1996 was over $660,000, compared to the average challenger expenditure of $255,000. Only 25 challengers—eighteen Republicans and seven Democrats—outspent their incumbent opponents, and an additional thirteen spent the same as the incumbent. Another 87 challengers were outspent by only 2:1. However, a majority of challengers found themselves to be financially completely outclassed, being outspent by the incumbent by more than 5:1; a plurality (159 or 43.6% of challengers) were outspent by more than 10:1. Most incumbents enjoyed a definite spending advantage, and for many, the advantage was overwhelming to the point that the opposition was literally buried in an avalanche of incumbent spending.

ON FUND-RAISING AND DETERRENCE: THE RENT-SEEKING LEGISLATURE

The ability of incumbents to attain safe reelection depends on deterring challengers and suppressing the ability of opponents to raise and spend large amounts of money. To no small extent this ability derives from the connections incumbents make in the fund-raising community. Challengers in congressional elections rely heavily on individual contributions to finance their campaigns. In the 1980s challengers typically raised less than 20 percent of their money from PACs; by comparison, incumbents garnered almost one-half of their campaign cash from PACs, and PACs gave over 75 percent of their money to incumbents.

According to all of the major research on PACs, they prefer incumbent legislators because they are better positioned to affect legislation, influence bureaucracies, and generally help interest groups obtain their political and policy goals. The division of the House of Representatives into highly specialized committees corresponds closely to the structure of the regulatory bureaucracy and to the organization of interest groups. For example, the Environmental Protection Agency is under the principal oversight of four House committees. Contributions by PACs affiliated with polluting industries that bear the weight of costs for air pollution control tend to track to those principal oversight committees.[9] PACs give money in a manner reflecting the concerns of George Stigler's economic theory of regulation: they give to legislators who can affect the bureaucracy overseeing industry regulation.[10]

PACs tend to be pragmatic in their campaign contributions; they donate money to incumbents of both political parties. A recent study of the changes in allocation strategies by corporate political action committees in the 1990s uncovered evidence that, despite the changes in the majority party in Congress, corporations continue to pursue a bipartisan strategy to protect incumbents in both parties while largely ignoring challengers.[11] Interviews with corporate PAC directors echoed what previous research had indicated before the change in party control: PACs have friends in both parties who can affect policy, and, while they have partisan preferences that make Republicans more attractive, the reality of a helpful incumbent is of greater value than the possibility of an even more helpful challenger.

The work of Kevin Grier and Michael Munger warrants close scrutiny by scholars interested in how PACs structure behavior.[12] Their tests of Denzau and Munger's thesis of rent-seeking behavior by legislators on four broad categories of economic PACs—corporations, labor unions, trade associations, and cooperatives—lent systematic, empirical evidence to support the argument that institutional advantages to incumbents structured political action.[13] The results of their analysis indicated institutional power was especially important in structuring donations to House members. The extensive committee system and formal rules of debate reinforce the influence of the majority party and committees on the shape of legislation as it passes through the House. The works of Eismeier and Pollock, Gopoian, and Wright also support the argument economic political action committees act in a strategic manner when giving to congressional candidates.[14] The strategy of pragmatic actors makes incumbents a safe investment and makes challengers a risk. We should expect strategic challengers to wait for a better opportunity, such as an open seat, when organized interests will be more willing to invest in their candidacies.[15]

INCUMBENT ADVANTAGE AND LEVELS OF SPENDING

We have seen that incumbents outspend challengers, often by astounding sums of money, and they can secure PAC contributions to a much greater extent than can challengers. Now we need to know how spending relates to incumbent security. Here we ask, How does spending relate to the performance of an incumbent compared to the effects of the baseline competitiveness of a district? In other words, how does money relate to the size of the incumbency advantage?

Before we can test a relationship between spending and an incumbent's advantage, we must establish a baseline of competition to compare with an incumbent's electoral performance. Previous research has relied on normal vote measures (i.e., averages of district partisanship across several elections and offices), sophomore surge or ''slurge'' measures (the change from the first election of an incumbent to the next), or frequencies of ''marginal'' districts to ascertain the incumbency advantage. Part of the debate surrounding whether incumbency benefit has increased or decreased over time arises from the differing methods employed to measure the advantage.

There is no consensus in political science as to the best way to measure the incumbency advantage, although the Gelman/King technique has attracted widespread attention.[16] This technique uses a multiple regression analysis to estimate the influence of a normal vote measure and incumbency on the congressional vote where incumbency is represented by a dummy variable coded 1 for Democratic incumbent, -1 for Republican incumbent, and 0 for an open seat. The slope of the incumbency variable represents the size of the incumbency advantage in a given year. In Figure 7.2 we present the track of the Gelman/King index estimates of the aggregate incumbency advantage since 1972. According to these estimates, incumbency has been worth as much as fourteen points in a given year, and, overall, the value of incumbency has increased substantially in the postwar era. The Gelman/King technique indicates that incumbency was worth 9.5 percent of the vote in 1996.

The Gelman/King measure is useful in that it advances a replicable technique that tracks the phenomenon of the increased value of incumbency and uncovers an increase in the value of incumbency generally associated with the increase in baseline, incumbent spending graphed in Figure 7.1. However, the Gelman/King measure produces a value for incumbency that is constant for a given year. Possible variations in the value of incumbency for different incumbents are not detected by this technique. Gelman and King significantly advanced the debate

Figure 7.2
The Gelman/King Incumbency Advantage, 1972–1996

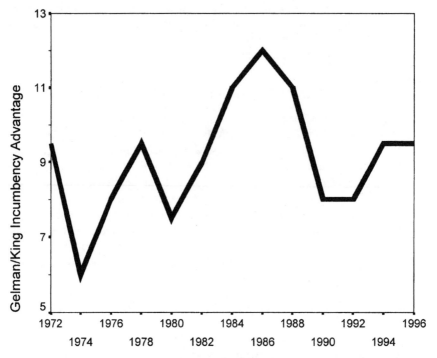

by using all elections in a given year as the basis for a regression estimate of incumbency in that year. But their approach does not account for variations in the value of incumbency for different incumbents in the same year.

The measure that comes closest to approximating the difference in competition is the sophomore surge and retirement slump. It is reasonable to expect the initial election of a legislator and the election after his or her retirement are more competitive. The surge of support for a first-termer and the subsequent falloff after retirement allow us to measure the change in party competition that surrounds incumbency. This approach gets at the personal advantage of an incumbent and separates the effects of "personal incumbency advantage" from party advantage. Alford and Brady cited the benefits from this method:

By focusing on a single district and a set of adjacent elections, it controls for district characteristics. By determining the difference between an incumbent performance and an open-seat performance, the measurement removes from gross incumbency advantage that portion attributable to partisan advantage, as reflected by the party's performance in an open-seat contest. The remainder is the net personal advantage enjoyed by the incumbent, above and beyond that which comes from the partisan or party organizational strength of the district itself.[17]

Surge/slump analysis tells us how a party did in a district preceding and following an incumbent, but it does not necessarily tell us how that party would do in a given year absent the incumbent. It also limits the scope of cases to be examined because most incumbents do not retire or seek initial reelection every year (the largest number of open seats in the last half century was 80 in 1992). Our analysis requires a direct estimate of the baseline of competitiveness in a district that does not rely entirely on normal vote measures and that can be estimated for all districts.

Our solution to this problem is found in the emergent literature on open seats that lends insight into the structure of competitiveness and advantage in House elections. Some districts are highly competitive in the absence of an incumbent; others are safe, from a partisan perspective, regardless of whether an incumbent runs or not. We expect open-seat elections to be generally more competitive than incumbent elections, but it does not mean that all open seats are competitive. Competitiveness and advantage are indeed two separate concepts.[18] While competitiveness may occur in open-seat and incumbent races, incumbency advantage is not a factor in open-seat races.[19] The incumbency advantage is the difference between the incumbent's vote and the vote that would have occurred had a seat been open, much like the surge/slump measure. Our measure must answer the question, How competitive is a district absent the incumbent?

In order to answer this question, we applied the findings of the research on open seats. Research on open seats has produced a statistical model that is very effective in predicting the vote in nonincumbent races. These models are developed using the statistical technique of multiple regression, which estimates the relationship between independent variables—in this case, the factors that explain election outcomes—and a dependent variable—in this case, the vote in the open-seat election. In another study, we used open-seat elections from 1988 to 1996 to estimate a regression equation for competition for those districts. Then we entered data on all elections into the regression equation to produce estimated votes for all districts *as if they were open*. A full description of this technique is beyond the space available, although a brief description and demonstration appear in the notes to this chapter.[20] The difference between the estimated open-seat vote for each district and the actual vote with the incumbent present indicates the magnitude of the incumbency advantage.[21]

Of the 384 incumbents who sought reelection in 1996, 19 were unopposed for reelection, and only 21 were defeated. Incumbents were not only returned to office but returned by large margins. As indicated in Figure 7.3, fewer than 15 percent of incumbent contests fell in Mayhew's marginal range (GOP candidate vote between 45% and 55%). If we expand the marginals to include the 40 percent to 60 percent range, just over one-third of contests were marginal. The average difference between the incumbent's reelection vote and the open-seat prediction was 8.5 percent, which is slightly lower than the 9.5 percent advantage detected using the Gelman/King technique.

How do these contests compare to the estimated levels of two-party compe-

Figure 7.3
Competition with and without Incumbents, 1996

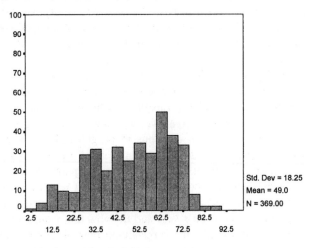

Std. Dev = 18.25
Mean = 49.0
N = 369.00

GOP Share of Two-Party Vote

A. Competition in Incumbent Races in 1996

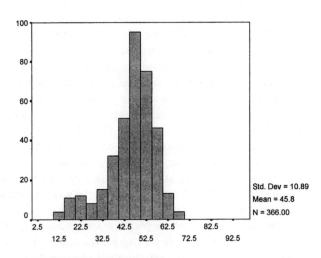

Std. Dev = 10.89
Mean = 45.8
N = 366.00

Predicted GOP Two-Party Vote

B. Predicted Competition without Incumbents

Figure 7.4
**The Distribution of the Incumbency Advantage and Incumbent Reelection
Margins in 1996**

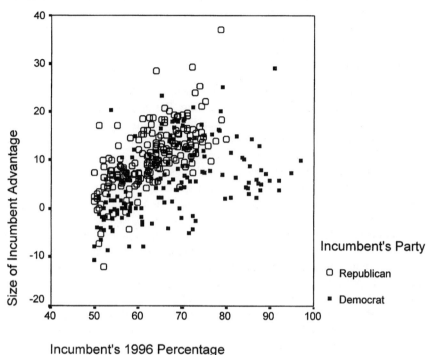

Incumbent's 1996 Percentage

tition in those districts generated by the model? As indicated in the second part
of Figure 7.3, the technique we used to estimate competition produced a distribution that has a mean skewed toward the Democratic Party. Almost one-half
of the incumbent contests from 1996 would have been marginal open seats,
according to the model. Despite the removal of incumbency, there are still about
80 very safe Democratic districts (Democrats receive over 70% of the vote), but
only about 20 districts where the Republican would garner over 60 percent of
the vote. These figures indicate Republicans in 1996 derived substantial benefits
from incumbency.

There are partisan differences evident in the distribution of the incumbency
advantage. In Figure 7.4, the incumbent's share of the two-party vote in 1996
is plotted along the x-axis; the size of the incumbency advantage (the incumbent's vote minus the estimated vote in the absence of an incumbent) is plotted
along the y-axis. Democratic incumbents are indicated by solid squares; Republicans, by open circles. The cloud of Republican points is less dispersed than
the cloud of Democratic points. In several districts the Democratic incumbent
received over 70 percent of the vote, but no substantial incumbency advantage

was evident. There are also Democratic districts where the incumbents ran behind the open-seat projection, despite receiving pluralities that lie outside the marginal range. Many of these seats are simply very safe Democratic constituencies in which the incumbent has little incentive to try to build his/her partisan reelection constituency.[22]

INCUMBENT SPENDING AND DISTRICT COMPETITION

We observed that in the aggregate, incumbent spending is increasing even in the absence of substantial challenger spending. Further, we noticed challengers still pale when compared to incumbents on the spending dimension. Finally, we see there is a baseline of competitiveness within districts that accounts for some of incumbents' retention rates. In this part of the chapter we examine the pattern of incumbent and challenger spending and look for relationships between the partisan security of a district and candidate spending. We next demonstrate the relationship between the incumbency advantage and spending by incumbents and challengers.

Incumbents who ran for reelection in highly competitive districts spent significantly more money than incumbents running in safer districts. To decide which districts were, at base, marginal or nonmarginal, we examined the predicted vote generated from our regression analysis in the last section. If we segregate the congressional districts by Mayhew's marginal criteria—more or less than 55 percent of likely vote (see Table 7.1)—we see that, among both Democrats and Republicans, incumbents running in districts with a marginal partisan base spent an average of $300,000 more than did incumbents in the districts with nonmarginal expected composition. Challenger spending is also discriminating along these lines. In districts where the out-party has a larger potential base, challengers of both parties spent more money, especially with Republican challengers, who spent an average of over $430,000 in districts where the incumbent party's expected vote, absent the incumbent, was less than 55 percent. In districts where a Democratic incumbent's expected baseline vote was over 55 percent, Republican challengers spent an average of just over $200,000. The relative financial advantage of the incumbent also is related to the partisan baseline: incumbents who have nonmarginal districts outspent their challengers, on average, by 2.5:1 (Democrats) and 3.6:1 (Republicans); in "marginal" districts the ratio still favored incumbents, although the average was reduced (1.9:1 for Democrats, 2.9:1 for Republicans).

Incumbent and challenger spending are related to the potential vulnerability of the district. Incumbents who do not have large partisan bases to draw on spend substantially more money seeking reelection; the challengers they face spend more money, on average, because the potential basis of support for their campaign is greater than in the safe districts of the incumbent party.

Does spending translate into large incumbency advantage? The descriptive data in Table 7.2 indicate the opposite is the case. When incumbents have small

Table 7.1
Campaign Spending and District Partisan Base

Incumbent Spending

	Incumbent's Party	
Estimated Incumbent Base	Democrats	Republicans
< 55%	823897 (N = 57)	738785 (N = 130)
> 55%	516455 (N = 118)	624918 (N = 60)

Challenger Spending

	Challenger's Party	
Estimated Incumbent Base	Democrats	Republicans
< 55%	265786 (N = 130)	431557 (N = 57)
> 55%	171525 (N = 60)	202352 (N = 118)

Cell entries are average expenditures, expressed in 1996 dollars.

advantages over the partisan base, they and their opponents spend large amounts of money. When incumbents' advantage is large, between 10 and 20 points, incumbents spend on average about one-half of what their less secure colleagues spend. The spending by challengers falls off even more. Challengers to incumbents with advantages between 10 and 20 points spent less than one-third of the money spent by challengers with small advantages (see Table 7.2).

The relationship between the size of the incumbency advantage, the incumbent's reelection percentage, and candidate spending becomes clearer when we compute the average incumbent reelection percentage and the average incumbency advantage, based on levels of incumbent and challenger spending, respectively (see Table 7.3). The highest incumbent reelection percentages are associated with low levels of incumbent and challenger spending; the lowest levels of incumbent reelection percentage are evident in the most expensive races. The range of the average incumbent reelection percentage is the same for incumbent and challenger spending: incumbents who spend less than $250,000 run, on average, fifteen points ahead of incumbents who spend more than $1 million. Incumbents who face challengers spending less than $100,000 run, on average, seventeen points ahead of incumbents who face challengers spending more than $750,000.

Table 7.2
Campaign Spending and the Size of the Incumbency Advantage in 1996

	Incumbent Spending	
Incumbent's Advantage	Democrat	Republican
< 10%	678738 (N = 121)	885053 (N = 85)
10-20%	513767 (N = 42)	591970 (N = 89)
> 20%	391756 (N = 6)	430352 (N = 8)

	Challenger Spending	
Incumbent's Advantage	Democrat	Republican
< 10%	387531 (N = 85)	355915 (N = 121)
10-20%	131613 (N = 89)	102143 (N = 42)
> 20%	7415 (N = 8)	186764 (N = 6)

Cell entries average spending by candidate type (incumbents or challengers).

Source: Federal Election Commission (1996) Candidate Summary Statistics File (http://www.fec.gov).

This descriptive analysis verifies the speculation of Jacobson and others regarding the peculiar relationship between incumbent expenditures and the size of the incumbent reelection margin. Research on House elections consistently has found that a linear estimation of the relationship between incumbent spending and the incumbent vote share is either (1) statistically insignificant or (2) negatively related. More incumbent spending usually is not associated with a larger vote for the incumbent. Jacobson remained especially focused on this problem, because a troubling question remained. Why would incumbents spend more money if that activity is not associated with success? Jacobson's approach was to reconsider the nature of the relationship between money and votes. Incumbent spending had a diminishing return for the incumbent. Therefore, an estimation of the relationship is needed to account for the curvilinear relationship of spending and votes. Jacobson initially estimated this relationship with a quadratic decay before settling on a natural log of incumbent and challenger spending.[23] The natural log produced a significant and intuitively pleasing relationship between spending and incumbent vote share.

A similar, counterintuitive pattern is evident with regard to the incumbency advantage; low-spending races are associated with large incumbency advantages.

Table 7.3
Incumbent Spending, Challenger Spending, and the Incumbency Advantage

	Incumbency Advantage		Average Reelection %	
	Category Means	Standard Deviation	Category Means	Standard Deviation
Incumbent Spending Level				
< 250,000 (N = 42)	8.87	8.05	74.48	10.26
250,000–500,000 (N = 110)	10.60	6.89	69.85	8.35
500,000–750,000 (N = 93)	9.41	6.47	63.30	7.21
750,000–1,000,000 (N = 50)	5.99	6.70	59.93	8.18
> 1,000,000 (N = 71)	5.00	6.34	59.40	8.92
Challenger Spending Level				
< 100,000 (N = 185)	11.48	6.54	71.58	8.32
100,000–250,000 (N = 53)	8.37	5.80	65.86	7.23
250,000–500,000 (N = 61)	5.50	5.24	57.96	4.37
500,000–750,000 (N = 37)	3.18	6.83	54.74	3.44
> 750,000 (N = 31)	2.67	6.61	54.25	2.89

Incumbents who spent between $250,000 and $500,000 had an incumbency advantage, on average, five points higher than incumbents who spent more than $1 million. However, the magnitude of the incumbency advantage is more sensitive to challenger spending. When a challenger spends less than $100,000, incumbents enjoy an incumbency advantage of over eleven percentage points, but when challengers spend over $500,000, the incumbency advantage virtually disappears, falling to just over three percentage points. Challenger spending clearly is more strongly associated with the incumbency advantage than is incumbent spending. The impact of money on the incumbent advantage is one of deterrence. Keeping potentially well funded candidates on the sidelines allows incumbents to avoid high-cost campaigns. Once a well-heeled challenger emerges, incumbents are capable of escalating their spending, and they do so accordingly.[24] But the well-heeled challenger already has compromised the large incumbency advantage. It is apparent that the incumbency advantage is a function of incumbents' avoiding well-funded challengers, rather than a function of incumbents' spending large amounts of money.

CONCLUSIONS

Incumbent safety does respond to money; however, challenger spending affects the size of the incumbency advantage. As a general rule, when incumbents spent a large amount of money on reelection, it was because they faced well-funded challengers or represented districts that, at base, were highly competitive and therefore more likely to be marginal. When incumbents faced no real threats to their reelection, expenditures were logically lower. This relationship holds up whether we consider the relationship between spending and the incumbent's vote share or between spending and the size of the incumbency advantage. Challenger spending is the engine that drives the size of the incumbency advantage. If an incumbent is going to have a "safe" reelection, he or she needs either to (1) represent a district that is naturally safe from a partisan perspective or (2) to act to ensure challengers of high financial quality do not enter the contest. Building the incumbency advantage therefore is a product not of the campaign-year politics of outspending the opposition (although that does not hurt) but of the actions that ensure the strategic politicians whom Gary Jacobson, Samuel Kernell, and Thomas Kazee describe so aptly remain out of the active campaign. In consequence, incumbents in part will cultivate their constituency to maintain their perception of impregnability and also maintain good relations with the economic and special interests sufficiently fickle to support candidates of either party.

The consequences for electoral competition are many. To the extent that money influences incumbent safety, it is because incumbents succeed in keeping well-financed challengers out of their districts. In this respect the congressional elections of 1996 were similar to previous elections. Incumbents who were safe were safe because no well-funded opposition emerged to oppose the incumbent. Our analysis indicated challenger spending over $250,000 halved the magnitude of the incumbency advantage; challengers who spent over $500,000 reduced the incumbency advantage by two-thirds of that enjoyed by incumbents without significant financial opposition (less than $100,000). Based on this analysis and the findings of other scholars whose work is cited in this chapter, the key to reducing the incumbency advantage appears to be increasing the financial quality of the challengers in congressional elections.

With regard to increasing challenger financial quality, much has been said, and little has been done. To increase challenger financial quality requires that we either change the perception of challengers among moneyed interests and cause them to shift to a challenger-based strategy of contributing money or change the rules to place more money in the hands of challengers. With regard to the former, such a fundamental change can occur only if moneyed interests are so disgusted with incumbents that they will finance challengers to those incumbents, even if it brings them into conflict with legislators who have oversight in their regulatory community. This possibility is not likely to happen. Even in 1994, when disgust with the Democratic Congress ran high, corporations gave more on average to Democratic incumbents than to Republicans and largely ignored Republican challengers. If corporations cannot be shaken loose of bipartisanship even during a change in political control, the prospects for future disruptions are unlikely.

The latter alternative, changing the rules, has received attention from political scientists and economists for decades, but rule changes confront the economic reality that surrounds reform; any change in the campaign finance rules necessarily will have to pass through the very Congress that benefits from the current campaign finance regime. The efforts at reform in 1992 and 1994 were affected largely by the prospects for success. In 1992 large numbers of Democrats and Republicans voted for sweeping campaign finance change, safe in the knowledge that President George Bush would veto the bill. With a new president in 1994, incumbent House members proved far more reluctant to consider propositions such as spending limits, matching funds, public financing, or PAC reform. The new president was willing to change the law; ergo, the costs of supporting reform were raised because incumbents no longer could vote for reform safe in the knowledge reform would never come about.

NOTES

The authors thank the Carl Albert Center for Congressional Studies at the University of Oklahoma and its director, Professor Ronald F. Peters, for providing support for this research. We also thank Professor Gary Copeland for assistance in completing this research.

1. David W. Mayhew, "Congressional Elections: The Case of the Vanishing Marginals," *Polity*, Summer 1974, pp. 295–317.

2. L. Sandy Maisel, "Quality Candidates in House and Senate Elections, from 1982 to 1990," in Allen D. Hertzke and Ronald M. Peters, Jr., eds., *The Atomistic Congress: An Interpretation of Congressional Change* (Armonk, NY: M. E. Sharpe, 1992), p. 142.

3. See, for example, Alan I. Abramowitz, "Incumbency, Campaign Spending, and the Decline of Competition in U.S. House Elections," *The Journal of Politics*, February 1991, pp. 34–57; Bruce Cain, John Ferejohn, and Morris Fiorina, *The Personal Vote: Constituency Service and Electoral Independence* (Cambridge, MA: Harvard University Press, 1987); Gary C. Jacobson, *The Electoral Origins of Divided Government: Competition in U.S. House Elections, 1946–1988* (Boulder, CO: Westview Press, 1990); Gary C. Jacobson and Samuel Kernell, *Strategy and Choice in Congressional Elections* (New Haven, CT: Yale University Press, 1983); Monica Bauer and John R. Hibbing. "Which Incumbents Lose in House Elections: A Response to Jacobson's 'The Marginals Never Vanished,' " *American Journal of Political Science*, March 1989, pp. 262–72; Paul S. Herrnson, *Congressional Elections: Campaigning at Home and in Washington*, 2nd ed. (Washington, DC: CQ Press, 1997).

4. Jacobson, *The Electoral Origins of Divided Government*.

5. The term "rent seeking" is a relatively recent addition to the lexicon on economics and politics. First described by Gordon Tullock, rent seeking is the practice by firms of seeking regulation that constrains competition and supply and thereby provides additional profits above the marginal cost of production. Several political scientists and economists recently used this concept to describe the behavior of incumbent legislators toward moneyed political interests, particularly Glenn R. Parker, *Congress and the Rent Seeking Society* (Ann Arbor: University of Michigan Press, 1995), and James L. Regens and Ronald Keith Gaddie, *The Economic Realities of Political Reform: Elections and the U.S. Senate* (New York: Cambridge University Press, 1995).

6. Kevin Grier and Michael C. Munger, "Comparing Interest Group PAC Contributions to House and Senate Incumbents, 1980–1986," *The Journal of Politics*, August 1993, pp. 615–44; Regens and Gaddie, *The Economic Realities of Political Reform*.

7. See the case studies in Thomas A. Kazee, ed., *Who Runs for Congress?* (Washington, DC: CQ Press, 1994).

8. Jacobson, *The Electoral Origins of Divided Government*, pp. 68–71.

9. James L. Regens, Euel W. Elliott, and Ronald Keith Gaddie, "Regulatory Costs, Committee Jurisdictions, and Corporate PAC Contributions," *Social Science Quarterly*, December 1991, pp. 751–60.

10. George Stigler, "The Economic Theory of Regulation," *Bell Journal of Economics and Management Science*, Spring 1971, pp. 1–21. See also Morris P. Fiorina, *Congress: Keystone to the Washington Establishment* (New Haven, CT: Yale University Press, 1977).

11. Ronald Keith Gaddie, Jonathan D. Mott, and Shad D. Satterthwaite, "The Partisan Dimension of the Corporate Realignment in Political Action," paper presented at the annual meeting of the American Political Science Association, Boston, September 5, 1998.

12. See, for example, Kevin B. Grier and Michael C. Munger, "Committee Assignments, Constituent Preferences, and Campaign Contributions," *Economic Inquiry*, Spring 1991, pp. 24–43.

13. Arthur T. Denzau and Michael C. Munger, "Legislators and Interest Groups: How Unorganized Interests Get Represented," *The American Political Science Review*, March 1986, pp. 89–106.

14. Theodore J. Eismeier and Philip H. Pollock III, *Business, Money, and the Rise of Corporate PACs* (Westport, CT: Quorom Books, 1988); David J. Gopoian, "What Makes PACs Tick? An Analysis of the Allocation Patterns of Economic Interest Groups," *American Journal of Political Science*, June 1984, pp. 259–81; John R. Wright, "PACs, Contributions, and Roll Calls: An Organizational Perspective," *American Political Science Review*, June 1985, pp. 400–414.

15. Ronald Keith Gaddie, "Investing in the Future: Economic PAC Contributions to Open Seat House Candidates," *American Politics Quarterly*, July 1995, pp. 339–55; Linda L. Fowler and Robert D. McClure, *Political Ambition* (New Haven, CT: Yale University Press, 1989).

16. Andrew Gelman and Gary King, "Estimating Incumbency Advantage without Bias," *American Journal of Political Science*, November 1990, pp. 1142–65.

17. John Alford and David Brady, "Personal and Partisan Advantage in U.S. Congressional Elections, 1846–1986," in Lawrence C. Dodd and Bruce I. Oppenheimer, eds., *Congress Reconsidered*, 4th ed. (Washington, DC: CQ Press, 1989), pp. 147–48.

18. Robert K. Goidel and Todd G. Shields, "The Vanishing Marginals, the Bandwagon, and the Mass Media," *Journal of Politics*, August 1994, pp. 802–10.

19. Melissa P. Collie, "Incumbency, Electoral Safety, and Turnover in the House of Representatives, 1952–1976," *The American Political Science Review*, March 1981, pp. 119–31.

20. The model incorporates the experience measures for both candidates (dichotomous variables indicating whether the candidate held prior elective office), an indication of which candidate has the spending advantage (a nominal variable coded 1 if the GOP candidate has the advantage, and 0 otherwise), a normal vote control for the baseline partisanship of the district, and controls for the black and Hispanic populations in the

district. A series of year-shift control variables were included for the years 1988, 1990, 1992, and 1994. The equation is:

$$Y = a + b_1X_1 + b_2X_2 + b_3X_3 + b_4X_4 + b_5X_5 \quad\quad [1]$$
$$+ b_6X_6 + b_7X_7 + b_8X_8 + b_9X_9 + b_{10}X_{10} + e$$

where: X_1 = Republican spending advantage (1 = GOP spending advantage; 0 otherwise); X_2 = Democratic political experience (1 = experienced; 0 otherwise); X_3 = Republican political experience (1 = experienced; 0 otherwise); X_4 = percent black population; X_5 = percent Hispanic population; X_6 = normal GOP vote; X_7, X_8, X_9, X_{10} = control variables for the 1988, 1990, 1992, and 1994 election years, respectively (coded 1 for the particular year; 0 otherwise); and e = error term of the regression. The model parallels results of analyses of incumbent elections in that candidate attributes (experience and spending advantage) and constituency factors, such as partisan history and racial composition, are significantly related to electoral outcomes.

The robustness of the model (adjusted R-square = .74) indicates that it should generate relatively accurate estimates of open-seat outcomes; therefore, it is reasonable to use the parameters of this equation to generate hypothetical election results in the absence of incumbents, so that:

$$\text{Expected Open Seat Vote} = 21.95 + 2.84X_1 + -3.25X_2 \quad\quad [2]$$
$$+ 3.47X_3 + -.14X_4 + -.09X_5 + .56X_6$$

where X_1 = Republican spending advantage; X_2 = Democratic political experience; X_3 = Republican political experience; X_4 = percent black population; X_5 = percent Hispanic population; and X_6 = normal GOP vote. We are generating predicted election results for 1996; therefore, the slope coefficients for the year controls were multiplied by a value of 0 and drop out of the estimate. A full demonstration of this technique is available in Ronald Keith Gaddie and Lesli McCollum, "Estimating the Incumbency Advantage: A New Approach to an Old Problem," paper presented at the annual meeting of the Southwestern Political Science Association, Corpus Christi, Texas, March 18, 1998.

21. See Ronald Keith Gaddie, "Is There an Inherent Democratic Party Advantage in Congressional Elections? Evidence from the Open Seats," *Social Science Quarterly*, March 1995, pp. 203–12. This approach was also used by Erikson and Palfrey to develop their "par" control variable for baseline competition. See Robert S. Erikson and Thomas R. Palfrey, "Campaign Spending and Incumbency: An Alternative Simultaneous Equations Approach," *Journal of Politics*, May 1998, pp. 355–73.

22. Richard Fenno in his 1978 book examined four types of constituency that are important to the incumbent: core, primary, reelection, and physical. See his *Home Style: House Members in Their Districts* (Boston: Little Brown, 1978). When the general reelection constituency is so skewed to one party that it does not merit the effort of expansion, we might find that incumbent efforts at deterring challengers and building a personal following are focused on the party and the primary electorate. See Kazee, ed., *Who Runs for Congress?* An incumbency advantage will likely play a role within a very safe partisan constituency, but an exploration of that thesis is beyond the scope of this chapter.

23. Gary C. Jacobson, "Money and Votes Reconsidered: Congressional Elections, 1972–1982," *Public Choice*, Spring 1985, pp. 7–62; Jacobson, *The Electoral Origins of Divided Government*.

24. See Kazee, ed., *Who Runs for Congress?*

Chapter 8

The Voting Rights Act and Supreme Court Restrictions on Majority-Minority Districts

Mark E. Rush

In the 1990s the U.S. Supreme Court restricted the use of ''majority-minority'' districts to enhance minority representational opportunities. In three controversial cases—*Shaw v. Reno, Miller v. Johnson*, and *Vera v. Bush*—the Court limited the lengths to which states could go to create such districts.[1] By doing so, it also limited the pressure the Justice Department could bring to bear upon states covered by the Voting Rights Act (VRA).

When viewed in light of Congress' decision in 1982 to amend the Voting Rights Act (thereby enhancing the ability of minority voters to challenge discriminatory electoral structures) and the Court's 1986 decision in *Thornburg v. Gingles*, these more recent decisions appear to be a break with precedent.[2] However, when viewed as part of the Court's 40-year struggle with issues of voting rights and representation, the restrictions on majority-minority districts do not appear to be an aberration. Instead, they embody one more controversial attempt by the Court to wrestle with the many conflicting and contradictory issues inherent in voting rights cases.

Critics of the Court argue its recent decisions not only overturn precedents that ought to have been left intact but also leave voting rights jurisprudence fraught with tension, inconsistency, and confusion.[3] In this chapter, I demonstrate the tensions and confusions existed long before the controversial decisions of the 1990s. In *Shaw, Miller*, and *Vera*, the Court simply confronted the tensions that had festered in its jurisprudence throughout the previous 40 years.

RESTRICTING THE USE OF MAJORITY-MINORITY DISTRICTS

In *Shaw*, the Court ruled that while states could, under the auspices of the VRA, enhance minority representational opportunities by creating majority-minority districts, they could not—even at the behest of the U.S. Justice Department—let race be the overwhelming factor in the creation of legislative and congressional district lines. Speaking for the Court in *Shaw v. Reno*, Justice Sandra Day O'Connor opined:

A reapportionment plan that includes in one district individuals who belong to the same race, but who are otherwise widely separated by geographical and political boundaries, and who may have little in common with one another but the color of their skin, bears an uncomfortable resemblance to political apartheid. . . . The message that such districting sends to elected representatives is equally pernicious. When a district obviously is created solely to effectuate the perceived common interests of one racial group, elected officials are more likely to believe that their primary obligation is to represent only the members of that group, rather than their constituency as a whole. This is altogether antithetical to our system of representative democracy.[4]

Thus, the Court argued, simply, that gerrymandering the political system to favor minorities (or any other interest) was no more justifiable than gerrymandering it in order to discriminate against them.

Justice John Paul Stevens responded the "antigerrymandering" principle underlying the majority opinions was actually unfair and unnecessarily burdensome to minority interests. While gerrymandering was reprehensible (and unconstitutional) when used by a majority to prevent a minority from exercising its fair share of political power, Stevens argued the same could not be said about a majority's charitably handing power back to a minority:

The duty to govern impartially is abused when a group with power over the electoral process defines electoral boundaries solely to enhance its own political strength at the expense of any weaker group. That duty, however, is not violated when the majority acts to facilitate the election of a member of a group that lacks such power because it remains under-represented in the state legislature—whether that group is defined by political affiliation, by common economic interests, or by religious, ethnic, or racial characteristics. The difference between constitutional and unconstitutional gerrymanders has nothing to do with whether they are based on assumptions about the groups they affect, but whether their purpose is to enhance the power of the group in control of the districting process at the expense of any minority group, and thereby to strengthen the unequal distribution of electoral power. When an assumption that people in a particular minority group (whether they are defined by the political party, religion, ethnic group, or race to which they belong) will vote in a particular way is used to *benefit* that group, no constitutional violation occurs.[5]

This difference of opinion was by no means novel. In fact, the inconsistencies in the Court's voting rights jurisprudence are the result of its ongoing inability to accommodate both views of organizing the political process. While proponents on both sides agree it is wrong to gerrymander political groups *out* of power, they disagree regarding whether a conscious attempt by the group in power to help its political opposition can be justified. Whereas critics such as

Stevens have sought to accommodate minority political interests by allowing benevolent gerrymandering, the Court majority of the 1990s asserted voting rights jurisprudence must be grounded on a consistent principle of political fairness.

THE UNCERTAIN LEGACY OF *GOMILLION V. LIGHTFOOT*

The Court confronted the issue of gerrymandering in *Gomillion v. Lightfoot* (1960).[6] In that case, the Alabama legislature had transformed the city of Tuskegee from a square into an "uncouth," 23-sided figure that fenced the black majority out of the city. As a result, they were unable to vote in (and control the outcome of) city elections.

While *Gomillion* was a giant step forward in the protection of minority voting rights, the decision left open an important question concerning the scope of the franchise. Justice Felix Frankfurter argued the Tuskegee gerrymander violated the 15th Amendment because, in denying black citizens the right to vote in municipal elections, the state legislature had, for all intents and purposes, denied their right to vote *in toto*.

Clearly, the black residents had not lost their right to vote. They had simply been forced to vote somewhere else. In this respect, the *impact* of the Tuskegee gerrymander could not be distinguished from that of the normal, decennial process of reapportionment in which voters may be moved from one voting district to another to balance their populations. What mattered in *Gomillion* was the *motivation* of the state legislature.

In his concurrence, Justice Charles E. Whittaker emphasized this distinction. He argued the case was characterized more accurately as a 14th Amendment equal protection claim because the legislation was clearly designed to have a discriminatory impact on black voters.[7] While the legislature was guilty of discrimination, it could not be charged with denial of the franchise:

[I]nasmuch as no one has the right to vote in a political division, or in a local election concerning only an area in which he does not reside, it would seem to follow that one's right to vote in Division A is not abridged by a redistricting that places his residence in Division B *if* he there enjoys the same voting privileges as all others in that Division, even though the redistricting was done by the State for the purpose of placing a racial group of citizens in Division B rather than A.[8]

Thus, the *Gomillion* Court unanimously condemned gerrymandering, but it did not clearly establish the constitutional basis for the decision. If Whittaker was right, gerrymandering involved only the 14th Amendment (not the 15th), because the scope of the franchise does not include the right to vote in a particular place. If Frankfurter was right, gerrymandering cases embody 14th *and* 15th Amendment claims, because the scope of the franchise is much broader than Whittaker acknowledged. It includes not only free access to the polls but the right to an opportunity to elect particular candidates as well.

The question of the scope of the franchise lay dormant throughout the next two decades of jurisprudence. In ensuing cases, the Court wrestled instead with the controversy surrounding benevolent gerrymandering that was intended to enhance the representational opportunities of minority voters.

GOOD GERRYMANDERING VERSUS BAD

During the 1960s the Court sustained attempts by states to create legislative districts that would *enhance* minority representational opportunities. In *Wright v. Rockefeller* and *United Jewish Organizations of Williamsburg v. Carey (UJO)*, the Court struck down challenges to New York's congressional and state legislative redistricting plans, respectively.[9] Both involved the creation of special majority-minority districts, and both caused divisions within the Court.

In *Wright*, Justice William O. Douglas condemned the Court for sustaining New York's use of majority-minority districts because they were the product of the same racial considerations that produced the Tuskegee gerrymander. Douglas, along with Justice Arthur J. Goldberg, therefore argued:

The principle of equality is at war with the notion that District A must be represented by a Negro, as it is with the notion that District B must be represented by a Caucasian, District C by a Jew, District D by a Catholic, and so on . . . Of course race, like religion, plays an important role in the choices which individual voters make from among various candidates. But government has no business designing electoral districts along racial or religious lines.[10]

In *UJO*, the Court struck down a challenge by Hasidic voters in the Williamsburgh section of Brooklyn to the state legislative redistricting scheme. In order to create districts that would enhance the voting power of other racial and ethnic minorities, the state had divided the Hasidic community, thereby preventing it from electing a Jewish representative.

UJO forced the Court to confront the tensions inherent in the Voting Rights Act. The redistricting process is inherently zero-sum; that is, enhancing one group's representational opportunity will come at the expense of some other group's electoral fortunes. The act tolerates gerrymandering only if it is aimed at protecting specific minority groups recognized by Congress. Other groups—such as Hasidics—that were not congressionally recognized were not protected from vote dilution.

In this respect, the *UJO* decision—in particular, Justice William J. Brennan's concurrence—is especially unsettling. Did the Court simply refuse to address Justice Douglas' assertion in *Wright* there was no principled distinction between gerrymandering that helped some groups and harmed others? Or, had the Court become comfortable with a gerrymandering principle that allowed the Congress to decide which groups qualified for special electoral considerations and which did not?

In rejecting the Hasidic plaintiffs' complaint, Justice Brennan dismissed their assertion they had discrete political interests. Instead, he declared that their interests would be protected by other "white" legislators because the Hasidic

petitioners have not been deprived of their right to vote, a consideration that minimizes the detrimental impact of the remedial racial policies governing the § 5 reapportionment. *True, petitioners are denied the opportunity to vote as a group in accordance with the earlier districting configuration, but they do not press any legal claim to a group voice as Hasidim.* In terms of their voting interests, then, the burden that they claim to suffer must be attributable solely to their relegation to increased nonwhite-dominated districts. Yet, to the extent that white and nonwhite interests and sentiments are polarized in Brooklyn, the petitioners still are indirectly "protected" by the remaining white assembly and senate districts within the county, carefully preserved in accordance with the white proportion of the total county population. While these considerations obviously do not satisfy petitioners, I am persuaded that they reinforce the legitimacy of this remedy.[11]

What is most striking about this passage is that Brennan's description of the Hasidics' claim would apply accurately to the plaintiffs in *Gomillion*. In both cases, the petitioners were "denied the opportunity to vote as a group in accordance with the earlier districting configuration." But, whereas black voters had the Court's sympathy in *Gomillion*, Hasidics were unable to gain it in *UJO*.

The difference, of course, is that black voters are the intended beneficiaries of the Voting Rights Act, while Hasidics are not. Nonetheless, Brennan's opinion affirmed the importance of Douglas' criticism: redistricting intended to *help* one group can be just as pernicious as redistricting designed to discriminate against a group. On what principled grounds could redistricting intended to enhance the electoral prospects of congressionally preferred groups be condoned while redistricting intended to help others was condemned?[12]

REVISITING THE SCOPE OF THE FRANCHISE

In *Mobile v. Bolden*, the Court revisited the debate between Justices Whittaker and Frankfurter concerning the scope of the right to vote and the constitutional grounds on which a vote dilution claim could be made.[13] In this case, the Court addressed whether a claim could be brought against an electoral arrangement that had a discriminatory impact against black voters, even though it had not been designed to do so.

The Court ruled minority voters had to show a challenged electoral scheme was the product of discriminatory legislative intentions. Writing for the Court's majority, Justice Potter Stewart echoed Justice Whittaker's concurrence in *Gomillion* and noted:

The appellees have argued in this court that . . . the at-large system of elections in Mobile is unconstitutional. . . . The answer to the appellees' argument is that . . . their freedom to vote has not been denied or abridged by anyone. The Fifteenth Amendment does not entail the right to have Negro candidates elected. . . . That Amendment prohibits only purposefully discriminatory denial or abridgment by government of the freedom to vote "on account of race, color, or previous condition of servitude."[14]

In his dissent, Justice Thurgood Marshall restated Frankfurter's assertion the right to vote included protections against vote dilution regardless of legislative intent. He sought to address the inconsistency inherent in the *UJO* decision by asserting protection against vote dilution should extend only to those groups "whose discreteness and insularity allow dominant factions to ignore them."[15] While Marshall wished to protect the gains made by minority voters, his reasoning offered no principled basis for distinguishing between marginalized Hasidic voters in Williamsburgh and marginalized black voters in Tuskegee.

Marshall lost the battle of *Mobile v. Bolden*, but his opinion ultimately carried the day. Congress amended the Voting Rights Act in 1982 to allow vote dilution challenges whenever, based on the "totality of the circumstances," it could be shown

the political processes leading to nomination or election in the State or political subdivision are not equally open to participation by members of a class of citizens . . . in that its members have less opportunity than other members of the electorate to participate in the political process and to elect representatives of their choice. The extent to which members of a protected class have been elected to office in the State or political subdivision is one circumstance which may be considered: *Provided*, That nothing in this section establishes a right to have members of a protected class elected in numbers equal to their proportion in the population.[16]

The amended VRA thus made it much easier for minority groups to challenge an electoral scheme. But the Court's interpretation of the act in *Thornburg v. Gingles* limited the manner in which a vote dilution claim could be made.[17]

Writing for the Court's majority in *Gingles*, Justice Brennan read the amended VRA to require plaintiffs to meet the following three criteria:

First, the minority group must be able to demonstrate that it is sufficiently large and geographically compact to constitute a majority in a single-member district. . . . Second, the minority group must be able to show that it is politically cohesive. . . . Third, the minority must be able to demonstrate that the white majority votes sufficiently as a bloc to enable it—in the absence of special circumstances, such as the minority candidate running unopposed—usually to defeat the minority's preferred candidate.[18]

The criteria elicited widespread criticism. Writing in dissent, Justice O'Connor responded Brennan had, for all intents and purposes, created a right to proportional representation—despite the VRA's assertion that no such right existed.

In contrast, voting rights advocates argued Brennan's criteria placed unfair limits on the type of group that could file a vote dilution claim. Regardless of their size or political cohesion, geographically dispersed minority groups could not file a vote dilution claim because they could not meet the first of the *Gingles* criteria. As a result, the *Gingles* criteria conditioned vote dilution claims on residential segregation.[19]

THE SUPREME COURT "REVERSES" COURSE

Thus, by the end of the 1980s, the Court found itself caught on the horns of a dilemma: it could not maintain a principled stand against gerrymandering and vote dilution if it took the position maintained by Justice Stevens in *Shaw*. Something was clearly wrong if gerrymandering was constitutional only if it was designed to help "the right groups." Furthermore, if the scope of the franchise was as broad as Frankfurter and Marshall argued and if—per the amended VRA—a viable vote dilution claim did not depend on proof of discriminatory intent, it would be impossible to design an electoral system immune to challenge.[20]

The Court addressed this issue in *Holder v. Hall* in striking down a challenge to the Bleckley County, Georgia, single-commissioner system of government.[21] Plaintiffs acknowledged the single-commissioner system clearly had not been established to discriminate against black voters. However, they contended it failed the "totality of circumstances" test set forth in the amended VRA because its majority-vote requirement made it impossible for *any* minority to elect the commissioner. The Court responded there must be a clear benchmark for determining the proper level of representation for a plaintiff group. Thus, in the same manner *Gingles* limited the scope of vote dilution to geographically compact groups, *Holder* limited it to situations where a clear representational benchmark could be established.

Critics argued the decision was a setback for minority voting rights.[22] In response, Justice Clarence Thomas explained the *Holder* decision was the only possible course the Court could have taken:

[T]he assumptions that have guided the court reflect only one possible understanding of effective exercise of the franchise, an understanding based on the view that voters are "represented" only when they choose a delegate who will mirror their views in the legislative halls. But it is certainly possible to construct a theory of effective political participation that would accord greater importance to voters' ability to influence, rather than control, elections.[23]

To avoid the endless litigation that would accompany such a conception of representation and vote dilution, it was necessary, Thomas argued, to establish a benchmark to determine just how difficult it *ought* to be for any group to elect a representative. Insofar as this decision is an inherently political choice, the

Court's jurisprudence did little more than ensure that its decisions would be controversial.

The controversies surrounding the Court's voting rights decisions were exacerbated by its reliance on the single-member district system of representation. "There is," Thomas stated, "no principle inherent in our constitutional system, or even in the history of the Nation's electoral practices, that makes single member districts the 'proper' mechanism for electing representatives to governmental bodies or for giving 'undiluted' effect to the votes of a numerical minority."[24] But, he argued, if the Court continued to support the use of single-member districts, it would never escape the "political thicket" of gerrymandering litigation.

CONCLUSION

The restrictions placed by the Court on minority voting rights claims were necessitated by its inability to set forth a coherent, consistent vision of fair representation. Its propagation of a broad vision of the voting right, coupled with its reliance on single-member districts, resulted in cases such as *Shaw* where districts as bizarre as the one struck down in *Gomillion* were being drawn in order to comply with the VRA. The Court chose to follow the path outlined by Thomas in *Holder* and restricted both the scope of the franchise and the creation of majority-minority districts. The alternative would have been to follow Stevens and turn a blind eye to the doctrinal inconsistencies that underpin his position.

Thomas' concurrence in *Holder* holds out the possibility the adoption of a system of proportional representation (PR) might help to resolve the controversy surrounding majority-minority districts. But, as I argue elsewhere in this volume, PR will not resolve the vote dilution controversy.[25] Instead, it simply will recast it in a different manner. Regardless of the system of representation, the redistricting process is inherently zero-sum and involves political choices. As a result, judicial attempts to regulate it will always be as divisive as the actions of the legislative bodies that the Court reviews.

NOTES

1. *Shaw v. Reno*, 509 U.S. 630 (1993); *Miller v. Johnson*, 515 U.S. 900 (1995); *Vera v. Bush*, 517 U.S. 952 (1996).
2. *Thornburg v. Gingles*, 478 U.S. 30 (1986).
3. Critics fall into two camps. On one hand, critics such as Pamela Karlan and Lani Guinier condemn the Court for forsaking minority interests despite the clear intention of Congress to enhance them in the Voting Rights Act. See, for example, Lani Guinier, *The Tyranny of the Majority* (New York: Free Press 1994); Pamela Karlan, "The Right to Vote: Some Pessimism about Formalism," *Texas Law Review*, June 1993, pp. 1705–40. Other critics focus on the Court's attempt to establish clear standards for identifying

gerrymanders. Specifically, they focus on the Rehnquist Court's attempts to distinguish when the shape of a district is so bizarre it indicates a clearly unconstitutional racial motivation on the part of mapmakers. See, for example, "Symposium: The Future of Voting Rights after *Shaw v. Reno*," *Michigan Law Review*, December 1993, pp. 483–682.

4. *Shaw v. Reno*, 509 U.S. 630 at 649 (1993).

5. Ibid. at 677.

6. *Gomillion v. Lightfoot*, 364 U.S. 339 (1960).

7. Justice Stevens later confirmed this opinion in *Karcher v. Daggett*, 462 U.S. 725 at 748 (1983).

8. Ibid. at 749.

9. *Wright v. Rockefeller*, 376 U.S. 52 (1964); *United Jewish Organizations of Williamsburg v. Carey*, 430 U.S. 144 (1977).

10. *Wright v. Rockefeller*, 376 U.S. 52 at 66–67.

11. *United Jewish Organization of Williamsburg v. Carey*, 430 U.S. 144 at 178; emphasis added.

12. The question of "which groups count" still is unresolved and a source of ongoing scholarly debate and controversy. See Guinier, *The Tyranny of the Majority*; Mark E. Rush, "In Search of a Coherent Theory of Voting Rights: The Supreme Court's Vision of Fair and Effective Representation," *The Review of Politics*, Summer 1994, pp. 504–23.

13. *Mobile v. Bolden*, 446 U.S. 55 (1980).

14. Ibid. at 64.

15. Ibid. at 122.

16. *Voting Rights Act Amendments of 1982*, 96 Stat. 131, 42 U.S.C. § 1973.

17. *Thornburg v. Gingles*, 478 U.S. 30 (1986).

18. Ibid. at 36.

19. See, for example, Pamela S. Karlan, "Maps and Misreadings: The Role of Geographic Compactness in Racial Vote Dilution Litigation," *Harvard Civil Rights–Civil Liberties Law Review*, vol. 24, 1989, pp. 173–248.

20. In fact, vote dilution is inherent in every electoral system. See, for example, Richard S. Katz, "Malapportionment and Gerrymandering in Other Countries and Alternative Electoral Systems," in Mark E. Rush, ed., *Voting Rights and Redistricting in the United States* (Westport, CT: Greenwood Press, 1998).

21. *Holder v. Hall*, 512 U.S. 874 (1994).

22. See, for example, Lani Guinier, "(E)racing Democracy: The Voting Rights Cases," *Harvard Law Review*, vol. 108, 1994, pp. 109–37.

23. *Holder v. Hall*, 512 U.S. 874 at 900.

24. Ibid. at 897.

25. See Rush, "Making the House More Representative: Hidden Costs and Unintended Consequences" in this volume.

Chapter 9

The Low Voter Turnout Problem

Mark Franklin and Diana Evans

This chapter addresses turnout in House elections. Even a cursory glance at turnout figures over time raises a number of questions that for years have troubled observers of American politics. Why do fewer people vote in House elections than in presidential elections? Why is House turnout so much lower in mid-term elections than in presidential election years? Is House turnout declining, and should we be concerned about any such decline? These questions and others are addressed with data relating to House and presidential elections over all the years since good records have been kept, beginning in 1828. We argue that features of House elections that have elicited *ad hoc* theories, unique to the American case, mimic in important respects the characteristics of a certain type of elections held in countries other than the United States. Such elections have been called second-order national elections, and we will be using some of the findings from second-order election research to shed light on the nature of House elections in the United States.[1]

In the comparative literature, second-order elections are elections purporting to be about a level of government other than the one responsible for directing the activities of the nation-state (first-order elections) but whose outcomes are structured entirely by considerations relevant to the outcomes of first-order elections.[2] Elections to local councils in Britain or to equivalent local bodies in other countries are second-order elections, as are elections to the European parliament in countries that are members of the European Union. Indeed, it is elections to the European parliament whose study has provided most of the insights that have come to be known as second-order election theory and that we apply in this chapter to the American case. In our view, elections for the House of Representatives can be regarded in essential respects as second-order elections tied as with an umbilical cord to elections for the presidency (which are clearly first-order elections) and reflecting features of the national (presidential) context. Of course, there is likely also to be a local component to turnout. Variables primarily local in their origin include measures of competitiveness such as whether an incumbent has a challenger and the level of spending in the race.[3] We, however, concentrate on the national component. Later in this chapter we spell out some of the findings from second-order election research in Europe that we believe apply to mid-term (and increasingly, in our opinion, to presidential-year) House elections.

TURNOUT IN HOUSE AND PRESIDENTIAL ELECTIONS

The literature on voter turnout has been dominated by two related questions. First, what induces a citizen to expend the time and effort to go to the polling place and cast a vote? Second, what accounts for declining rates of voting over the past 40 years? With respect to the decision to vote, socioeconomic and social psychological explanations figure prominently in the literature. Many scholars have investigated voter turnout at this level, and we note some of the major findings. One principal predictor of turnout is the voter's level of education. Wolfinger and Rosenstone characterized its importance as "transcendent."[4] In addition, older voters are significantly more likely to vote than younger ones, while southerners are less likely to vote than residents of other regions. In the most comprehensive study of overall political participation to date, Verba, Schlozman, and Brady found that turnout also is predicted by voters' political interest, information, and efficacy, as well as the strength of their partisanship.[5]

In addition, some scholars have gone beyond voters' internal inducements to participate, arguing for the importance of contextual factors such as registration requirements and mobilization of the electorate. The latter is a function traditionally performed by local party organizations and labor unions; in modern, candidate-centered elections it is done by the candidates' organizations.[6] With regard to registration requirements, the more restrictive such laws are in any given jurisdiction, the lower the turnout.

The second question that dominates the literature, the puzzle of declining voter turnout, is a matter of ongoing debate. However, traditional forms of voter mobilization have declined over the years; Rosenstone and Hansen attributed much of the decline in turnout between 1960 and 1980 to that factor alone.[7] They also found that social psychological variables played a role. The reduction in turnout over that period was related to declines in a number of the individual-level variables that predict turnout—voters' political efficacy, attachment to political parties, and degree of satisfaction with the choice of candidates in elections. Additionally, the 26th Amendment to the Constitution, which lowered the voting age to 18 beginning with the 1972 elections, dramatically reduced the average age of the voting population overall: "The size of the voter group least likely to participate increased by 40 percent overnight, accounting for the substantial drop in voter participation in that one year."[8] Nevertheless, the largest share of turnout decline was attributable to the reduction in mobilization efforts by parties, unions, and social movements. Those negative forces were so powerful they swamped the positive impact on turnout of increased levels of education and the liberalization of voter registration laws during that period.

The fact social psychological factors should have been overwhelmed in this way by features of the electoral context (election rules and mobilization efforts) points us toward another tradition in turnout research—one existing primarily outside the United States. Among scholars who study differences between countries, the importance of institutional and contextual differences in affecting turnout has been a major theme in the political participation literature since the earliest studies, and a link can be made between institutions and voter motivations if we consider differences between elections in how much is at stake.[9] An election that does not decide the disposition of executive power (e.g., an election for the European parliament or a U.S. mid-term election) can be expected to prove less important and therefore less apt to motivate voter turnout than a national election in Europe or an American presidential election. If executive power is at stake, we would expect more people will turn out—especially if the election is a close one, the outcome seems likely to determine the course of public policy, and there are large perceived differences between policy alternatives.[10]

Taking such differences to their extreme in a country like Switzerland—where the outcome of parliamentary elections has no discernible policy implications (because the same coalition will take office whatever the outcome, and all important policies are subject to referendum)—we see turnout rates only about one-half of those in a country, such as Malta, where every important political decision is affected by the outcome of a single electoral contest.[11] This type of contest is one reason that mobilization shows up as being so important in individual-level studies: important elections stimulate more electoral activity by parties and candidates. Differences such as those between Malta on the one hand and Switzerland on the other are far greater than differences between educated and uneducated Americans (the most powerful individual-level predictor of turnout differences), emphasizing it is not education that is transcendent, but contextual factors—the focus of this chapter.[12]

We start by considering the evolution of turnout levels in House and presidential elections since reliable records started to be kept in 1828.[13] Figure 9.1 shows that, until 1840, turnout in House elections was higher than in presidential elections and that there was no systematic difference between House turnout in presidential years and at mid-term. Presidential turnout after 1840 almost invariably exceeds House turnout even in presidential election years; and, from this time on, presidential-year House turnout invariably exceeds mid-term turnout. Indeed, what seems to have happened in 1840 is that presidential elections started to bring more voters to the polls—voters who might not have turned out merely for a House contest but most of whom did vote for a House candidate

Figure 9.1
Presidential and House Turnout at Presidential and Mid-Term Elections

while they were in the polling booth. Turnout in mid-term elections also increased at this time, but not by nearly so much.

Until 1880 the gap between House and presidential turnout, while maintaining these general disparities, seemed to fluctuate in size without any discernible trend. But from about 1880 onward, House turnout in presidential years (though continuing to track presidential turnout very closely) begins to diverge, with votes for House candidates even in presidential years falling increasingly below the number of votes for presidential candidates. The difference between turnout in House elections in presidential years and in the subsequent mid-term election waxes and wanes over time with no discernible trend since the difference first was established in 1842.

Both presidential and House turnout drop precipitously after 1896, a development often attributed to the tightening of election laws and the coming of voluntary voter registration—reforms designed to reduce or eliminate the "graveyard vote" and to make it difficult to "vote early, vote often."[14] As shown in Figure 9.1, a progressive decline in turnout started in 1898 that may well have coincided with the tightening of electoral laws in successive states.[15] The changes in election laws generally are supposed to have been completed by 1916, and the further drop in turnout thereafter is supposed to have been due to low turnout among recently enfranchised women, who gained the vote for the first time in 1920. The overall accuracy with which mid-term and presidential turnout track each other is remarkable, albeit with lower turnout in mid-term elections. Not surprisingly, House and presidential turnout in presidential election years covary even more closely, thereby leading us to suppose that turnout in House elections must respond to similar forces as turnout in presidential contests.

Our Expectations

Changes in turnout reflect changes in the costs and benefits of voting. Evidently, the changes in election laws referred to earlier constituted changes in the costs of voting, but, aside from developments of that kind, costs remain relatively fixed over the short term.[16] What changes from election to election are primarily the benefits of voting. Some elections are more important than others, and more important elections have higher turnout. What makes an election important? For one thing, an important election should present voters with the opportunity to choose policies that, if enacted, would bring major changes in their lives. Of course, the Framers of the U.S. Constitution in their wisdom designed a political system in which no "faction" easily could capture the whole of the apparatus of government and elections only definitively decide who will make policy, not what policies they will make—in contrast to elections in most other democratic countries—and it has been argued turnout is consequently lower in the United States than elsewhere.[17] But U.S. elections see large variations in turnout between different types of elections and over time for the same type of election, as noted. In presidential elections, recent research has shown that a very large proportion of the over-time variance can be explained by a simple model positing higher turnout when the race is a close one and lower turnout in conditions of divided government.[18] These two considerations impact directly the importance of an election by making every vote count (in a close race) or by reducing the likely ability of a winning candidate to enact his or her program into law (in conditions of divided government).[19]

Determinants of House Election Turnout

If turnout in House elections tracks turnout in presidential elections as well, as we see it doing in Figure 9.1, we would expect the same effects to be important in elections of both types, though in House elections we might also expect additional influences from such variables as the number of close House contests and number of incumbent candidates. But the most important variable to add to the set employed in explaining presidential election turnout is whether the House election is a mid-term election, since it is quite clear from Figure 9.1 mid-term elections see lower turnout after 1840. In the following analyses we focus on elections from 1840 onward because the relationships of interest clearly did not exist before that time.

The first column in Table 9.1 presents a simple model that predicts House turnout from some of the contextual variables found to be important in predicting presidential turnout with the addition of a dummy variable to take account of the lesser importance of House elections in mid-term election years. The predictors are the closeness of the race (percentage distance between the first and second parties in House elections nationwide), whether the election was held at mid-term, whether 18-year-olds had been given the vote, and a variable used in previous research to indicate the increasing costs of voting resulting from reform of election laws after 1896 (coding of all the independent variables is described in notes to Table 9.1). Certain variables that might have been expected to be important on the basis of individual-level studies proved to have effects that were not significant. Most importantly, one variable found to be important in predicting presidential turnout (number of prior years of divided government) did not prove significant in predicting House turnout.[20] Still, model 1 of Table 9.1 explains so much variance in House turnout (over 90%) that it does not seem likely features of individual races (such as number of close races or incumbents running) could add much explanatory power. Indeed, the power of variables connected with the national context raises the question whether House election turnout does any more than track presidential election turnout in the sense that whatever draws voters to the polls for presidential elections largely determines their decision to vote in congressional races as well.

The second column in Table 9.1 replaces the reform, 18-year-old vote, and party distance independent variables with a single variable indicating turnout in the concurrent or most recent presidential election. This model explains a spec-

Table 9.1
Four Models Explaining Percentage Turnout in House Elections since 1840

Independent variable	Model 1	Model 2	Model 3	Model 4
INTERCEPT	77.23***	-7.24**	5.42	
	(0.98)	(2.51)	(4.47)	
Mid-term election	-12.00***	-12.41***	-12.04***	-11.94***
	(0.90)	(0.79)	(0.69)	(0.48)
Distance between parties	-0.192*			
	(0.09)			
Electoral reform[a]	-21.35***			
	(1.05)			
18-year-old voting	-4.589***			
	(1.33)			
Presidential turnout		1.06***	0.92***	0.99***
		(0.04)	(0.05)	(0.01)
Trend in House turnout[b]			-6.12**	-4.68***
			(1.95)	(0.68)
Nationalization of elections[c]				3.80***
				(0.42)
Adjusted R^2	0.909	0.930	0.946	0.974[d]
N	79	79	79	74

*Significant at $p < .05$; ** sig. at $p < .01$; ***sig. at $p < .001$ (all one-tailed).

a. A variable registering the progressive tightening of electoral laws by taking on a value of 0 until 1896, 0.1 in 1898, 0.2 in 1900, and so on until reaching 1.0 in 1916, which value is retained thereafter. Any effect of this variable can be interpreted as the entire reduction in turnout occurring between 1896 and 1916.

b. A variable that starts at 0 in 1840 and increases by just less than 0.07 per year to reach the value of 1.0 at the end of the series. Any effect of this variable can be interpreted as the overall change in House turnout occurring during the entire period of our study that is not accounted for by other variables.

c. A variable applying the sign of each residual to (1-trend), where trend is described in note b.

d. Variance explained is not normally computed when the intercept is omitted. This coefficient is the variance explained when the predicted Ys from model 4 are regressed on House turnout.

Note: Standard errors in parentheses.

tacular 92.6 percent of variance in House turnout—meaning that the model predicts actual turnout with considerable accuracy—simply by positing that House turnout would duplicate presidential turnout, though with a twelve-point reduction at mid-term elections. However, there are various indications (not shown) that model 2 is incomplete. The most obvious predictor not yet taken into account is the apparent tendency of House turnout to increasingly diverge from presidential turnout over the years. The third column in Table 9.1 consequently adds a trend variable to take account of declining House turnout relative to presidential turnout; but this variable does not appear to resolve the difficulty.

As an aid to diagnosing the problem, Figure 9.2 plots the residual differences between actual turnout and the turnout predicted by model 3. The plot shows a remarkable tendency for the residual differences to decline with the passage of time (maximum and minimum values get closer and closer to 0). In other words, turnout in presidential elections has in recent years become an increasingly accurate predictor of turnout in House elections. The highly accurate predictions made by models 2 and 3 of Table 9.1 would have been even more accurate had all House elections been conducted in the conditions pertaining since 1960. This finding makes it all the less likely a search for additional predictor variables at the level of the constituency would prove fruitful in terms of explained variance. If we had been able to explain historical variations with constituency-level predictors, any such explanations would have become largely redundant in recent years.

What we see in Figure 9.2 seems to be a turnout perspective on the nationalization of electoral forces Donald Stokes documented long ago.[21] Stokes showed how the swing from one party to another occurring at successive elections could be partitioned into national, state, and local effects; and that, while in the early 1800s local effects had dominated, by 1960 the effects had become largely national. In other words, the swing between parties in each separate district in modern times tends to follow a national trend. Applying this logic to turnout, a totally nationalized electorate would show the same change in turnout in each constituency, and such a situation would give us a turnout in House elections whose variation from one election to the next was explained totally by national forces of the kind employed in Table 9.1. What Figure 9.2 tells us is that such a situation progressively has been coming into being in elections since 1840. The nationalization of electoral forces has applied to turnout as well as to the balance of the two-party vote.

Figure 9.2 also suggests a means for correcting our model so as to yield accurate coefficients. The decline in the extent of residual differences over time needs to be taken into account. We can do this by including a term that models the nationalization of election forces. The figure also shows the presence of two extreme outliers (occurring in 1838 and 1942). The first falls before the period from which we are computing our effects, but the latter can and should be eliminated before we proceed.

Our nationalization variable is intended to reflect the progressively reduced dispersion over time of the errors around the prediction of House turnout. The variable varies from 1 to 0, declining in magnitude over time. For each case in the data matrix this trend is given the sign of the residual term for that case, minus if the residual is negative and plus if the residual is positive (see Figure 9.2).[22] The findings are shown in model 4, which also suppresses the intercept term.[23]

Models that incorporate information from their own errors are suspect. Variance explained is inflated and may have no meaningful interpretation. But such models can still make more accurate predictions. In this instance, various di-

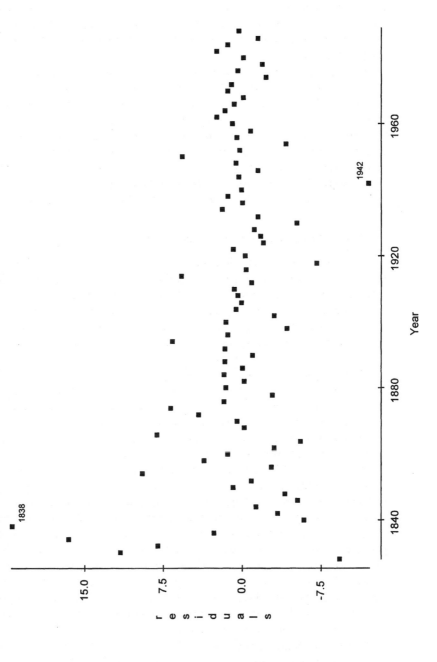

Figure 9.2
Residuals from House Turnout Predicted According to Model 3, with Two Outliers Identified

agnostics (not shown) tell us that model 4 is indeed quite satisfactory. Moreover, this model does have substantive interpretations both for the coefficient applying to the nationalization of turnout and for the overall variance explained. The latter—97.4 percent—is the variance we would have explained had the nationalization of electoral forces been complete at the start of our time period and continued unchanged.

The coefficient for the nationalization of turnout can be interpreted as the extent to which errors were reduced over the period. Not shown is the average residual at the end of the time series, 1.0, meaning that since the 1960s predictions of House turnout were accurate to within plus or minus 1 percent on average, a span of two percentage points. The nationalization coefficient indicates that at the start of the series the span of the average error was 3.8 percent greater than that, or almost 6 percent. Thus, the nationalization of electoral forces since 1840 has had the effect of reducing by two-thirds the extent of error in predictions of House turnout made on the basis of national effects.

House Elections as Second-Order National Elections

If turnout in House elections can be explained virtually completely on the basis of turnout in concurrent or immediately preceding presidential elections, together with a small number of simple trend variables, does this explanation mean that House elections are nothing more than pale reflections of presidential elections? We already know that in terms of the two-party vote this conclusion is not valid. House elections can yield results radically at odds with concurrent or previous presidential elections.

Table 9.2 provides suggestive evidence that House turnout is not totally dependent on presidential turnout any more than House outcomes totally reflect presidential outcomes. There we see that when turnout in the previous House election is plugged into an equation predicting turnout in presidential elections, in lieu of turnout in the previous presidential election, the result is a considerably more powerful prediction of turnout in presidential elections. This result is shown in Table 9.2 by the fact that, while turnout in the previous presidential election has no significant effect on turnout in the current election (model 2), turnout in the previous House (mid-term) election has an enormous impact (model 3). Diagnostic tests show this model to be poorly specified, but this chapter is not concerned to find the correct specification for a model predicting presidential turnout from House election turnout. The purpose of Table 9.2 is simply to demonstrate that presidential turnout is not independent of House turnout. The two form part of a complex and mutually dependent system in which House turnout is largely a function of turnout in the current or previous presidential election, while presidential turnout is partly a function of turnout in the previous (mid-term) House election.[24]

Scholars of congressional elections long have theorized House election outcomes represent a "normal vote" from which presidential outcomes deviate.[25] This theory has fallen into disrepute in recent years because of its inability to

Table 9.2
Three Models Explaining Turnout in Presidential Elections since 1840

Independent variable	Model 1	Model 2	Model 3
INTERCEPT	80.47***	73.94***	30.87***
	(1.35)	(9.58)	(3.41)
Divided government (years)	-0.49*	-0.48*	-0.39*
	(0.24)	(0.25)	(0.20)
Distance between parties (percent)	-0.27*	-0.26*	-0.25**
	(0.10)	(0.10)(0.09)	
Election reform[a]	-18.40***	-16.86***	
	(1.54)	(2.73)	
Presidential turnout$_{t-1}$		0.08	
		(0.12)	
House turnout$_{t-1}$			0.75***
			(0.05)
Adjusted R^2	0.862	0.865	0.895
N	39	38	38

*Significant at $p < .05$; **significant at $p < .01$; ***significant at $p < .001$ (all one-tailed).

a. A variable that takes on a value of 0 until 1896, 0.2 in 1900, 0.4 in 1904, 0.6 in 1908, 0.8 in 1912, and 1 thereafter to register the progressive tightening of electoral laws.

Note: Standard errors in parentheses. Models 1 and 2 are taken from Mark N. Franklin and Wolfgang P. Hirczy de Mino, "Separated Powers, Divided Government, and Turnout in U.S. Presidential Elections," *American Journal of Political Science*, January 1998, pp. 316–36; model 3 was computed for this chapter.

account for certain features of mid-term election outcomes.[26] We argue that neither presidential nor mid-term election results can be considered "normal." Both reflect aspects of the national political situation as seen through different lenses. We make this argument by analogy to second-order elections outside the United States. We feel justified in advancing this argument because every feature of mid-term congressional elections we have painstakingly identified corresponds to features of second-order national elections in parliamentary contexts.

In the first place, second-order elections reflect the context of the national political arena and do not bring any additional context to bear that is unique to the electoral arena ostensibly involved. In the results reported in Table 9.1 above and the following analysis, we show how little room there was in the variance unexplained by national political forces for turnout in U.S. House elections to be reflecting anything but these national forces. Of course, the manner in which these national forces operate certainly will involve local effects (e.g., get-out-the-vote efforts) that will be more marked when the election is an important one.[27]

In the second place, second-order elections are less important than national elections. This lower importance is reflected in lower turnout unless the second-order election occurs in conjunction with a first-order election. This pattern is precisely what we observe when we compare House elections occurring at mid-term with those that occur in presidential election years. Indeed, the second-order effect on turnout in mid-term House elections (11.94% in model 4 of Table 9.1) is very close to what would have been found in an election to the European parliament occurring two years before the next first-order national election.[28] In the third place, second-order elections are leading indicators of first-order elections. Turnout and the balance of party forces in elections to the European parliament can serve as better predictors of turnout and party balance for the next first-order parliamentary election than can equivalent features of the previous first-order election.[29] Table 9.2 shows us that the same is true (at least in terms of turnout) of U.S. mid-term elections in relation to presidential elections.

Interpreting House Elections in the Light of Second-Order Election Theory

If elections to the House are best seen as second-order elections, how does this view help us to interpret their characteristics? One characteristic common to second-order elections everywhere is the tendency for these elections to show less support for government parties than a first-order election would have shown. This swing against the government is partly a matter of people's voting differently in a second-order election than they would have voted had the election been a first-order election, but it is also partly a matter of turnout. When turnout is lower, the people who vote are not necessarily a random sample of those who would have voted had turnout been higher. So the lower turnout in U.S. mid-term elections is one reason the outcome of these elections sometimes contrasts with the outcome of the previous presidential contest.

A cottage industry has grown up in the United States to attempt to explain the phenomenon of mid-term loss. When the idea of mid-term elections reflecting a normal vote was shown to be untenable, a controversial theory suggested that people vote to balance the outcome of the previous presidential election, wanting more centrist policies than either party alone would give them.[30] The idea was that some voters seek to achieve divided government by voting differently in House than in presidential elections, and that sometimes they succeed.

We suggest this idea is fanciful. It calls for more calculation on the part of voters than even the most sanguine studies of voter rationality have observed empirically. But, more importantly, the idea is unnecessary. The same phenomenon of a swing against the party (or parties) that controls the executive is a ubiquitous feature of second-order elections everywhere, but few countries if any have the possibility of creating a divided government. So mid-term loss, as it is called in the United States does not require a uniquely U.S. explanation and can be explained on the same basis as the same phenomenon elsewhere.

Elections to the European parliament are the second-order elections that have been most researched. These elections almost invariably register a swing against national governments in all countries taking part.[31] The reason seems to be a combination of two different motivations. The first, described as "voting with the heart," is what happens when voters bring to bear no considerations other than their ideal party preferences and is very close to the behavior described by U.S. commentators as the "normal vote." But there is another behavior that occurs in European Parliament elections. This behavior has been described as "voting with the boot" and happens when voters use the opportunity of an election with no serious implications to vent their frustration with government performance or policies. The exact mix of these two behaviors in European elections depends on their timing relative to adjacent first-order elections and on the political situation of the moment.[32] Timing is not at issue in mid-term elections that always occur exactly two years before the next presidential election, but other factors can arise that turn such elections into opportunities to protest.

Arguably, the best way to think about the mid-term election outcome in 1994 is as a cry of frustration directed at the multitude of failures that characterized President Clinton's first two years in office. Democrats stayed home in large numbers, too irritated to be bothered to vote and contributing to the particularly low turnout of that election, while turnout among Republican voters, particularly members of the Christian Right, was higher than in the previous election.[33] This result may have been possible only in a country where many regard mid-term elections as having no important consequences for the conduct of government— as being second-order elections. If Democrats had anticipated the results of staying home, they might well have behaved differently. Such a mix of behaviors, consistent with second-order election theory, would have produced precisely the observed outcome (a massive swing to the Republicans), an outcome that otherwise has to be seen as a mid-term course correction.

Leaving differential turnout aside, second-order election theory tells us lower turnout in second-order elections is inevitable unless they occur in conjunction with first-order elections. So there is no reason to be concerned about the low turnout in mid-term House elections beyond any concern we might have about the low turnout in U.S. elections generally.[34]

It is true that House turnout has declined even relative to the low (and perhaps declining) levels of presidential turnout. We do not comment in this chapter upon the decline in presidential turnout other than to note that this decline has occurred since a 20th-century high point in 1960. The decline in House turnout relative to the presidential baseline seems to us to have been due most likely to the very nationalization of electoral forces documented earlier. If House election turnout, like House election outcomes, has become increasingly determined by national forces, it follows it increasingly has brought less to bear from the local context. It is evident that before 1840 House elections were fought on grounds different from those pertaining in presidential elections, and these different grounds were clearly important to voters, bringing more of them to the polls than would vote in presidential elections. After 1840 it seems likely that many of these local considerations remained. But over the years since that time the nationalization of electoral forces progressively has reduced the local component in House elections. We should not be surprised if turnout has declined as a consequence.

CONCLUSIONS

We began this chapter with several questions. Why do fewer people vote in House elections than in presidential elections? Why is House turnout so much lower in mid-term elections than in presidential election years? Is House turnout declining over time, and should we be concerned about any such decline? The answers flow straightforwardly from our analysis of House elections as evincing second-order characteristics. House turnout is lower than presidential turnout because House elections are viewed by many as less important. Turnout is especially lower at mid-term because in those years there is no presidential contest to bring people to the polls who might vote for a House candidate at the same time. House turnout has been declining because there has been a trend toward greater nationalization of turnout in House elections, removing from House elections some of the factors that gave them an independent importance and focusing voter attention on their least important aspects. That the trend is consistent with the previously documented nationalization of partisan performance in congressional elections increases our confidence in the results presented here.

To provide these answers, we have interpreted House elections comparatively in the context of second-order election theory. Of course, House elections are not really second-order elections. They do have clear consequences for national policy making: by determining the existence and size of the president's party's legislative majority, House elections can enhance presidential power or cripple it. The elections of 1994 are only the most recent example of the potential for mid-term elections to have a dramatic impact on the governance of the nation. But to the extent that voters were sensitized to that fact through the collective impact of their own actions in 1994, ensuing congressional elections will have fewer second-order characteristics. Indeed, in the very next mid-term elections, voters in 1998 increased the size of the president's party's contingent in the House for only the second time at a mid-term election in this century. Such behavior is quite inconsistent with second-order election theory. The outcome generally was thought to have been due to disgust at House Republicans for pursuing the impeachment of the president, in which case it will have been the supposedly second-order arena that supplied the motivations for party choice.

With regard to the trend in turnout in House elections since 1840, although our models explain nearly all of the variance, we do not pretend to have a theoretically general model of turnout. To say that House turnout tracks presidential turnout and vice versa leaves much unanswered: specifically, what accounts for declines in turnout overall? We have shown House election turnout seems to be in decline because presidential election turnout is in decline. Additionally, true to the theory of second-order elections, turnout in the previous mid-term election presages turnout in the next presidential election. When we exit that interdependent system, we see (from model 1 in Table 9.1) that changes in turnout at House elections over time are partly a function of changes in election laws—changes prior research tells us also affected presidential turnout.

Clearly, House turnout is declining and is doing so in tandem with declining turnout in presidential elections. Should we worry about this general decline in turnout? It has been argued widely low turnout results in political inequality that takes the form of a class bias in election results and in subsequent public policy.[35] Thus, to the extent we care about political equality in a democracy, the answer is we *should* be concerned, and we *should* take seriously prescriptions for how to remedy low turnout, for example, by easing voter registration requirements, by enacting campaign finance reform, or, much more controversially, by making voting compulsory.[36]

NOTES

1. Karlheinz Reif and Hermann Schmitt, "Nine Second-order National Elections—A Conceptual Framework for the Analysis of European Election Results," *European Journal of Political Research*, March 1980, pp. 3–44.

2. Ibid.; Cees van der Eijk, et al., *Choosing Europe? The European Electorate and National Politics in the Face of Union* (Ann Arbor: University of Michigan Press, 1996).

3. Gregory A. Caldeira, Samuel C. Patterson, and Gregory A. Markko, "The Mobilization of Voters in Congressional Elections," *The Journal of Politics*, May 1985, pp. 490–509.

4. Raymond E. Wolfinger and Steven Rosenstone, *Who Votes?* (New Haven, CT: Yale University Press, 1980), p. 102.

5. Sidney Verba, Kay Schlozman, and Henry Brady, *Voice and Equality: Civic Voluntarism in American Politics* (Cambridge: Harvard University Press, 1995), p. 358.

6. Caldeira et al., "The Mobilization of Voters"; Steven J. Rosenstone and John M. Hansen, *Mobilization, Participation, and Democracy in America* (New York: Macmillan, 1993).

7. Rosenstone and Hansen, *Mobilization*, p. 215.

8. Ibid., p. 218.

9. Herbert Tingston, *Political Behavior* (London: King, 1937); G. Bingham Powell, Jr., "American Voter Turnout in Comparative Perspective," *The American Political Science Review*, March 1986, pp. 17–43.

10. Mark N. Franklin, "Electoral Participation," in Laurence Leduc, Richard Niemi, and Pippa Norris, eds., *Comparing Democracies: Elections and Voting in Global Perspective* (Thousand Oaks, CA: Sage, 1996), pp. 214–33.

11. Wolfgang Hirczy, "Explaining Near-Universal Turnout: The Case of Malta," *European Journal of Political Research*, February 1995, pp. 255–72.

12. Arendt Lijphart, "Unequal Participation: Democracy's Unresolved Dilemma," *The American Political Science Review*, March 1997, pp. 1–14; Franklin, "Electoral Participation."

13. Our data are taken from Thomas T. Mackie and Richard Rose, *The International Almanac of Electoral History*, 3rd ed. (Washington, DC: Congressional Quarterly Press, 1991).

14. Philip Converse, "Change in the American Electorate," in Angus Campbell and Philip Converse, eds., *The Human Meaning of Social Change* (New York: Sage, 1972), pp. 263–337.

15. See also Walter Dean Burnham, "The Changing Shape of the American Political Universe," *The American Political Science Review*, March 1965, pp. 7–28.

16. Factors such as education, mobility, and leisure change, but over a period of decades rather than years.

17. Franklin, "Electoral Participation"; Ruy Teixeira, *The Disappearing American Voter* (Washington, DC: Brookings Institution Press, 1992), p. 8.

18. Mark N. Franklin and Wolfgang P. Hirczy de Mino, "Separated Powers, Divided Government, and Turnout in U.S. Presidential Elections," *American Journal of Political Science*, January 1998, pp. 316–36.

19. Even though rational choice considerations led theorists to expect it, previous research in the United States had failed to find unambiguous evidence for this effect. See Teixeira, "The Disappearing American Voter," p. 54. But recent research (Franklin and Hirczy) has shown that the effect was masked in the United States by the fact that many close races result in divided government, and divided government reduces turnout (see models 1 and 2 of Table 9.2). This proposition was used by Franklin and Hirczy as a critical test for a more general proposition—separated powers reduce turnout. The theory propounded in that article is that lower turnout in U.S. elections than elsewhere results from precisely the fact separated powers reduce the stakes of an election by making it more difficult for a winning party to enact its program. Divided government was seen as a critical test of this proposition because if separated powers matter, more separated powers (in conditions of divided government) should matter more. But a by-product of the research was a properly specified model of the determinants of turnout in presidential elections over time.

20. Franklin and Hirczy, "Separated Powers."

21. Donald Stokes, "Parties and the Nationalization of Electoral Forces," in Walter Dean Burnham, ed., *The American Party System* (London: Oxford University Press, 1967), pp. 182–202.

22. In technical terms, a binary variable taking on the values $+1$ or -1 to match the sign of each residual is multiplied by (1-trend) where trend is the "trend in House turnout" employed in models 3 and 4 of Table 9.1. The result is the variable called "nationalization of turnout" in Table 9.1. A comparable result is given by a quasi-two-stage methodology in which the residuals from the first stage are estimated in a second stage by the nationalization variable, and the predicted values from that second stage are used as an independent variable in model 4, in lieu of the nationalization variable itself.

In that case the coefficient on the predictor has no ready interpretation, but other coefficients are virtually identical to those shown in model 4.

23. If the intercept is not suppressed, even though it is not significantly different from zero, its value biases the estimation of other coefficients.

24. Evidently, the two sets of elections should be linked by a simultaneous equation model, but such a model is beyond the scope of the present chapter.

25. Angus Campbell, "Surge and Decline: A Study of Electoral Change," in Angus Campbell et al., eds., *Elections and the Political Order* (New York: John Wiley, 1966), pp. 40–62.

26. Robert Erikson, "The Puzzle of Mid-Term Loss," *Journal of Politics*, November 1988, pp. 1011–29.

27. Well-funded races will evince such efforts more than poorly funded races; but, for the most part, such differences will wash out in the aggregate, giving us the national effects that we observe.

28. Van der Eijk et al., *Choosing Europe*, pp. 318–25.

29. Michael Marsh and Mark N. Franklin, "The Foundations: Unanswered Questions from the Study of European Elections, 1979–1994," in ibid., pp. 11–32.

30. Alberto Alesina and Howard Rosenthal, "Partisan Cycles in Congressional Elections and the Macroeconomy," *The American Political Science Review*, June 1989, pp. 373–98; Morris P. Fiorina, *Divided Government* (New York: Macmillan, 1992), pp. 64–85.

31. Reif and Schmitt, "Nine Second-Order National Elections"; van der Eijk et al., *Choosing Europe*.

32. In the immediate aftermath of a first-order election there is apparently little point in protest voting since second-order elections occurring at such times are given little attention. In the period preceding a first-order election, however, voting with the boot is much more likely to occur since the media and party leaders pay considerable attention to such elections, which are seen as barometers or bellwethers of public opinion. See Christopher J. Anderson, "When in Doubt, Use Proxies: Attitudes toward Domestic Politics and Support for European Integration," *Comparative Political Studies*, October 1998, pp. 569–601.

33. Clyde Wilcox, *The Latest American Revolution?* (New York: St. Martin's Press, 1995), pp. 14–16.

34. We already pointed out our own conviction low turnout in presidential elections merely reflects the mechanics of the U.S. political system. Americans are seldom asked to decide matters of great moment at their elections, so turnout is seldom high.

35. Lijphart, "Unequal Participation."

36. Wolfinger and Rosenstone, *Who Votes?*, pp. 61–88; Lijphart, "Unequal Participation."

Chapter 10

Comparing Systems of Election and Representation

Wilma Rule

An underdeveloped election system brought representation to the U.S. House of Representatives when it first convened in 1789. In the early years that followed, there were no national pattern for financing House elections and no problem with incumbents' serving term after term. Turnover of members was about 50 percent.[1] There were no national political parties. Where parties existed within some states, they were characterized—as are those in some developing democracies today—as spokesmen for special interests given to bribery and corruption.[2]

House election procedures numbered two, common to England both then and now.[3] There were election of a representative by a majority or plurality in a single-member district (SMD) and election of several representatives by plurality vote in a large, multi-member district (MMD). These two election procedures resulted, for that time, in a relatively diverse group of white, male representatives among the 10 percent of the population with the proper qualifications for voting (see Chapter 2 in this volume). It was probably the highest vote of "the people" among the countries of the world with national legislatures. However, free women and slaves were excluded in those days from voting and representation in the U.S. House.

Enactment of the Reapportionment Act of 1842 requiring only SMDs started the U.S. House on a downward trend to further unrepresentativeness, contrary to the views of James Madison and other Constitution founders and supporters.[4] What began as an underdeveloped, fairly open system for the House in 1789 resulted more than 200 years later in a highly developed, nearly closed system infusing and dispensing millions of dollars to reelect 93 percent of incumbent House members by scarcely 50 percent of eligible voters.[5]

THE GOALS OF THE FOUNDERS FOR THE HOUSE

The House of Representatives was conceived as "the people's house," elected biennially, sensitive to shifts in public opinion, with considerable turnover in its membership. Alexander Hamilton, who otherwise favored nonpopular government, wrote the elected representatives constituted the "democratical" part of government.[6] However, it should be borne in mind that the elected representatives were subject to the legislative qualifications of their home states (see Chapter 2 in this volume).[7]

The House was to act somewhat like a jury open to the appeal of interest groups, James Madison's "factions," but capable of objective decisions for the public good. Madison, the major architect of the U.S. Constitution, wrote in the *Federalist Number 10* the "unequal distribution of property" was the most common and durable source of factions.[8] With large electoral territories, the influence of economic factions, corrupt political parties, and overbearing majorities could be controlled, according to Madison, who explained: "Extend the sphere and you take in a greater variety of parties and interests; you make it less probable that a majority of the whole will have a common motive to invade the rights of other citizens."[9]

In correspondence with Thomas Jefferson and others, Madison advised a similar arrangement for the election of state legislators. He was responding to observations state legislators were self-serving and did not promote the general good. The most effective remedy for this local bias in small election districts was to enlarge the electorate, according to Madison. In comments on Thomas Jefferson's draft of the Virginia Constitution, Madison advised Jefferson to provide for one statewide senatorial district instead of several. "If an election by districts be unavoidable . . . the evil will be diminished in proportion to the extent given to the districts," Madison added.[10] He urged that only a few senators be chosen from districts and the remainder be elected at large.[11]

John Adams, prior to adoption of the U.S. Constitution, called for "equality of representation" and advocated that "equal interests among the people should have equal representation" in legislatures.[12] This idea was a popular one. It was based on observations of extreme disproportionality and unrepresentativeness in the English House of Commons and the colonial legislatures before the Revolutionary War.[13]

While Madison's preference was for large, multi-member districts for elections, he and the other supporters of the U.S. Constitution were agreed on a House elected by the people and representative of them and subject to frequent change (Madison called this "representative democracy"). Adams and other like-minded leaders did not pursue their ideas for achieving broad representation in the House. The Constitution did not specify election formulas but left the matter to the individual states.

THE TWO-PARTY SYSTEM AND MULTI-MEMBER DISTRICTS

The movement for male suffrage and the election of Andrew Jackson as president in 1828 emphasized popular rule and resulted in the establishment of two national parties—Whigs, who later were called Republicans, and Democrats. Within the context of partisanship the 1842 statute mandating majority/plurality elections in SMDs was enacted. A valid argument activated the political party leaders: a well-organized majority of Democrats or Republicans in a multi-member district could win all the House seats, leaving the minority party voters unrepresented.

Yet SMDs could have been devised where needed, together with MMDs (as Madison advised Jefferson). In the latter, some minority party candidates could be elected as well as representatives from the two major political parties. Thus, a House seat could be won with just more than 20 percent of the vote in a five-member district. However, it was nearly impossible for nonmajor party candidates to be elected in the single-member district. They ordinarily had to win a majority of just more than 50 percent of the votes, or the highest plurality vote that usually was won by major party candidates.

While MMD elections were not allowed for election to the House, they flourished at the state legislative level well into the next century. In the 1970s and 1980s researchers discovered MMDs offered considerable more opportunity for women to be elected to the state legislature than SMDs.[14] Moreover, women legislators elected from MMDs had valuable experience with which they could compete for a House seat. However, it also was documented that black and Latino men's legislative recruitment in multi-member districts was close to nil. Apparently, some white voters would give one of their legislative choices in an MMD to a minority woman, but not to a minority man. Lawsuits brought under the Voting Rights Act of 1965 resulted in the abandonment of MMD elections in states covered by the act, largely for state legislatures, leaving the SMD electoral formula dominant throughout the nation.[15]

A NONDIVERSE U.S. HOUSE

The low-diversity, unrepresentative House membership is shown in Figure 10.1. The year is 1996, but subsequent elections have the same pattern. Latinos constitute approximately 10.0 percent of the population but have only 4.4 percent representation in the House. African Americans, with 12.6 percent of the population, have a higher representation of 8.5 percent. Their representation/population ratio is also higher at .67 than the Latinos' .43. These contrast markedly with the nonminority men's representation/population ratio, which is more than 100 percent at 1.13. Women (nonminority and minority) are the least represented, constituting 12 percent in the House, while their population is 51 percent, resulting in a representation/population ratio of .23. While exact rep-

Figure 10.1
U.S. House of Representatives, 1996: Ethnic and Gender Representation and
Representation/Population Ratios

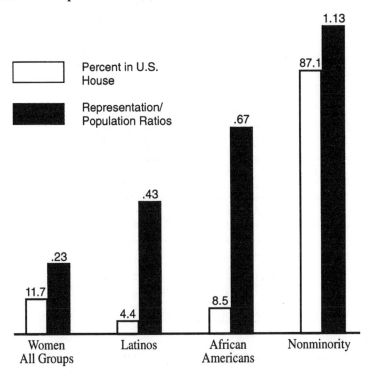

Note: Representation/population ratio example: Women were 51 percent of the national population.
   Dividing their population into the 11.7 percent of women representatives yields a ratio of .23,
   about one-fourth of parity, which would be 1.00.
Sources: Based on U.S. Department of Commerce, *Statistical Abstract of the United States* (Wash-
   ington, DC: U.S. Government Printing Office, 1996), p. 279, Table 1.2; Center for the American
   Women in Politics, "Women in Elective Office, 1997," a Fact Sheet, Eagleton Institute, Rut-
   gers University, 1997; *New York Times,* "Results of the U.S. House," November 7, 1996, pp.
   B8–B9.

resentation of various population groups in the nation is not essential for fair
representation, a reasonable resemblance to the diversity of the population is
required to accord with the Founders' goal of a people's House.

SEVEN STEPS TO UNREPRESENTATION

What explains this lopsided under- and overrepresentation? Figure 10.2 sets
forth general empirical models of the election systems of the U.S. House and
several European parliaments, including those in Austria, Denmark, Finland,
Germany, Netherlands, Norway, and Sweden.[16] The models represent ongoing

Figure 10.2
General Models of Election Systems of the U.S. House and European Parliaments

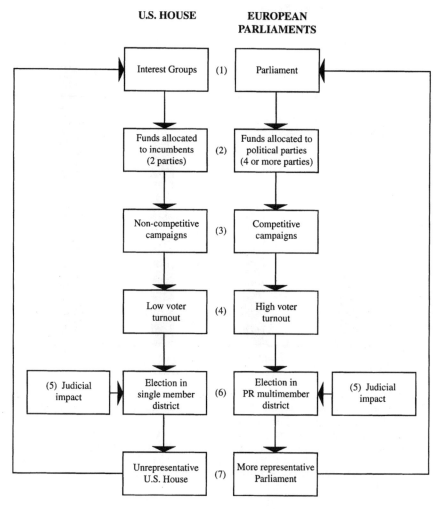

patterns of behavior causally linked, sequential (parts 1–4, 6–7), and composed of six highly correlated and interactive steps that result in the continued election of an unrepresentative U.S. House and in a more representative set of parliaments in Europe.[17] The European parliamentary system is presented for comparative purposes, including its contrasts with the House system on campaign finance and election formula, examined later.

The House election sequence in Figure 10.2 begins with interest groups at step 1 since they are the major contributors to individual election campaigns.[18] In contrast, the preponderance of campaign funds for elections in Europe derives

Table 10.1
Interest Group Contributions to U.S. House Candidates, 1993–1994

Interest Group	Amount	Percent
Corporations and Trade Associations (e.g.; tobacco, health, insurance, gaming)	$82.3	62
Labor Unions	33.4	25
Advocacy Groups (*e.g.*: American Medical Association, Sierra Club)	11.8	9
Unreported	4.5	4

Source: U.S. Bureau of the Census, *Statistical Abstract of the United States* (Washington, DC: U.S. Government Printing Office, 1996), p. 219.

from national parliaments that allocate funds directly to political parties. Individual contributions to candidates and political parties are authorized both in the United States and in Europe. However, in the former it is primarily interest group money that goes to reelecting incumbents who have dominated the House since 1978. A total of $132 million in "hard" (reported, regulated) money was contributed to these candidates in 1993–1994 (see Table 10.1).

Business interests gave the most "hard" money, and labor less than one-half as much; advocacy groups gave only 9 percent of the total. House members also indirectly received millions of dollars in "soft" money (not reported, unregulated) from various interests. These unlimited funds ostensibly are for political party building. However, campaign funds in 1991–1992 were channeled indirectly to House candidates through national and state party organizations or through other means.[19] The amount of money donated by interest groups has been increasing exponentially in subsequent elections (refer to Chapters 6 and 7 in this volume).

Step 2: in Europe, public funds are distributed to four to seven political parties in proportion to the parliamentary seats they won in the last election.[20] In the U.S. House, incumbents receive two-thirds to four-fifths of all the campaign funds contributed by political action committees. In turn, party organizations also concentrate their additional moneys on incumbent candidates, whose rate of reelection has increased since 1976. Incumbency was 66 percent in nine European countries with the party-list form of proportional representation (List-PR), and political funds were spent on electing the parties' slate of candidates.[21]

Steps 3 and 4: U.S. House elections are usually one-sided events with foregone conclusions, whereas the European parliamentary contests typically are extremely competitive. Voter turnout in mid-term elections for the House was 45 percent in 1994, and during the presidential elections of 1996 it was 54 percent of registered voters.[22] The young, poor, and the uneducated are nonvoters as well as others who decline to vote in noncompetitive House elections.[23]

As a consequence, elections for the House are decided without the participation of most eligible voters. In European elections, the turnout for the seven countries studied averages 85 percent.[24] A high voter turnout is correlated positively with the importance of the election to the individual voter (salience), as found in a study of 29 nations.[25]

Step 5: Judicial decisions are an important causal factor for the unrepresentativeness of the U.S. House and the representativeness of European parliaments. U.S. judicial decisions not only have perpetuated dominance of the SMD election formula but have ruled in favor of the *status quo ante* before the Voting Rights Act was amended in 1982.[26] These amendments emphasized minority representation. However, neither minority nor nonminority women were included as a discrete class. The amended Voting Rights Act encouraged state and local governments to revise their SMD boundaries in order to create "majority minority" districts in which a majority of blacks or Latinos could elect candidates of their choice. By 1982 the number of minorities in the House had increased considerably, but only halfway to population parity. Subsequently, the U.S. Supreme Court (*Shaw v. Reno*, 1993, to *Bush v. Vera*, 1996) ruled deliberately drawn "majority minority" districts were unconstitutional (see Chapter 8 in this volume).

Although minority House incumbents were reelected in 1996 in four white-dominated, redrawn districts, the overwhelming number of minority members was elected first from "majority minority" districts.[27] Thus, the "majority majority" white districts reinstituted by the U.S. Supreme Court appear to prevent substantial gains for minorities in the future, given no change in the SMD election formula or the Court's opinion. In contrast, the impact of the European judiciary has been to support party-list proportional representation, described in a subsequent section.[28]

Steps 6 and 7: Each of the foregoing five steps is explanatory and significant in determining who is elected. In House elections when the numbers of the young, poor, and uneducated nonvoters are added to those of other minorities and women, there is a majority of the population that largely is unrepresented directly. Instead, white males, who are 40 percent of the nation's population, are the typical election winners in House elections.[29] Although 40 incumbents declined to run again for election since 1978, and only about 26 incumbents were defeated, the 66 newcomers constitute only 15 percent of the average new House. That proportion is low compared to approximately one-third newcomers in Europe's parliaments. Because the House is not representative of most Americans, it is questionable whether it can be sufficiently responsive to changing concerns within the population.

Feedback: at the conclusion of the House election cycle (as presented in Figure 10.2, steps 1–7), the interest groups that funded the election receive some "payoffs." Anecdotal evidence indicates the "payoffs" may range from access to influential House members, from Speaker, to committee chairs, to legislation or amendments, to bills favoring their corporate, trade, or advocacy groups.[30]

(See Chapter 6 in this volume.) These favors make it worthwhile for interest groups to donate campaign funds for the next contest. In so doing, the House election system keeps cycling again and again.

In Europe, according to one comparative study, some individual political contributions from plutocrats and corporations could result in "payoffs" for individual donors. Yet these contributions constitute an estimated 10 to 30 percent of the parties' budgets along with the balance provided by public funds and members' dues.[31] Consequently, part of the feedback to European parliaments is the generally high esteem that the public has for them, for their election system, and for the proportional representation formula's fairness and equity. This favorable public opinion toward parliaments and the salience of elections helps keep the European election cycling. In the United States, according to a generally representative Gallup poll taken in 1994, 41 percent of the respondents stated that they had little confidence in Congress, while the same percentage had only some confidence.[32] Nevertheless, the U.S. House election system continues as presented earlier and in Figure 10.2.

CONCLUSIONS

One can be proactive before a system breaks down so that one may restore, reform, and rebuild it. (See Chapters 15 and 18 in this volume.) Reform proposals include limiting the amount of money interest groups may contribute to House candidates and political parties and improving the disclosure of campaign contributors.[33] Another proposal would give greater opportunity for challengers to win over incumbents by providing public "seed money" for all House candidates. These proposals, if constitutional, would limit only the scale of financial contributions of interest groups and would leave intact the interest groups' practice of giving much more money to incumbents (see Chapter 7 in this volume).[34] Challengers with "seed money" would have little likelihood of winning against incumbents with such overwhelming campaign funds. One solution might be consideration of Europe's successful campaign funding, publicly financed with private contributions kept to a minimum.

Term limits have been proposed as an alternative to high levels of incumbency in the House. Such limits were not included in the Constitution, for it was held that limiting terms was a prerogative of the people in each House district.[35] Such limits alone would leave the present financial arrangements intact (see Chapter 14 in this volume). Moreover, it is likely that a district's partisan majority or plurality would remain. The result would be a circulation of elites with little alteration in partisan viewpoints, even though the personnel in the House would be changing.

Returning briefly to the Founders' ideas for representation in the House, subsequent adaptation in modern times is pertinent here. "The people's house" was to reflect the at-large population and to be responsive to it. Multi-member districts, Madison wrote, would lessen the influence of economic factions, corrupt political parties, and overbearing majorities in single-member districts. Fifty years later and throughout the 19th century, reformers in Europe had similar ideas. They began to develop multi-member, proportional representation districts to allow legislative representation for minority voters and minority parties even when there was an entrenched majority.[36] Candidates would be elected on the basis of the votes obtained by one of several political parties. For example, if Party X received 20 percent of the votes, Party X candidates would get 20 percent of the seats in parliament. The party-list proportional representation electoral formula was adopted first by countries in Europe with ethnic or religious divisions.[37] It was viewed as a stabilizing measure since nearly all groups would be included in the parliament. Later, as male suffrage became universal, people without representation in majoritarian districts sought to have proportional representation adopted for electing their parliaments. Another development allowed "preference voting," whereby voters could choose among the parties' candidates if they did not want to accept the party's slate.[38] Thus, parliaments become more representative of Europe's citizens in the 19th and 20th centuries.

This slow, evolutionary journey to proportional representation is one way to a more representative House. A more expeditious way is through national electoral commissions and national referenda, as in New Zealand.[39] Chapter 13 in this volume tells how Scotland changed its election formula. Both these examples of electoral reform took place in former United Kingdom jurisdictions with inherited SMDs districts that later added party-list proportional representation.[40] South Africa, by contrast, elects all of its new parliament by proportional representation.[41] In the latter and in New Zealand, a more representative national legislature that includes substantial numbers of women and other minorities was achieved. Likewise, a more representative House is achievable and would accord with the goals of the Founders of the nation and the U.S. Constitution.

NOTES

1. "Systems of election," or "election system," refers to a pattern of intercorrelated behaviors that result in the election of legislative candidates and in the representational outcome. It differs from "electoral systems," a general term that includes the electoral formula (e.g., majority, proportional representation, etc.), district magnitude (number of representatives per district), and threshold (the minimum votes needed to win a seating). See Arend Lijphart, *Electoral Systems and Party Systems* (New York: Oxford University Press, 1994), p. 1; Andre Blais and Louis Massicotte, "Electoral Systems," in Lawrence LeDuc, Richard G. Niemi, and Pippa Norris, eds., *Comparing Democracies, Elections, and Voting in Global Perspective* (Thousand Oaks, CA: Sage, 1996), p. 50.

2. Scott Mainwaring, "Electoral Volatility in Brazil," *Party Politics*, October 1988, pp. 523–46.

3. Enid Lakeman, "Comparing Political Opportunities in Great Britain and Ireland," in Wilma Rule and Joseph F. Zimmerman, eds., *Electoral Systems in Comparative Perspective: Their Impact on Women and Minorities* (Westport, CT: Greenwood Press, 1994), pp. 45–49.

4. *Reapportionment Act of 1842*, 5 Stat. 491.

5. For incumbency, see U.S. Bureau of the Census, *Statistical Abstract of the United States* (Washington, DC: U.S. Government Printing Office, 1996), p. 279; Peter Mair, "Party Systems and Structures of Competition," in LeDuc, Niemi, and Norris, eds., *Comparing Democracies, Elections, and Voting in Global Perspective*. Mair wrote, "Closed structures of competition are clearly characteristics of traditional two-party systems" (p. 96). The average turnout for U.S. mid-term elections was 35 percent (1982–1994); for presidential years it was 53 percent (1976–1992) of the eligible voters. See the *Statistical Abstract of the United States*, p. 287.

6. Gordon Wood, *The Creation of the American Republic 1776–1787* (Chapel Hill: University of North Carolina Press, 1969), p. 197.

7. *U.S. Constitution*, Article 1, § 2.

8. James Madison, *The Federalist Number 10*, in Richard D. Heffner, ed., *A Documentary History of the United States* (New York: New American Library, 1958), p. 43.

9. Ibid.

10. Julian P. Boyd, ed., *The Jefferson Papers* (Princeton, NJ: Princeton University Press, 1952), vol. 6, pp. 308–9. See also Wood, *The Creation of the American Republic*, pp. 510–11.

11. Boyd, *The Jefferson Papers*, pp. 308–9.

12. Wood, *The Creation of the American Republic*, p. 170.

13. Ibid.

14. Robert Darcy, Charles D. Hadley, and Jason Kirksey, "Election Systems and the Representation of Black Women in American State Legislatures," *Women and Politics*, vol. 13, no. 2, 1993, pp. 73–90. See also Wilma Rule, "Multimember Legislative Districts: Anglo and Minority Women and Men's Recruitment Opportunity," in Wilma Rule and Joseph F. Zimmerman, eds., *United States Electoral Systems: Their Impact on Women and Minorities* (Westport, CT: Greenwood Press, 1992), pp. 57–72.

15. Wilma Rule, "Why More Women Are State Legislators," *Western Political Quarterly*, June 1990, pp. 437–48.

16. Omitted are Belgium, Italy, Spain, and Switzerland, for which sufficient data on political finance are unavailable. See Karl-Heinz Nassmacher, "Comparing Party and Campaign Finance in Western Democracies," in Arthur B. Gunlicks, ed., *Campaign and Party Finance in North America and Western Europe* (Boulder, CO: Westview Press, 1993), pp. 247, 263.

17. David Easton, *A Systems Analysis of Political Life* (New York: John Wiley and Sons, 1965), p. 18.

18. A comparison of early studies with the most recent ones reveals tactics of campaign funding appear to vary with changes in the political environment. However, the strategy for preservation of incumbents remains intact. Paul S. Herrnson, "High Finance of American Politics: Campaign Spending and Reform in Federal Elections," in Gunlicks, ed., *Campaign and Party Finance*, p. 26; Herbert Alexander and Anthony Corrado, *Financing the 1992 Election* (Armonk, NY: M. E. Sharpe, 1995). For the 1996 campaign, see, for example, Leslie Wayne, "Business Biggest Campaign Spender," *New York Times*, October 18, 1996, p. 1; David E. Rosenbaum, "The Political Money Game, the Year of Big Loopholes," *New York Times*, December 26, 1996, p. 1. See Chapters 6 and 7 in this volume for further information.

19. Diana Dwyre, "Spinning Straw into Gold: Soft Money and U.S. House Elections," *Legislative Studies Quarterly*, August 1996, pp. 409–24.

20. Karl-Heinz Nassmacher, "Comparing Party and Campaign Finance in Western Democracies," in Gunlicks, ed., *Campaign and Party Finance*, pp. 241–43.

21. Richard Katz, "Intraparty Preference Voting," in Bernard Grofman and Arend Lijphart, eds., *Election Laws and Their Political Consequences* (New York: Agathon, 1986), p. 98. Also consult in the same volume Karl-Heinz Nassmacher, "Comparing Party and Campaign Finance in Western Democracies," pp. 247–48, and Gudrun Klee, "Financing Parties and Elections in Small European Democracies," p. 195.

22. *Statistical Abstract of the United States, 1997*, p. 288.

23. Task Force on Campaign Reform, *Campaign Reform, Insights and Evidence* (Princeton, NJ: Woodrow Wilson School of Public and International Affairs, 1998), p. 41.

24. Mark L. Franklin, "Electoral Participation," in LeDuc, Niemi, and Norris, eds., *Comparing Democracies, Elections, and Voting in Global Perspective*, pp. 215, 227. Other factors include frequency of elections (negative), convenience of voting, compulsory voting, Sunday voting, and proportionality of national legislature.

25. Ibid.

26. *Voting Rights Act Amendments of 1982*, 96 Stat. 131, 42 U.S.C. § 1973.

27. Wilma Rule, "Women, Representation and Political Rights," in Mark E. Rush, ed., *Voting Rights and Redistricting in the United States* (Westport, CT: Greenwood Press, 1998), p. 41.

28. The German Constitutional Court has ruled against aspects of public financing. See Peter Losche, "Problems of Campaign Financing in Germany and the United States, Some Comparative Reflections," in Gunlicks, ed., *Campaign and Party Finance*, pp. 219–330. In contrast, Pilar del Castillo noted problems without public funding. See his "Problems in Spanish Party Financing," in Herbert Alexander and Rei Shiratori, eds., *Comparative Political Finance among the Democracies* (Boulder, CO: Westview Press, 1994), pp. 97–104.

29. Task Force on Campaign Reform, *Campaign Reform, Insights and Evidence*, p. 41; *Statistical Abstract of the United States, 1996*, p. 279.

30. Daniel M. West and Burdett A. Loomis, *The Sound of Money* (New York: W. W. Norton, 1998).

31. Nassmacher, "Comparing Party and Campaign Finance in Western Democracies," in Gunlicks, ed., *Campaign and Party Finance*, pp. 253–55.

32. *Statistical Abstract of the United States, 1996*, p. 285.

33. Task Force on Campaign Reform, *Campaign Reform*, pp. 6–9.

34. See Adam Clymer, "Justices Reject Bid to Limit Party Spending," *New York Times*, June 27, 1996, p. B-6.

35. *U.S. Constitution*, Article 1.

36. Stein Rokkan relates the origins of proportional representation in *Citizens, Elections and Parties* (New York: David McKay, 1970), pp. 157–68.

37. Denmark (1855), Swiss cantons (1891), Belgium (1899), and Finland (1906) (ibid., p. 157).

38. Matthew S. Shugart, "Minorities Represented and Unrepresented," in Rule and Zimmerman, eds., *Electoral Systems in Comparative Perspective*, pp. 31–41.

39. Jack Nagel, "Constitutional Reform and Social Difference in New Zealand," *Cardoza Journal of International and Comparative Law*, vol. 4, no. 2, 1996, pp. 373–94.

40. Andrew Reynolds, *Electoral Systems and Democratization in Southern Africa* (London: Oxford University Press, 1998).

41. Wilma Rule, "Electoral Systems, Contextual Factors, and Women's Opportunity for Election to Parliament in Twenty-three Democracies," *Western Political Quarterly*, September 1987, pp. 477–98.

Chapter 11

Too Much of a Good Thing: More Representative Is Not Necessarily Better

John R. Hibbing and Elizabeth Theiss-Morse

Reform sentiments are much in evidence on the American political scene at the end of the century, and improving the way public opinion is represented in political institutions is often the major motivation of reformers. This conclusion is clear from the activities of contemporary political elites and from the mood of ordinary people. Gross dissatisfaction exists with the nature of representation perceived to be offered by the modern political system. People believe the political process has been commandeered by narrow special interests and by political parties whose sole aim is to contradict the other political party. Given the centrality of representation in the U.S. polity, the editors of this volume are to be commended. It is laudable to want to consider ways of improving the system and, therefore, making people happier with their government. Many of the ideas described in the chapters have considerable merit.

We do, however, wish to raise two important cautions: one briefly and the second in greater detail. Perhaps these cautions are not needed; most of the other contributors are almost certainly aware of them. Still, general debate often neglects these two points. Therefore, quite apart from whether it is a good idea or a bad idea, say, to reform campaign finance, enact term limits, or move toward proportional representation and away from single-member districts, it is important for readers to be reminded that (1) ''because the people want them'' is not a good justification for why procedural reforms should be adopted and (2) enactment of the reforms craved by the people will not necessarily leave us with a system that is more liked even by the people who asked for them in the first place. We take each point in turn.

IGNORING THE PEOPLE'S VOICE ON PROCESS MATTERS IS NOT EVIL

It would be easy at this point to slip into a discussion of the level of political acumen possessed by the American public and, relatedly, of the extent to which elected officials and political institutions should listen to the people. But such a discussion has been going on at least since the time of Plato, and it is unlikely we would add much to it here. Instead, we merely wish to point out that, whatever the overall talents of the rank and file, political change in the realm of process should *not* be as sensitive to the public's wishes as political change in the realm of policy.

It is one thing to maintain that in a democracy the people should get welfare reform if they want it. It is quite another to maintain those same people should get term limits if they want them. Process needs to have some relative permanence, some stickiness, or it would not meet the definition of an institutional process. Without this trait, policy legitimacy would be compromised. The U.S. Constitution (like all constitutions) drives home this contention by including much on process (vetoes, impeachments, representational arrangements, terms of officials, minimum qualifications of officials, etc.) and precious little about policy. What policy proclamations *are* to be found in the Constitution have faced a strong likelihood of being reversed in subsequent actions (slavery and the 13th Amendment; tax policy and the 16th Amendment; prohibition and the 21st Amendment). Constitutions are written not to enshrine policy but to enshrine a system that will then make policy. These systemic structures should not be subjected lightly to popular whimsy.

The Framers took great efforts to insulate process issues from the momentary fancies of the people; specifically, they made amending the Constitution difficult. It is not unusual for reformers, therefore, to run up against the Constitution and its main interpreters, the courts. Witness recent decisions undermining the ability of citizens to impose legislative term limits on members of Congress save by constitutional amendment. This uphill battle to enact procedural reform is precisely what the Founders intended—and they were wise to do so.

It may be that the people's will should be reflected directly in public policy, perhaps by way of initiatives or, less drastically, by way of citizen legislators who act as delegates rather than Burkean trustees. But it does not follow that the rules of the system themselves should change with public preferences in the same way health care policy should change with public preferences. There may be many good reasons to change the processes of government, possibly by making government more representative, but a persuasive defense of process reforms is *not* embedded in the claim that the people are desirous of such reform. Just as the Bill of Rights does not permit a simple majority of the people to make decisions that will restrict basic rights, so the rest of the Constitution does not permit a simple majority of the people to alter willy-nilly the processes of government. There are good reasons for such arrangements.

BE CAREFUL WHAT YOU WISH FOR

One important reason we should be glad ordinary people are not in a position to leave their every mark on questions of political process and institutional design is the very good possibility people will not be happy with the reforms they themselves advocate. The people generally clamor for reforms that would weaken institutions and strengthen the role of the people in policy decisions. They advocate people's courts, an increased number of popular initiatives and referenda, devolution of authority to institutions "closer" to the people, term limits, staff cuts, emaciating the bureaucracy, elimination of committees, cessation of contact between interest groups and elected officials, and a weakening of political parties. These changes would clear the way for people to have greater influence on decisions, and this is what the people want, right?

Our research suggests greater influence is *not* what the people really want. The public does not desire direct democracy; it is not even clear people desire democracy at all, although they are quite convinced they do. People want no part of a national direct democracy in which they would be asked to register their preferences, probably electronically, on important issues of the day. Proposals for such procedures are received warmly by a very small minority of citizens. Observers who notice the public's enthusiasm for virtually every populist notion sometimes go the next step of assuming the public wants direct democracy. This assumption is simply an inaccurate one.

However, the public *does* want institutions to be transformed into something much closer to the people. The public sees a big disconnect between how they want representation to work and how they believe it is working. Strong support of populist government (not direct democracy) has been detected in innumerable polls conducted during the last couple of decades. That the public looks favorably upon this process agenda is beyond dispute. A national survey we conducted in 1992 found strong support for reforms that would limit the impact of the Washington scene on members of Congress.[1] For example, seven out of ten respondents supported a reduction in congressional salaries, eight out of ten supported term limitations, and nine out of ten supported a balanced-budget amendment. What ties these reforms together is the public's desire to make elected officials more like ordinary people. In focus groups we conducted at the same time as the survey, participants stated many times that elected officials in Washington had lost touch with the people. They supported reforms believed to encourage officials to start keeping in touch. Elected officials, just like the people back home, should balance the budget. Elected officials, just like the people back home, should live off modest salaries. Elected officials should face the prospect of getting a real job back home rather than staying in Washington for years and years. These reforms would force elected officials to understand the needs of their constituents rather than get swept up in the money and power that run Washington.

If these reforms were put into place, would the public suddenly love Congress? We do not think so. Certain reforms, such as campaign finance reform, may help since they would diminish the perception that money rules politics in Washington. But the main reason the public is disgruntled with Congress and with politics in Washington is the processes inherent in a democratic political system—debates, compromises, conflicting information, inefficiency, and slowness. This argument may seem odd on its face, so in the next few paragraphs we provide our interpretation of why the public questions the need for democratic processes.

The public operates under the erroneous assumption the majority of the American people agree on policy matters. In focus groups we conducted in 1997 it was common to hear participants make claims such as this one: "Eighty percent of the American people agree on what needs to be done [about serious societal problems], but it's the other twenty percent who have the power." This pervasive and persistent belief in the existence of popular consensus on tough policy issues is, of course, grossly mistaken. Virtually every well-worded survey question dealing with salient policy issues of the day reveals deep divisions in the American public. From welfare reform to health care; from remaining in Bosnia to the taxes-services trade-off; from a constitutional amendment on flag desecration to the situations in which abortion is believed to be properly permitted, the people are at odds with each other.

This level of popular disagreement would be quite unremarkable except for the fact that the people will not admit that the disagreement actually exists. Instead, people project their own particular views, however ill formed, onto a clear majority of other "real" people. Those (allegedly) few people who allow it to be known that they do not hold these views are dismissed as radical and noisy fringe elements that are accorded far too much influence by polemical parties, self-serving special interests, and spineless, out-of-touch elected officials. Thus, the desire to move the locus of decision making closer to the people is based on a faulty assumption right off the bat. Many believe that if decisions emanated from the people themselves, we would get a welcome break from the fractious politics created by politicians and institutions. Pastoral, commonsensical solutions will instead quietly begin to find their way into the statute books. The artificial conflict to which we have unfortunately become accustomed will be no more, and we can then begin to solve problems.

Given people's widespread belief in popular consensus, it is no wonder they despise the existing structure of governmental institutions. All that these institutions—and the people filling them—do is obscure the will of the people by making it look as though there is a great deal of divisiveness afoot. Who, then, can condone debate and compromise among elected officials if these processes only give disproportionate weight to nefarious fringe elements intent upon subverting the desires of healthy, red-blooded Americans? Who, then, can condone inefficiency and slowness when we all agree on what needs to be done, and politicians ought just to do it? Democratic processes merely get in the way. People react positively to the idea we ought to run government like a business—

it would be efficient, frugal, and quick to respond to problems. Of course, what people tend not to realize is that it would also be undemocratic.

Too many people do not understand political conflict; they have not been taught to deal with it; they have not come to realize it is a natural part of a culture such as ours. When they are confronted with it, they conclude it is an indication something is woefully amiss and in need of correction. They jump at any solution perceived to have the potential of reducing conflict, solutions such as giving authority over to potentially autocratic and hierarchical, businesslike arrangements or to mythically consensual ordinary people.

Our fear is that, if the people were actually given what they want, they might soon be even more disillusioned with the political system than ever. Suppose people *were* made to feel more represented than they are now; suppose authority *were* really pushed toward the common person. The first thing people would learn is that these changes will have done nothing to eliminate political conflict. The deep policy divisions polls now reveal among the citizenry would be of more consequence since these very views would now be more determinative of public policy. Conflict would still be pervasive. Popular discontent would not have been ameliorated. Quite likely, people would quickly grow ever more cynical about the potential for reform to accomplish what they want it to accomplish.

Instead of allowing the people to strive for the impossible—an open and inclusive democracy devoid of conflict—we need to educate the people about the unrealistic nature of their desires. Instead of giving the people every reform for which they agitate, we need to get them to see where their wishes really are headed. The people pay lip service to democracy, but that is the extent of it. They claim to love democracy, but they love only the concept. They do not love the actual practice of democracy because it suggests differences; because it is ponderous; because it revolves around debate (bickering) and compromise (selling out) and divisions (gridlock).

CONCLUSION

We hasten to point out that we are not opposed to reforms. For what it is worth, we believe the U.S. polity could certainly benefit from selective modifications in current institutional arrangements. But we *are* opposed to the tendency of many ordinary people to try to enact reforms intended to weaken political institutions, even though these same people evince no real plan involving where that power should be transferred. It is often assumed the people are populists and therefore want power in their own hands. As we have indicated, they do not in actuality want power. They only want to know they could have this power if they wanted it. They only want to know this power is not being exercised by those who are in a position to use it to their own advantage. They only want decisions to be made nonconflictually. They are willing to entertain a variety of possible structures (some far from democratic) if those reforms appear to offer hope of bringing about all these somewhat contradictory desires.

Altering representational arrangements should be considered. The current system can and must be improved. The campaign finance system is an embarrassment, and the dispute over drawing oddly shaped districts for the purpose of obtaining majority-minority districts lays bear the very real problems of single-member districts. But we should not jump at all reforms simply because the people think they want them. No one said that in a democracy the people would get to shape process into whatever they want. It is not inconsistent to have democratic governmental structures that are rather impervious to popular sentiments for change in those procedures. What makes the system democratic is the ability of people's opinions to influence policy, not the ability of people's opinions to influence process.

This inability of citizens to greatly influence process is fortunate because the people's ideas about process are fundamentally flawed. People (understandably) think well of the American public writ large, and people (understandably) dislike conflict, so people (nonsensically) assume the two cannot go together in spite of the impressive array of factual evidence indicating conflict and the American people—indeed, any free people, as Madison so eloquently related in *Federalist Number 10*—go hand in hand. As a result of their misconception, the people will undoubtedly be quite dissatisfied with the actual consequences of most attempts to expand representation via campaign finance, term limits, or proportional representation. There may be good reasons to enact such reforms, but, we submit, neither a public likely to be suddenly pleased with the postreform political system nor a public somehow deserving of a direct voice in process reform is one of them.

NOTES

This chapter is a revised version of an article that appeared in *PS: Political Science and Politics*, vol. 31, no. 1, March 1998, pp. 28–31. The findings described are based on research supported by the National Science Foundation under grants SES-21–22733 and SBR-97–09934.

1. John R. Hibbing and Elizabeth Theiss-Morse, *Congress as Public Enemy: Public Attitudes toward American Political Institutions* (Cambridge: Cambridge University Press, 1995).

Part IV

Reform Possibilities

Chapter 12

Reforming the House:
Three Moderately Radical Proposals

Arend Lijphart

Most observers of the U.S. House of Representatives undoubtedly agree that in many respects, large and small, the House does not perform its representative function very well. Not being an expert on the details and intricacies of House operations, I leave the smaller matters—such as incremental steps to reform the financing of election campaigns—to the specialists. Let me focus instead on three major characteristics that make the House insufficiently representative: (1) its election by plurality, which does not provide adequate representation for minorities and minority views; (2) its election by an unrepresentative electorate, especially in mid-term elections, when only about one-third of the eligible voters make use of their right to vote; and (3) its comparatively small size of only 435 members.

The three reforms that would greatly alleviate these defects are the introduc tion of proportional representation (PR) for House elections, adoption of a four-year term for representatives, and enlargement of the House by about 50 percent to roughly 650 members. Many political scientists and other informed observers would regard these proposals as quite radical. I call them only moderately radical for two reasons. One is that I can think of considerably more drastic proposals that I believe also would improve the representative quality of the House, such as a shift from our presidential system to a parliamentary form of government. Second, my three proposals may look radical from a purely national point of view, but, in comparative terms, they are not radical at all: they merely would bring the House in line with the lower (or only) houses in most of the established democracies.

PROPORTIONAL REPRESENTATION

That PR provides more accurate representation than majoritarian election methods is not controversial. What opponents of PR fear, however, is that this advantage is outweighed by serious disadvantages, particularly the fragmentation of the party system. I agree that this concern is valid in presidential systems. Scott Mainwaring called the combination of presidentialism and multipartism, common in Latin American democracies, "the difficult combination" because multipartism increases the likelihood that the president's party will not have a congressional majority and hence also the likelihood of executive-legislative deadlock.[1]

On the other hand, political scientists also have found that, in presidential systems, the use of PR for congressional elections tends not to lead to a high degree of fragmentation of the party system under two conditions: the election of the president by plurality instead of majority runoff and the concurrence of presidential and congressional elections.[2] The reason is that plurality in presidential elections discourages minor parties from participating and advantages and especially the two largest parties, and that this advantage for the largest parties spills over into congressional elections if these are held simultaneously. Both of these conditions are fulfilled in the United States in presidential election years. The Electoral College method for presidential elections is a rough functional equivalent of the plurality method, and both presidential and congressional elections take place at the same time in early November, which means that the adoption of PR for House elections may well lead to the end of our almost pure two-party system but that it is unlikely to lead to excessive fragmentation.

Another important consideration, of course, is the type of PR that would be adopted. PR comes in a multitude of forms that have an effect on the number of parties. Of particular importance is the so-called district magnitude, that is, the number of representatives elected in the election district: the smaller the districts, the more difficult it is for small parties to gain representation, and the less fragmented the party system is likely to be.[3] On the assumption of the most straightforward kind of PR system in which the 50 states would serve as the election districts for House elections, the average district magnitude would be only 8.7 (435 divided by 50), which is a relatively low number by comparative standards and is not likely to produce extreme multipartism.

Another way to look at the restrictive effect of district magnitude is to calculate what the equivalent electoral threshold would be. Thresholds are used often in PR systems in order to deny representation to very small parties. District magnitudes and electoral thresholds can therefore be seen as two sides of the same coin, and a reasonable approximation of their relationship, suggested by Rein Taagepera, is $T = 75\%/(M+1)$, in which T is the threshold, and M is the average district magnitude.[4] This means that the average magnitude of 8.7 representatives per district calculated for House elections earlier is the equivalent of an electoral threshold of about 7.7 percent—indicating that parties smaller than about 7.7 percent will be disadvantaged seriously, if not barred altogether. Such a 7.7 percent threshold is considerably higher than the legal threshold of 4.0 to 5.0 percent applied in many European PR systems.

In short, while the combination of PR and presidentialism may be a "difficult combination" in other countries, it is highly unlikely to lead to major problems in the United States.

FOUR-YEAR TERMS

One qualification needs to be added at once to the preceding conclusion insofar as it is based on the concurrent election of president and House: it applies only to presidential election years, since mid-term congressional elections are not concurrent elections. In order to make all House elections concurrent, the term of office of representatives would have to be increased from two to four years (or, of course, presidential terms would have to be decreased from four to two years, but I think that the latter possibility does not need to be seriously considered). If PR were introduced for House elections, therefore, it should ideally be combined with a shift to four-year terms for House members.

However, four-year terms are worth adopting even in the absence of PR. The reason is that voter turnout in House elections in presidential election years is considerably better—or, more accurately, considerably less poor—than in mid-term congressional elections: raising voter participation from about one-third of the eligible voters, typical of mid-term elections, to about one-half in recent presidential elections means an increase of about 50 percent. Generally speaking, more privileged voters—those with higher incomes, greater wealth, and better education—turn out to vote in greater numbers than less advantaged citizens, and the lower the turnout, the greater this difference tends to become. Unequal turnout spells unequal representation and unequal influence. Four-year terms, coinciding with the four-year presidential terms, therefore, would make the House appreciably more representative. It also should be pointed out that four-year terms are close to the norm for lower or only houses in the established democracies. There are a few countries with three-year terms (Australia, New Zealand, and Sweden), but most democracies use four-year or five-year terms. In parliamentary systems, these terms are maximum rather than fixed terms, but the average actual legislative term of office in the established democracies is still close to four years.

This argument in favor of four-year terms is based on the desirability of making the House more representative by raising the turnout in House elections and thereby making turnout more equal. This advantage can be achieved by four-year terms without any other changes in the system, such as the introduction of PR. However, another advantage of adopting both PR and four-year terms is that PR also has the effect of raising turnout—by roughly ten percentage points.[5] Other measures that can further boost turnout are automatic registration and especially, as I have argued at length elsewhere, compulsory voting.[6]

ENLARGING THE HOUSE

Finally, the House of Representatives could be made more representative if its membership would be enlarged. The general pattern in democracies is for the size of lower (or only) houses to increase with population size: small countries tend to have smaller legislatures than large countries. As Rein Taagepera discovered, this pattern can be expressed in a neat formula: the size of a country's national assembly tends to approximate the cube root of its population size.[7] According to this norm, the House with its 435 members is unusually small for a country with a population of about 270 million people; it "should" have a House with about 650 members. (The exact cube root of 270 million is 646.) The fact that both the United Kingdom and Germany have lower houses of approximately this size shows that a membership of 650 is not too large for the effective operation of a legislature.

Having 650 representatives would improve representation in two major ways. First, increasing the membership of the House by about 50 percent entails a decrease in the population size of the average congressional district by about 50 percent, which lessens the distance between voters and their legislators. Second, assuming that plurality elections would be maintained, smaller congressional districts make it easier to draw these districts in such a way as to provide representation for geographically concentrated minorities without having to fashion the outrageously shaped districts that the Supreme Court dislikes.

If the 650 representatives would be elected by PR under the conditions outlined earlier (i.e., in districts coinciding with the 50 states), the average district magnitude would go up from 8.7 to 13.0, and the equivalent electoral threshold would go down from about 7.7 to about 5.4 percent. This change could be considered an advantage in that it would increase the proportionality of the election results; it would probably also reduce the number of very small states with only one representative—and hence necessarily without PR. Moreover, a threshold of 5.4 percent is still higher than the 4.0 to 5.0 percent threshold used in many European PR systems. On the other hand, if the new district magnitudes would be regarded as too permissive for small parties, a legal threshold of say 6 or 7 percent could be imposed.

FEASIBILITY

I am well aware of the political science law that the probability of reform varies inversely with the magnitude of the proposed reform. Therefore, even though I consider the previous proposals only moderately radical, I am not overly optimistic that they have an excellent chance of being adopted in the foreseeable future. At the same time, the most radical—or the least moderate— of my three proposals, the adoption of PR, together with the enlargement of the House, actually may have a somewhat better chance than the less drastic proposal to shift from two-year to four-year terms. For one thing, four-year terms for representatives would require a constitutional amendment, whereas PR as well as increasing the size of the House can be accomplished by law.

Second, the three proposals differ in the degree to which they can be introduced step by step. It is hard to see how a four-year term could be adopted incrementally, for instance, at first for some representatives but not for others or an initial increase to a three-year term to be followed later by a four-year term; a three-year term also would aggravate the problem of nonconcurrence between House elections and presidential elections. However, both the enlargement of the House and the adoption of PR could be adopted incrementally. This is very obvious in the case of the former proposal, although for practical reasons increases in membership would have to coincide with decennial reapportionments; as a result, unless relatively large increases were adopted every ten years, it would take a long time to reach the goal of 650 House members.

As far as the gradual adoption of PR is concerned, the United States is unusual among Western democracies in having a tradition in which different jurisdictions may elect their representatives by different election methods. For instance, most states in the United States currently use plurality, single-member districts for electing their representatives, but majority-runoff elections are used in Louisiana (where the first round of the election is referred to as the ''nonpartisan primary'') and were used in Georgia until recently; moreover, until 1970, several states had at-large instead of single-member district elections or elected one at-large representative in addition to representatives chosen in single-member districts. The elimination of the legal requirement mandating single-member districts, as Representative Cynthia McKinney (D-GA) has proposed, would enable some states to adopt proportional or semi-proportional systems, while others could retain plurality, single-member district elections while waiting to see how the PR or semi-proportional experiments worked out.

In the final analysis, major reforms may be less, perhaps much less likely than minor ones, but they also have the potential of improving the House a great deal more. It therefore would be a pity if we believed in the political science law stated earlier to such an extent that we would not even think seriously about major reforms like the three proposed in this chapter—thereby making this pessimistic law into a self-fulfilling prophecy.

NOTES

This chapter first appeared in *PS: Political Science and Politics*, vol. 31, no. 1, March 1998, pp. 10–13 and is reprinted with the permission of The American Political Science Association.

1. Scott Mainwaring, ''Presidentialism, Multipartism, and Democracy: The Difficult Combination,'' *Comparative Political Studies*, July 1993, pp. 198–228.

2. Matthew S. Shugart and John M. Carey, *Presidents and Assemblies: Constitutional Design and Electoral Dynamics* (Cambridge: Cambridge University Press, 1992); Mark Jones, *Electoral Laws and the Survival of Presidential Democrats* (Notre Dame, IN: University of Notre Dame Press, 1995).

3. Rein Taagepera and Matthew S. Shugart, *Seats and Votes: The Effects and Determinants of Electoral Systems* (New Haven, CT: Yale University Press, 1989), pp. 112–25; Arend Lijphart, *Electoral Systems and Party Systems: A Study of Twenty-Seven Democracies, 1945–1990* (New Haven, CT: Yale University Press, 1994).

4. Lijphart, *Electoral Systems and Party Systems*, pp. 182–83.

5. Andre Blais and R. K. Carty, "Does Proportional Representation Foster Voter Turnout?" *European Journal of Political Research*, March 1990, pp. 167–81.

6. Arend Lijphart, "Unequal Participation: Democracy's Unresolved Dilemma," *The American Political Science Review*, March 1997, pp. 1–14.

7. Rein Taagepera, "The Size of National Assemblies," *Social Science Research*, December 1972, pp. 385–401.

Chapter 13

Building a Representative House in Scotland and the Role of Women

Alice Brown

The official opening ceremony of the new Scottish parliament was on July 1, 1999. The establishment of parliament is the result of a long campaign for reform and will mean that politics in Scotland never will be the same again.[1] The record-breaking United Kingdom general election in 1997 returned the Labour Party to power after eighteen years in opposition. The government lost little time in implementing one of its key election manifesto promises, namely, constitutional change, which included devolving power to Scotland and quickly publishing its White Paper on Devolution just two months after taking office. In the two-question referendum that followed in September 1997, people in Scotland voted to establish a Scottish parliament with tax-varying powers. The public endorsement of the government's proposals largely silenced those who had opposed constitutional change. The Scotland bill subsequently was published in December and introduced to the House of Commons early in 1998 before receiving royal assent later that year.

This chapter examines the background of the constitutional debate in Scotland and the development of plans to establish a more representative house run on fundamentally different lines from the Westminster model. The participatory role of women in the debate and developmental process also is examined.

BACKGROUND OF THE HOME RULE MOVEMENT

The year 1998 was not the first year in which a referendum was held in Scotland on constitutional change. A referendum on a Scottish Assembly took place in 1979 under a previous Labour government. At that time, the referendum contained just one question asking whether the Scottish people supported the setting up of a Scottish Assembly. Although 52 percent of votes cast favored an assembly at that time, the number of voters failed to reach the 40 percent of the total electorate set by the British government as a condition for constitutional change. The failure of the Scotland bill in 1979 contributed to the defeat of the Labour Party in the general election of that year. During the 1980s and up to the general election held on May 1, 1997, the Conservative Party was in power in Britain and opposed the establishment of a separate parliament for Scotland. While the Conservatives enjoyed over 50 percent of the votes in Scotland in the mid-1950s, they saw this support collapse to just 17.5 percent in 1997.

Throughout the 1980s and 1990s critics of the Conservative government claimed Scotland was suffering a "democratic deficit" on the grounds Scotland voters had not voted for the government but were subject to the policies being made in Westminster. For example, over the past two decades, the Conservatives held as few as 10 seats out of the 72 Scottish parliamentary seats before the loss of all their seats at the 1997 election. Women who joined the campaign for constitutional change argued they were suffering a "double democratic deficit" because of their significant underrepresentation in political office at local, central, and European levels. In the general election of 1992, 5 women were elected from Scottish constituencies from a total of 72, the same number as were elected in 1959. Although the increase to 12 women members of parliament (MPs) in the 1997 general election is a marked improvement, it still represents just 16.6 percent of the total number, in spite of the fact positive measures, in the form of all-women short lists, were operated by the Labour Party. At the local government level, women's representation is higher at around 22 percent but has not changed significantly over the last fifteen years; at the European level, just one of Scotland's eight members of the European parliament (MEPs) is a woman. Therefore, until the 1997 election, Scotland and the rest of the United Kingdom had one of the lowest representation rates of women in Europe.[2]

The Campaign for a Scottish Parliament

The campaign for home rule in Scotland gathered force during the 1980s and 1990s and was coordinated by the Campaign for a Scottish Assembly, which later was renamed the Campaign for a Scottish Parliament (CSP). It brought together a group of eminent Scots to consider the governance of Scotland, and they published *A Claim of Right for Scotland* in 1988, in which they asserted the sovereign right of the Scottish people to have control over their own affairs. They also recommended the setting up of a Scottish Constitutional Convention (SCC) to draw up plans for a Scottish parliament.

SCC had its first meeting in 1989, attended by representatives from the Scottish Labour Party, Scottish Liberal Democrats, Democratic Left, Green Party, voluntary sector, trade unions, churches, local government, business community, and a wide range of organizations and groups, including women's groups. The Scottish National Party (SNP) came to the first meeting of the convention but withdrew on the grounds the convention was in danger of being dominated by the Labour Party. The Conservative Party did not take part in proceedings and restated opposition to reform and continued support for the status quo. Noting the composition of the convention was around 90 percent male, a group of women submitted their own document, *A Woman's Claim of Right*, which drew attention to the relative exclusion of women from political decision making and made their case for a more democratic and representative legislature for Scotland.

The convention published its first document, *Towards Scotland's Parliament*, in 1990, endorsing the *Claim of Right* and setting out initial plans for a new-style Scottish parliament. Their proposals were based on a critique of the Westminster model of government they charged with being unrepresentative, undemocratic, highly centralized, and secretive and for operating at times and in ways that discouraged participation. Ideas began to develop for a new type of parliament operating on fundamentally different lines and involving as wide a range of representation as possible, especially of those traditionally excluded from political office.

With the return of the Conservative Party to power at the 1992 general election, hopes of constitutional change were dashed. However, the campaign for a Scottish parliament gathered momentum, and a number of new campaign groups were formed. A Scottish Civic Assembly was set up, and the SCC continued to meet. Other groups, such as the Scottish Education and Action for Development (SEAD), organized conferences and other events to explore ways of increasing democratic participation and representation at the grassroots level, and the campaign organization Charter 88 carried out a "Citizen's Enquiry" to gauge the level of support for a constitutional reform program. Women were involved in all of these groups but formed their own organization, the Women's Coordination Group, with the key aims of coordinating women activists from different parties, trade unions, and women's organizations and of improving the representation of women in political office.

A broad range of people from Scottish civil society participated in the campaign for a more representative legislature in Scotland, both within and outside the convention. The debates and political involvement surrounding a new parliament with improved representation were not confined to the political parties and included a broad range of organizations representing Scottish civil society. Another unusual aspect of the campaign was involvement of women *as* women and their willingness to cross party and ideological lines in a concerted campaign to improve their political representation.

Taking on board the development of the debates and the campaign post-1992, the Scottish Constitutional Convention published an updated document, *Scotland's Parliament, Scotland's Right*, on St. Andrew's Day, 1995. The convention partners agreed to a scheme for a Scottish parliament that would have a form of the additional member system for elections and included an Electoral Contract committing the parties to pursuing the principle of equal representation and putting forward an equal number of male and female candidates for election in winnable seats. They were able to reach this compromise in spite of the differences between the two main parties involved over the type of electoral system to be adopted and ways of ensuring gender balance.[3] This development was a significant one given the Labour Party's dominance in Scotland and the fact it has much to gain by retaining the first-past-the-post electoral system.[4]

The argument was also made that changing the electoral system alone would not necessarily enhance participation or make the parliament more representative or democratic. Consideration was given to other ways of encouraging participation, such as changing the times and location of parliamentary sittings and meetings, providing allowances and facilities for those with caring responsibilities, improving information for and involvement of the general public, and reforming the practices and procedures of the parliament.[5] The case for a Scottish parliament, therefore, has included a vision of a new type of politics and representative house involving new people while at the same time widening democratic engagement with the political process. The establishment of the parliament is seen as a unique opportunity to engender a different type of democratic and representative politics.

POST-ELECTION DEVELOPMENTS

When the Labour Party was in opposition and first announced its decision in 1996 to hold a two-question referendum on devolution should it be elected, many in Scotland feared the party was lessening its commitment to change.[6] However, the government kept their pre-election promise, introducing a referendum bill to the House of Commons within weeks of coming into office followed by the white paper *Scotland's Parliament*, setting out its plans for a Scottish parliament based on the scheme agreed to by the Scottish Constitutional Convention and incorporating amendments suggested by other organizations.[7] The government listed the powers to be retained by the United Kingdom parliament, stating that all other areas of policy will fall within the responsibility of a Scottish parliament. The Scottish parliament, therefore, will be able to make laws in relation to all devolved matters including health, education and training, local government, social work, housing, economic development, transport, law and home affairs, the environment, agriculture, fisheries and forestry, sport and the arts, and research and statistics. It also will be responsible for equal opportunities in all of these policy areas.

Crucially, the government endorsed the electoral system proposed by the convention and reiterated the commitment to establish a more representative house. The Scottish parliament will comprise 129 members elected under a form of the additional member system (AMS). The majority will be elected from Westminster parliament constituencies except Orkney and Shetland, which at the moment form one constituency. In addition to the 73 "constituent members," 56 "additional members" will be selected from party lists drawn up for each of the current European parliament constituencies. There will be seven additional members from each constituency. Each elector will be entitled to cast two votes—one for a member of the Scottish parliament (MSP) in a single-member constituency and one for the party of his or her choice. Votes for the 73 constituency MSPs will be counted on the current first-past-the-post basis. The 56 additional members will be chosen by proportional representation in the eight multi-member constituencies, with each electing seven members. In the final national allocation of seats, adjustment will be made according to the proportion of votes the parties won and the number of seats they obtained in the single constituencies.

In addressing the question of who will be eligible for selection and election to the Scottish parliament, the government stated it wanted to see a wide range of people putting themselves forward and attached great importance to equal opportunities for all—women, members of ethnic minorities, and disabled people. It urged all political parties to bear this goal in mind in their methods of selecting candidates for election. The government also envisaged a new type of parliament that adopted modern methods of working, was accessible, open, and responsive to the needs of the public, and encouraged wide participation in the decision-making process.

The government put its proposals to the people of Scotland in a two-question referendum on September 11, 1997. It received strong support on the two questions, with 74.3 percent of the electorate agreeing that there should be a Scottish parliament and 63.5 percent agreeing that a Scottish parliament should have tax-varying powers.[8] The Scotland bill was duly published in December 1997 before being introduced to the House of Commons in January 1998 and receiving royal assent at the end of the same year. In anticipation of the elections in May 1999, the political parties revised their selection processes and became heavily engaged during 1998 in selecting their candidates for the constituency seats and in deciding how to operate the party list element of the process.

In the spirit of building a new type of house of parliament, the secretary of state for Scotland, Donald Dewar, announced his decision in November 1997 to establish an all-party group to take forward consideration of how the Scottish parliament should operate.[9] The Consultative Steering Group (CSG) began its work in January 1998 before reporting to the secretary of state in December outlining draft standing orders for the parliament. To support the work of the group, expert panels were established relative to procedures and standing orders, financial issues, information and communications technology (ICT), and media issues. Research was commissioned on models of good practice in other countries, and the process of gathering views from a wide cross-section of Scotland society took the form of public meetings, focus group exercises, and written consultation.

In considering the evidence and preparing its report for the secretary of state, CSG worked on the basis of four key principles, stating that "we hope that they will be endorsed by the Scottish Parliament and stand as a symbol of all we hope for from our elected representatives'':

1. The Scottish parliament should embody and reflect the sharing of power between the people of Scotland, the legislators, and the Scottish Executive.

2. The Scottish Executive should be accountable to the Scottish parliament, and the parliament and executive should be accountable to the people of Scotland.

3. The Scottish parliament should be accessible, open, and responsive and develop procedures that make possible a participative approach to the development, consideration, and scrutiny of policy and legislation.

4. The Scottish parliament in its operation and its appointments should recognize the need to promote equal opportunities for all.

For example, in order to meet some of these objectives, CSG recommended committees of the parliament should be able to initiate as well as scrutinize and monitor proposals from the Scottish Executive and should include non-MSPs in their membership, draw evidence from advisory groups and civic forums, and meet in different parts of Scotland to involve those most immediately affected by their proposals. Recognizing that in a unicameral system the prelegislative process is crucial, the group suggested ways in which it should be possible for individuals and organizations to have input into the policy-making process at an early stage. Imaginative ways of using ICT to enhance democratic participation also are envisaged. Women campaigners were encouraged particularly by the recommendation to establish an equal opportunities committee charged with mainstreaming equal opportunities into all the workings of the parliament and its appointments and an equality unit responsible for providing gender disaggregated statistics and monitoring progress on equality policy.

In agreeing on a new, more proportional electoral system and proposing a more open and participative policy process, the aim is to ensure that the new Scottish parliament is much more representative in its composition of MSPs but also more representative in general of the views of the people in Scotland. It is anticipated "representation" will not be confined to electing parliamentarians, and it is hoped there will be other and varied channels through which the representation of ideas and proposals for legislation can be made. There is concern this representation of "interests" should not be defined narrowly and restricted to those who have sufficient financial assets to make their views heard. Responding, to some extent, to the allegations of sleaze and media publicity that surrounded the previous Conservative administration, there are proposals for codes of conduct for MSPs and for the operation of lobbying activities. One of the key aspirations is that the establishment of a new house operating on new rules and procedures will help engender a different kind of democratic process and representative political system.

THE ROLE OF WOMEN IN THE DEVELOPMENTAL PROCESS

Women have played an important role in the developmental process to ensure more women are elected to the new house, and there are new channels and opportunities for their concerns to be represented. Women political activists participated directly in the Scottish Constitutional Convention, the Scottish Civic Assembly, and other groups and organizations in Scottish civil society. New women's organizations, such as Engender, were established in the early 1990s, and new networks and coalitions were forged between women inside and outside the political parties. Much of the campaign was brought together by the Scottish Women's Coordination Group, set up after the 1992 general election. The group adopted different strategies in coordinating the campaign to keep the issue of women's representation high on the political agenda. They published information and campaign leaflets on women and politics, organized seminars and conferences, invited women from other countries to share their experiences and strategies for change with women in Scotland, conducted questionnaire surveys of political candidates for local, Westminster, and European elections, lobbied politicians and others in decision-making positions, and held press conferences publicizing the key objective to achieve gender balance in the Scottish parliament. A shorthand term for the activities of the group was the "50:50 campaign."[10]

A major achievement of the Coordination Group was success in brokering an agreement between representatives of the Scottish Labour Party and the Scottish Liberal Democrats to accept the principle of gender balance and give a commitment to field an equal number of male and female candidates in winnable seats at the first elections for the new parliament. This electoral contract subsequently was endorsed by the Scottish Constitutional Convention and included in their final report published in November 1995.

The pressure for gender equality in Scotland's first parliament for almost 300 years was sustained by the Women's Coordination Group during the general election campaign and the 1997 referendum campaign. They invited the newly elected minister for women issues, Henry McLeish, to a conference at which he reaffirmed the Scottish Labour Party's commitment to achieving gender balance in the elections for the Scottish parliament. Some of the women from the group were invited to act as advisers to the new minister and then to his successor, Helen Liddell.

A new initiative introduced by the minister was the setting up of a Women in Scotland Forum to provide a direct channel to government for women in Scotland. It is intended the forum should continue to exist and should help inform the policy-making process of the new parliament. Women's groups also responded to the consultation exercise carried out by the cross-party Consultative Steering Group by making specific recommendations for promoting wider representation and equal opportunities and for running the parliament in ways making it more possible for women and others with caring responsibilities to participate.

However, it should be noted women political activists also experienced setbacks. The Scottish Labour Party is alone in adhering to the commitment to adopt a positive measure to increase women's representation in the form of a "twinning" mechanism in the selection process, allowing a woman and a man to be selected for a pair of constituency seats. The Scottish Liberal Democrats have stepped back from implementing their proposal to use a "zipping" mechanism on the party list seats to achieve gender balance. In line with other parties, the Scottish National Party (SNP) continued to encourage more women to come forward for selection but decided against zipping the top-up list should there be an imbalance in the number of men and women elected in the constituency seats. A further disappointment was the decision equality legislation should continue to be a reserved power at Westminster and the absence of a clause in the Scotland bill exempting the selection processes of the political parties from the provisions of the Sex Discrimination Act. This act was used by two unsuccessful male candidates to challenge the British Labour Party's positive action measure of all-women shortlists in the period preceding the 1997 general election.

In spite of these setbacks, much has been gained, and the work of women activists continued in the period preceding the elections held in May 1999, and they will oversee the work of the new parliament and its parliamentarians in the future.

CONCLUSIONS

A number of factors combined in a way that offers a real prospect of a radical shift toward true representativeness in the future governance of Scotland. First, the constitutional question has opened up the discourse about democracy, representation, and accountability, and it is a discourse involving a wide spectrum of Scottish civil society. In this political climate, women have been able to make their specific claim for fair representation.[11] Second, the likelihood of a new institution provides a real political opportunity structure for establishing a Scottish parliament run on significantly different lines from those of the Westminster model. Third, the decision to move to a more proportional electoral system has allowed greater opportunity to improve the representation of different political parties and of people from different parts of Scotland and to change the gender balance and representation of ethnic minority groups. Fourth, active mobilization of women around the issue of gender balance has been instrumental in ensuring equal representation has been pushed up the political agenda. Finally, the experiences of other countries with devolved structures and proportional electoral systems and of emerging democracies such as South Africa have been relevant to the debate and have assisted the development of alternative plans in Scotland.

In exploring the issue of representation and recruitment to political office, Pippa Norris and Joni Lovenduski identified three main influences operating at what they describe as the systematic, political party, and individual level.[12] The "systematic" refers to the political, economic, social, and legal context in which selection and election take place; the "political party" covers the rules and procedures of parties in the process; and the "individual" covers the factors influencing the supply and demand for candidates, that is, the decisions of those who put themselves forward for selection and of those who select. In Scotland conditions have altered at all three levels with changes to the political context and electoral system, a shift in the attitudes and practices of some of the parties, willingness of candidates to come forward for selection, and changes to the methods of selection. There is a real chance, therefore, the combination of these factors could alter the composition of political office, with Scotland's first parliament since 1707 being more representative of all the people.

The proposals to make the parliament more open, accessible, and accountable and to work on the basis of power-sharing and equal opportunities also offer new possibilities for widening representation and participation in the policy and decision-making process.

There are, of course, less optimistic scenarios based on a more cynical view of the plans for change. After the new politicians make the final decisions on their standing orders and parliamentary procedures, it will be more possible to judge whether the aspirations of those who have campaigned to build a new house with more equal representation and more inclusive processes have been realized.

NOTES

This chapter is a revised version of an article published in *PS: Political Science and Politics*, vol. 31, no. 1, March 1998, pp. 17–20.

1. Alice Brown, David McCrone, Lindsay Paterson, and Paula Surridge, *The Scottish Electorate* (Houndmills, England. Macmillan, 1998).

2. Alice Brown, "Women and Politics in Scotland," *Parliamentary Affairs*, January 1996, pp. 26–40.

3. Alice Brown, "Scotland: Paving the Way for a Devolution," *Parliamentary Affairs*, October 1997, pp. 658–71.

4. The Labour Party won 45.6 percent of the votes in the 1997 general election in Scotland, gaining 56 of Scotland's 72 parliamentary seats. The Scottish Liberal Democrats obtained 10 seats with 13.0 percent of the vote. However, with over 22.0 percent of the vote the SNP gained just 6 seats, and the Conservative Party lost all its seats in Scotland in spite of receiving 17.5 percent of the vote. Under the electoral scheme proposed for the new Scottish parliament, it is unlikely any party will obtain an overall majority in the house. An opinion poll conducted by System 3 in November 1997 estimated the composition of the new parliament as follows: Labour 55 seats, SNP 42 seats, Liberal Democrats 18 seats, and the Conservatives 14 seats.

5. Bernard Crick and David Millar drafted new standing orders and other procedures for the Scottish parliament. See their *To Make the Parliament of Scotland a Model for Democracy* (Edinburgh: John Wheatley Centre, 1995).

6. These concerns related to the 1979 experience, particularly the operation of the 40 percent rule, and the belief by some that policy in Scotland was being driven by Tony Blair and those in the party south of the border who were less than committed to constitutional change.

7. Scotland's *Parliament* (Edinburgh: Scottish Office, 1997).

8. Alice Brown, David McCrone, and Lindsay Paterson, *Politics and Society in Scotland*, 2nd ed. (Houndsmills, England: Macmillan 1998).

9. The group comprised representatives from the four main political parties in Scotland—Henry McLeish, the Scottish office minister for devolution; George Reid from the SNP; leader Jim Wallace of the Scottish Liberal Democrats; and Paul Cullen representing the Conservative and Unionist Party—in addition to representatives from business, the trade union movement, local government, equal opportunities commission, consumers' council, and the Scottish Constitutional Convention. The author of this chapter was a member in the capacity of an academic adviser.

10. The term "50:50" originated from the Scottish Trade Union Congress (STUC) Women's Committee's proposal that gender equality in the Scottish parliament could be achieved most simply by devising a scheme whereby one man and one women represented each parliamentary constituency in Scotland (two-member constituencies). The policy later was adopted by the Labour Party in Scotland at its conference in March 1991. However, the decision to adopt the AMS for elections to the parliament with 73 constituency MSPs and 56 top-up seats meant different ways of achieving gender balance had to be considered. The Scottish Labour Party subsequently agreed to a policy of "twinning" or "pairing" constituencies whereby both men and women can stand for selection in a pair of constituencies. The woman with the highest number of votes will get one constituency, and the man with the highest number of votes will get the other. The Scottish Liberal Democrats intended to use the top-up list to redress any imbalance in gender representation in the constituency elections. SNP also said they would use the electoral system to ensure greater equality in representation. The Scottish Conservative and Unionist Party maintained their opposition to any form of positive action measure.

11. Alice Brown, "Deepening Democracy: Women and the Scottish Parliament," *Regional and Federal Studies*, Spring 1998, pp. 103–19.

12. Pippa Norris and Joni Lovenduski, *Political Recruitment: Gender, Race, and Class in the British Parliament* (Cambridge, England: Cambridge University Press, 1994).

Chapter 14

The Possible Effects of Term Limits on Congressional Diversity and Attrition

Stanley M. Caress

A widespread public debate developed in the 1990s about restricting the length of service of members of Congress. The movement to establish term limits began at the state level and soon stimulated a contentious, nationwide exchange of opinions. Term-limit advocates vigorously contended that putting limits on incumbents' tenure of office would make legislators more reflective of the public's will and would produce numerous other benefits.[1] The opponents of term limits were equally adamant in their objections and claimed term limits would make governing difficult and would give increased power to lobbyists and special interest groups.[2] The term-limit debate eventually led to political action in several states.

Initiatives were placed on the ballots in California, Oklahoma, and Colorado in 1990 that mandated term limits for state legislators. The initiatives passed in all three states, and many other states soon adopted similar measures. Some states attempted to place limits not only on the tenure of their state legislators but also on their congressional delegation. After the electorates of several states placed term restrictions on their members of Congress, the issue was thrown into the courts. The U.S. Supreme Court ultimately ruled in *United States Term Limits Incorporated v. Thornton* in 1995 that term limits could be placed on Congress only by an amendment to the U.S. Constitution and that state-imposed term limits on members of Congress were unconstitutional.[3]

The impetus for establishing term limits soon shifted to Congress and became a major issue in the 1994 election. The Republicans, who were the minority party in Congress at the time, made term limits a centerpiece of their ''Contract with America'' campaign platform. The Republican success in the 1994 election, which gave them majority status in both the House and Senate, brought the issue new prominence and eventually led to congressional consideration of a constitutional amendment. Efforts within Congress to establish term limits progressed rapidly, but eventually the constitutional amendment failed to receive enough support on a floor vote in 1995 and was dropped from active consideration (see also Chapter 15 in this volume).

While there has been no further major congressional action on adoption of term limits in the years that followed its initial congressional consideration, the debate about their desirability has continued. There is still a large segment of the public supporting congressional term limits, and it easily could emerge as a major issue in future election campaigns.

WOULD TERM LIMITS CHANGE CONGRESS?

The basic assumption inherent in the term-limit polemic is that restrictions on the ability of incumbents to run for reelection will alter Congress in several important ways. Both term-limit supporters and opponents agree that prohibiting the current pattern of incumbents continuously seeking reelection inevitably would change Congress as new members replaced long-term incumbents. The disagreement is whether these changes would be positive or negative. Ambiguous, value-laden claims such as "term limits will either produce better or worse laws" never can be substantiated definitively, but more realistic questions about the impact of limited congressional tenure can be answered with adequate research.

Would term limits change the nature of the membership of Congress? Would they impact what type of individuals obtain congressional leadership positions? Would they significantly alter congressional career patterns, and if so, how? What would be some of the major unanticipated consequences of term restrictions? These are all legitimate research questions that have been systematically examined by scholars. While credible research on term limits is still in its formative stages, some revealing answers are beginning to emerge.

EARLY ATTEMPTS TO PREDICT THE IMPACT OF TERM LIMITS

The early debate between advocates and opponents of term limits was purely speculative and based only on conjecture. Both sides used only logical arguments to support their claims and offered no substantive evidence to confirm their contentions. Beginning in 1992, however, a number of scholars began using credible methodological techniques to examine the potential ramifications of term limits on Congress. The techniques normally used by these scholars included the gathering of empirical data and the construction of mathematical models that could project the possible consequences of term-limit adoption. The preliminary research conducted by these scholars gave shape to a number of important questions but initially produced conflicting findings that did little to resolve the continuing debate on term-limit desirability.

One of the first questions scholars attempted to answer was, What would be the influence of term limits on the electability of minority and female congressional candidates? A secondary, but related, question—would term limits increase the number of minority and female incumbents selected to fill leadership positions within Congress?—also received scholarly attention. Additional research efforts attempted to determine if term limits would alter existing career patterns and create a tendency for incumbents to leave office before the end of their allowable tenure.

Thompson and Moncrief conducted one of the first academic studies on the impact of term limits on female and minority candidates.[4] They examined past legislator behavior and asserted term limits would facilitate greatly the election of minorities and women to legislative bodies. They reasoned the ascendance of women and minorities to public office was blocked by the tendency of incumbents to remain in office for long periods of time. They believed that since legislative incumbents had major advantages over challengers, open seats provided the best opportunities for women and minorities to be elected. Thompson and Moncrief concluded term limits routinely would create open seats and therefore help women and minorities get elected to legislative bodies in greater numbers.

Reed and Shansberg created an elaborate mathematical model, however, that produced results contradicting Thompson and Moncrief's findings.[5] Reed and Shansberg's model concluded term limits would hurt minority congressional candidates but could help female candidates. Their model indicated such limits create a disadvantage for candidates from groups that remain in office the longest and projected that since minority members of Congress as a whole stay in office longer than nonminority incumbents, term limits would create a disadvantage for minority candidates. Female congressional incumbents, however, stay in office for shorter durations than their male colleagues, and thus the model predicted term limits would give them an advantage. Reed and Shansberg did caution, however, their model may have overemphasized term limits' negative effect on minorities because such members typically represent minority districts and would be replaced by other minority candidates.

The question of leadership attainment was addressed by Hodson et al., who conducted a study that logically forecast the impact of term limits on minorities and females obtaining legislative leadership positions.[6] Their research suggested the rapid turnover created by term limits would produce new opportunities for minority and female incumbents and undoubtedly produce an increase in the number of members of both groups who would become legislative leaders. This conclusion was based primarily on logical inferences from empirical evidence.

The issue of congressional incumbent attrition rates also was considered by Reed and Shansberg, who conjectured term limits would create a massive wave of incumbents leaving office when the maximum allowable terms in office had expired. They concluded that this change would occur regardless of the number of allowable terms in office because they assumed incumbents would attempt to stay in office as long as possible.

Francis and Kenny examined the states with term limits and observed that limiting the career longevity of incumbents made them far more likely to leave office before the end of their allowable time to seek other career opportunities.[7] They therefore concluded term limits would increase incumbent early retirement rates, and a periodic, massive wave of incoming freshmen would not appear as predicted by Reed and Shansberg because of the continuous replacement of exiting incumbents.

APPLYING THE EXPERIENCE OF STATE LEGISLATURES TO THE CONGRESS

The original academic studies of term limits may have produced contradictory results because they based their predictions primarily on examining congressional and state legislative behavior patterns displayed prior to term-limit enactment. Members of a term-limited legislative body conceivably could act much differently than members of a non-term-limited one. Projecting future congressional electoral behavior under term limits from observing how Congress and other legislatures act without them is a risky endeavor that, despite the level of sophistication of the methodology, produces conclusions that must be treated as speculative.

As Francis and Kenny realized, a more fruitful method of forecasting the impact of term limits on Congress is to examine the experiences of states with term limits on their state legislators. Some states with term limits have part-time amateur legislative bodies and are not good indicators of what Congress could expect from term-limit enactment. Other states, however, have professional, full-time, two-party competitive legislatures analogous to Congress in their electoral dynamics. The California state legislature, for example, has districts approximately the size of congressional districts and has election patterns similar to those of congressional elections. It was also the first state legislature to feel the full impact from term limits because it was the first of the three original states that imposed term limits to experience a complete rotation of its incumbents. Examining the reactions of the California state legislature and other similar state legislatures to the imposition of mandatory term restrictions could give a prophetic picture of what might be expected if Congress adopted similar measures. There is always a measure of uncertainty in projecting the consequences of an action on a political institution from the experiences of another institution, but the evidence from some of the term-limits states is revealing and is the best available guide for understanding what would happen if the U.S. Constitution was amended to include tenure restrictions on members of Congress.

The experience of the states with term limits strongly indicates Congress could expect certain things to happen if tenure restrictions were implemented. Term limits could alter the gender and ethnic composition of Congress, but only

Table 14.1
California State Assembly Minority Membership

	1980	1982*	1990#	1992*	1994	1996**
BLACK	6.25%	6.25%	8.75%	7.5%	7.5%	5%
HISPANIC	2.5%	5%	5%	13.75%	15%	17.5%
ASIAN	0%	0%	0%	1.25%	1.25%	2.5%
NON-MIN	91.25%	88.75%	86.25%	77.5%	76.25%	75%

*Election after Reapportionment.
#Enactment of Term Limits.
**After Complete Rotation of Incumbents.
Source: California Secretary of State's Office.

if certain other factors were also present. Such limits would produce a more rapid turnover of leadership positions than otherwise would be the case. It can be anticipated term limits will change incumbent career patterns, which could produce some seldom-considered consequences.

IMPACT ON THE ELECTION OF MINORITY CANDIDATES

The conflicting conclusions found in the scholarly studies about the impact of term limits on the electoral fortunes of minority congressional candidates illustrate how difficult it is to draw valid conclusions on this subject. California's experience, however, is both interesting and ironic and may provide some useful insights. During California's original period of term-limit implementation (1990–1996), the number of minority legislators swelled (see Table 14.1). Minority membership in the legislature's lower house increased from 13.75 percent in 1990 (the year of term-limit passage) to 25 percent in 1996 (the year all incumbents were barred from running for reelection). The total figure tells only part of the story because while the number of legislators with Hispanic backgrounds grew dramatically (12.5%), the number of black legislators declined slightly (3.75%).[8] These unequal election outcomes for Hispanics and blacks suggest term limits will influence the electability of minority candidates in a complex manner, and other factors need to be considered.

Term limits may facilitate increased election opportunities for minority legislative candidates only if their minority group is grossly underrepresented in the legislative body. If the number of incumbents from a minority group is equivalent to the minority group's voting strength in the general population, term limits do not create any advantage. The number of Hispanic California state legislators increased only slightly in the decade prior to term-limit enactment, while the state's Hispanic population grew rapidly. The number of black legislators during the same time period also grew slightly, but the black population as a proportion of the state's overall population remained constant. Term limits unleashed the pent-up Hispanic voting power and produced a significant jump in the number of Hispanics elected to the legislature, while the number of blacks elected, reflecting the lack of their population growth, remained constant and eventually dropped.

The divergent election results for Hispanics and blacks in California suggest term limits would increase the number of minorities in Congress only if minorities were underrepresented in comparison to their population's percentage of the general voting public at the time of term-limit enactment. If the size of the minority delegation is already at parity with its group's proportion of the general population, there is no pent-up voting strength for term limits to release. If this situation is the case, term limits' removal of incumbents would not create any new opportunities for minority candidates.

The Senate is unlikely to experience a similar situation. The voting power of minority groups in the population of an entire state normally is diluted and insufficient to propel one of its own members to electoral success. Term-limit enactment could impact the increased election of minority candidates only if the group's numbers grew large enough to outweigh nonminority voting strength in a party's senatorial primary.

IMPACT ON THE SUCCESS OF FEMALE CANDIDATES

Women have been elected to Congress in an increasing number during the past three decades.[9] Would the adoption of congressional term limits accelerate this increase? An examination of the number of women elected to state legislatures with term limits gives some indication of the answer to this question.

The number of women elected to state legislatures varies considerably between states. When all states are examined together, the aggregate data for the 1990s show the rise in the number of females elected to legislative seats in states with term limits is no greater than in states that have not adopted such limits.[10] The rate of increase of female membership in state legislatures from 1990 to 1996 in states both with and without term limits is 3 percent (see Table 14.2).

There are several potential reasons that term limits appear to have no impact on the electoral success of female candidates. The proportion of females elected to state legislative seats increased dramatically from 1970 to 1990. Therefore, several of the states that enacted term limits in the 1990s already had a sizable portion of their state legislative seats held by women. In these states term limits will force a large number of females out of office along with their male colleagues. These female incumbents can be replaced either by other females or by males. Thus, once the proportion of female incumbents reaches a level where they would be forced out of office in large quantities, term limits no longer facilitate an increase in the number of women elected to a legislature.

Table 14.2
Percentage of Women in State Legislatures with and without Term Limits

	1980	1990	1992	1994	1996	% Change >90 to >96
With	13% (310)	21% (451)	23% (547)	23% (567)	24% (581)	**3%**
Without	11% (576)	17% (838)	19% (942)	19% (949)	20% (1003)	**3%**

Actual numbers in parentheses; percentages have been rounded.
Source: U.S. Bureau of the Census, *Statistical Abstract of the United States* (Washington, DC: U.S.
  Government Printing Office, 1997).

DOES REDISTRICTING NEGATE THE EFFECT OF TERM LIMITS?

The open seats created by term limits apparently provide increased opportunities for minorities to get elected only if other demographic factors are present. Because the effect of term limits is tied closely to population changes, the influence of redistricting cannot be ignored. The impact of term limits on state legislatures does not appear to be as great as some scholars had expected, because redistricting may have created many of the same opportunities.

The redistricting following the decennial census produces several consequences that tend to negate the anticipated impact of term limits.[11] While redrawing district boundaries seldom forces a large number of incumbents to leave office, and in fact often produces districts that protect incumbency, redistricting can produce conditions in some areas favorable for increased minority electoral success. These are typically the same areas where term limits also would be expected to help minority candidates. These areas are represented by nonminority incumbents but have undergone a significant growth of minority voters in the past decade. Term limits in these areas would force a nonminority incumbent out of office who probably would be replaced by a minority candidate. Redistricting, however, often does this first.

Redistricting can force incumbents in areas with changing populations to run in less familiar districts, thereby making them more vulnerable to challengers. Voluntary early retirement by incumbents usually increases in these situations, and the number of open seats normally rises. In California the major jump in minority candidates elected occurred in the election following redistricting (1992) and not in the one following the complete rotation of incumbents out of office (1996). The previous postredistricting election a decade earlier (1982) also produced an increase in minority candidates' winning seats. The end result of redistricting is that there is an increased potential for minority candidates to win seats that preempts any advantage that term limits would have created.

IMPACT ON MINORITIES AND WOMEN GAINING
LEADERSHIP POSITIONS

Hobson et al. believed term limits' constant forcing out of incumbents would create more legislative leadership vacancies that inevitably would produce more minority and female leaders.[12] Congressional term limits certainly will rotate leadership positions more rapidly than is the case today, but they would increase only the number of minorities and females gaining these positions if other conditions existed. Such limits also would have to significantly increase the numbers of minorities and women in Congress before they could impact the obtainment of leadership positions. Present election trends indicate the number of women and minorities elected to Congress has increased without term limits. If this trend continues, the accelerated rotation of leadership positions may produce at least more opportunities for minorities and females. Whether these opportunities will be realized or not is, however, uncertain.

A comparison of the experience of states that have adopted term limits with states that have not suggests these limits alone do not increase the likelihood of minority and female legislators' obtaining leadership positions. Many states with limits have witnessed minorities and females' moving into leadership roles, but this development also has been the case in other states that never enacted term limits. For example, in Rhode Island, which lacks term limits, June Gibbs became the state Senate's first female deputy minority leader, and Martha York became the first female chair of the powerful Health, Education, and Welfare Committee in 1994.[13]

Term limits in California may have produced an ironic impact on minorities' gaining leadership roles that never was anticipated. Willie Brown had become the state's first black Speaker of the California State Assembly (the legislature's lower house) a decade prior to term-limit enactment. The destabilizing influence of term limits may have contributed to the political turmoil that made him lose his leadership position. In the election that followed term-limit enactment a change in partisan control occurred in the California State Assembly. In the 1994 election, the Republicans became the majority party for the first time in decades. This shift of power reflected national political trends but may have been facilitated by an increase in the early retirements of incumbents resulting from impending term limits. Brown, a Democrat, maneuvered extensively to retain his office, but it eventually went to a Republican. The speakership was held briefly by a Republican female and then by a nonminority Republican. The Democrats regained control of the assembly in 1996, which was also the year of the complete rotation of incumbents under term limits. Since 1996 California has had two Speakers, both of Hispanic background. This peculiar leadership rotation was primarily the consequence of political factors and increased Hispanic voting power, but term-limit enactment should not be discounted as an indirect contributing factor.

Term limits force legislative leaders to vacate their positions before they otherwise would do so, thus creating new opportunities. These increased opportunities for minorities and women may not be realized, however, unless these groups also have increased influence within the legislative body. If term limits increase the minority or female membership in a legislative body, they can facilitate the movement of these two groups into leadership positions. If term limits do not produce this precondition, they create no real advantage for minorities or women.

WILL TERM LIMITS CREATE NEW LEGISLATOR CAREER PATTERNS?

In states that adopted term limits, a new legislator career-hopping pattern often became apparent. Incoming legislators normally commit themselves to their seat for a few terms, but as they enter the later stages of their allowable tenure, they begin to look for new positions. Few incumbents waited until the end of their allotted terms to leave office. Most legislators attempted to find a new office before they were forced out of office. Many legislators attempted to run for an office that would not require them to relinquish their present seat, thereby allowing them to retain their present seat if they were unsuccessful in obtaining the new position. If they won the new seat, they left office in mid-term, thus producing a vacancy. This career-hopping pattern created a consequence never considered in the formative debate on term-limit desirability—the increased need for special elections to fill the growing number of vacant seats.

The adoption of term limits in California, for example, created a significant rise in special elections that was the product of a domino, career-hopping pattern. This domino pattern was characterized by incumbents from the upper chamber of the state legislature, who could run in mid-term without losing their current seats, leaving office prior to the end of their terms to take other national or state offices. The vacancies created by this practice produced a need for several special elections. The candidates in these special elections for open, upper chamber seats often were incumbents from the other chamber who could run in special elections without giving up their current positions. If an incumbent from the lower chamber was successful in winning the upper chamber seat, a new lower chamber vacancy was created that also needed to be filled with a special election. This domino pattern resulted in an unanticipated and unprecedented increase in the number of special elections in California during its initial period of term-limit implementation (see Table 14.3).

Term limits certainly would make a congressional career far less stable. Members of Congress serving under the cloud of a finite stay in office undoubtedly would alter their current career patterns. Today, most members of Congress treat their position as their final vocation and seek reelection until they are ready to retire. If term limits were enacted, many members of Congress undoubtedly would adopt a career pattern similar to the one found at the state level. They would attempt to prolong their political career by seeking another office after

Table 14.3
California Special State Legislative Elections

	Total Special	Domino
1982	1	0
1983	0	0
1984	0	0
1985	0	0
1986	2	0
1987	3	0
1988	1	0
1989	3	0
1990*	7	1
1991	13	11
1992	3	0
1993	16	7
1994	3	1
1995	10	7
1996	2	0

*Enactment of term limits.
Source: California Secretary of State's Office.

their stay in Congress was concluded, thereby producing a pattern where incumbents would be willing to vacate office earlier than otherwise would be the case if they could find a promising new opportunity. Consequently, term limits could encourage members of Congress to begin searching for their next office after serving only a few of their allowable terms in office. Few incumbents would be willing to wait until the last moment to switch jobs, and thus attrition rates would rise. The two-year term served by members of the House of Representatives would tend to produce fewer mid-term vacancies than is evident at the state level, but more vacancies would occur if members of Congress successfully ran for local offices with elections that did not coincide with congressional terms.

WHAT WOULD BE THE EXPECTED IMPACT ON CONGRESS?

Term limits can be expected to change Congress in both anticipated and unanticipated ways. They may increase the number of minority candidates elected to the House, but only if the number of minority incumbents at the time of term-limit adoption is far below the level of their group's voting strength in the general population. If, however, the number of minority incumbents is approximately equivalent to their group's proportion of the voting public, it is unlikely that term-limits would facilitate the election of additional minority candidates. It is conceivable term-limit enactment could result in a decrease in the number of representatives from the minority group if their number is at parity with their group's voting strength in the population.

Term limits could accelerate the election of women to congressional seats, but an increase in females running and winning seats appears just as likely to occur either with or without term limits. If a term-limit constitutional amendment is ratified after women make up a large portion of the Congress' membership, the advantage it might provide would decrease substantially.

Constitutional term limits certainly would increase the rate of rotation of congressional leaders and consequently produce new leadership opportunities for minority and female incumbents. But these new opportunities would be realized only if the number of minority and female incumbents increased sufficiently to give them greater influence within the Congress.

The most significant potential consequence of term-limit ratification would be a change in incumbent career patterns. An increase in incumbents' leaving office prematurely to seek other positions would probably occur. Incumbents lacking job security almost certainly would be more inclined to give up their seat before being officially barred from reelection if another promising position emerged. This situation could increase the likelihood of vacant seats.

NOTES

1. Paul Jacobs, "For Voters Who Care," in Edward Crane and Roger Pilon, eds., *The Politics and Laws of Term Limits* (Washington, DC: Cato Institute, 1994), pp. 27–44.

2. Terry Eastland, "The Limits of Term Limits," *Commentary*, Summer 1993, pp. 53–55.

3. "Excerpts from Decision in Term Limits Case (*U.S. Term Limits vs. Thornton*)," *Congressional Quarterly Weekly Report*, May 27 1995, pp. 1528–29.

4. Joel A. Thompson and Gary F. Moncrief, "The Implications of Term Limits for Women and Minorities: Some Evidence from the States," *Social Science Quarterly*, June 1993, pp. 300–309.

5. Robert W. Reed and D. Eric Shansberg, "The House under Term Limits: What Would It Look Like?" *Social Science Quarterly*, December 1995, pp. 698–719.

6. Timothy Hodson, Rich Jones, Karl Kurtz, and Gary Moncrief, "Leaders and Limits: Changing Patterns of State Legislative Leadership under Term Limits," *Spectrum: The Journal of State Government*, Summer 1995, pp. 6–16.

7. Wayne L. Francis and Lawrence Kenny, "Equilibrium Projections of the Consequences of Term Limits upon Expected Tenure, Institutional Turnover, and Membership Experience," *The Journal of Politics*, February 1997, pp. 240–52.

8. *Official Election Returns Data Sheets* (Sacramento: Office of the Secretary of State, 1998).

9. Michael Barone, Grant Ujifusa, and Douglas Mathews, *The Almanac of American Politics* (New York: E. P. Dutton, 1980, 1996).

10. U.S. Bureau of the Census, *Statistical Abstracts of the United States, 1997*, vol. 117 (Washington, DC: U.S. Government Printing Office, 1997), p. 285.

11. Stanley M. Caress, "The Impact of Term Limits on Legislator Behavior: An Examination of a Transitional Legislature," *PS: Political Science and Politics*, December 1996, pp. 671–77.

12. Hodson et al., "Leaders and Limits," pp. 6–16.

13. Rita Thaemert, "Twenty Percent and Climbing—Women Legislators," *State Legislatures*, January 1994, pp. 28–32.

Chapter 15

Eliminating Disproportionate Representation in the House

Joseph F. Zimmerman

The U.S. House of Representatives is the only national governmental institution that by design in 1789 sprang directly from the voters and is subject to their control every two years, thereby suggesting it would be a citizen legislative body with the possibility of relatively frequent membership turnover. Under its original conception, the House was to be a popular and reformed House of Commons directly reflecting public opinion in the national policy-making process by acting as the protector and champion of the voters' cause.

The origin of the debate over the representative nature of the House of Representatives is traceable to the constitutional convention of 1787 and the letters written to editors of New York City newspapers by Federalists and anti-Federalists.[1] A leading Massachusetts anti-Federalist, John DeWitt, wrote an essay on representation published in the *Boston American Herald* on November 5, 1787, that is relevant today:

[T]here is a charm in politics. That persons who enter reluctantly into office become habitated, grow fond of it, and are loath to resign it.—They feel themselves flattered and elevated, and are apt to forget their constituents, until the time returns that they again feel the want of them.—They uniformly exercise all the powers granted to them, and ninety-nine in a hundred are grasping at more.[2]

Delegate Melancton Smith at the New York state convention considering ratification of the proposed U.S. Constitution contended on June 21, 1788, representatives should "resemble those they represent; they should be a true picture of the people; possess the knowledge of their circumstances and their wants; sympathize in all their distresses; and be disposed to seek their true interests."[3] Smith's call for descriptive representation was rejected by Alexander Hamilton, who in the *Federalist Number 35* addressed the charge the proposed 65-member House would not be large enough to represent the interests of all citizens and classes "to produce a true sympathy between the representative body and its constituents" but dismissed a body representing all classes as "altogether visionary."[4]

The debate over the representativeness of legislative bodies continued in the nineteenth century, when new voting systems—described in a subsequent section—were adopted in several states, including cumulative voting in Illinois to elect members of its House of Representatives and limited voting to elect city councillors in Ohio. The dissatisfaction with the single-member district (SMD) system, also known as the first-past-the-post or relative majority system, during this time period resulted from the fact the largest minority political party (as illustrated by the Republican Party in northern Illinois and the Democratic Party in southern Illinois) was grossly underrepresented, and in some cities the Republican Party had none of its candidates elected. There also was interest on the part of U.S. governmental reformers in the single-transferable vote form of proportional representation (STV-PR), developed by Thomas Hare of London in 1857, but the system was not adopted until the early decades of the twentieth century, when a number of cities incorporated an STV-PR provision in their respective charter.

More recently, Richard S. Childs, co-founder with Woodrow Wilson of the National Short Ballot Organization, in 1916 explained:

Although the people may be ready to vote overwhelmingly for a measure, their nominal agents and servants in the representative system will frequently maintain a successful indifference or resistance election after election. Our governments are less anxious to please the people than they are to please the politicians who thus become an irresponsible ruling class with a vast and marketable influence. Our representative system is misrepresentative.[5]

Childs drafted the first council-manager charter for municipalities in 1909 and was convinced that structural reform—adoption of a council-manager charter—and electoral reform—adoption of STV-PR to replace the ward or SMD system—were essential for making city governments responsible to the voters.[6]

Today, there is a democratic deficit in many legislative bodies in the United States. Nevertheless, such a deficit may not be a serious problem, as Heinz Eulau pointed out, provided the representative is "at least alert and sensitive to the preferences and wishes of the represented."[7] Eulau concluded: "It is an error ... to assume that the 'chosen'—whether elected or selected—are or can be 'like' their choosers" because the status of elected officers makes them "fundamentally different from their choosers."[8] In consequence, the relationship between the electorate and the representative is much more complex than that of a delegate or trustee, or combination of delegate and trustee.

While one can agree with Eulau on the complexity of the relationship between the representative and the represented, the importance of symbolic representation should not be underestimated. A healthy democracy should ensure that a united "minority" group above a "critical" mass has full opportunity to elect a number of its members to public offices for reasons of symbolic and policy substantive representation. Structural impediments to the election of candidates of such a group need to be removed or reduced.

The principal barriers to the election to the House of Representatives of members of grossly underrepresented groups are the SMD election system, incumbency, and inadequate campaign funds for challengers. These barriers suggest the need for adoption of a different electoral system, enlargement of the House, term limits, a new system of election campaign finance, and more effective regulation of campaign contributions and expenditures. This chapter focuses on alternative electoral systems, quotas for underrepresented groups, enlargement of the House, term limits, and two radical proposals for change. For details on campaign finance, consult Chapters 6, 17 in this volume.

ALTERNATIVE ELECTORAL SYSTEMS

Voting is a democratic mechanism to select government officers and to give legitimacy to a government. To produce a more representative House, the electoral system should be an egalitarian one ensuring that the effectiveness of ballots cast by any group of voters—be they women, "minorities," or the socioeconomically disadvantaged—is not diluted or canceled, rendering the group powerless to elect others or to have its members elected; maximize participation at the polls; promote representation of competing interests in the House; facilitate citizen access to House members; provide equity in representation for various groups; and help legitimate the authority of the House.[9]

The fairness of the representation produced by electoral systems is related directly to their respective complexity, with the more complex ones providing the most equitable representation for various groups and political parties. While the right to vote is enshrined in the political culture of the United States, the votes cast are filtered through the electoral system, which may produce major representational distortions. The plurality SMD system, for example, provides direct representation only for the group of voters who cast ballots for the winner, and they may constitute a minority of the voters if three or more candidates contested a seat and split the ballots cast. Furthermore, the selection of the winning candidate in a district dominated by one party may have been made in a political party primary election in which only a very small percentage of party voters participated. The result often is the largest political party is represented disproportionately by an exaggerated majority, and similarly a decline in voter support of candidates of a particular party may result in a disproportionate loss of seats, as witnessed by the Republican rout in 1974 as an aftermath of the Watergate scandal, when numerous state and local government officers seeking reelection were defeated. In addition, it is possible for a major political party to win more seats than the other major party whose candidates collectively received the most votes.

From a political party standpoint, the ideal candidate must be widely acceptable to voters, and this fact discourages a party in an SMD system from nominating a candidate who belongs to a "minority" group, even if it is a sizable one. Emphasizing the undemocratic nature of this system, Douglas J. Amy in 1993 wrote:

[I]magine for a moment that for some reason a large political minority was suddenly denied the right to vote in the United States. The public protest would be immediate and vociferous.... Yet while such formal disenfranchisement would be clearly intolerable, every one of our single-member plurality elections has virtually the same effect, producing a kind of *de facto* disenfranchisement of a substantial block of voters.[10]

Under the current electoral system, one of the most outstanding men or women in the United States stands no chance of election to the House of Representatives if the opposition political party controls his or her district, since only one member will be elected in a district. Even if the outstanding person is a member of the dominant political party in the district, his or her chance of election to the House is very slim if the incumbent seeks reelection under typical conditions. The Center for Voting and Democracy in 1998 issued a report highlighting the number of safe U.S. House seats and asking: "Which is worse: contributors giving money to candidates in a competitive race or contributors blatantly buying access by giving to candidates they know will win?"[11]

The general ticket electoral system (statewide or at-large system) for selecting a state's delegation to the House of Representatives was employed by six states—Alabama, Georgia, Mississippi, Missouri, New Hampshire, and New Jersey—until a 1842 congressional reapportionment act required the use of single-member districts.[12] This change was viewed at the time as a reform making the House a more representative body because under the general ticket system the political party with a bare plurality of the statewide votes for its candidates captured the entire delegation, and a party with localized strength was unable to elect even one of its members.

Congress, after each subsequent decennial census of population, enacted a reapportionment statute containing the SMD requirement, including the Reapportionment Act of August 8, 1911.[13] No reapportionment statute, however, was enacted immediately subsequent to the 1920 census of population, and Congress failed to include in its 1929 reapportionment act the terms "contiguous," "compact," or "equal" relative to congressional districts.[14] The U.S. Supreme Court in 1932 opined these requirements in the 1911 act "expired by their own limitation. They fell within the apportionment to which they expressly related," and the failure of Congress to include these requirements in the 1929 act "was deliberate."[15] Congress, however, restored the SMD requirement in 1967 out of fear certain southern states might use the general district system to dilute the black vote.[16]

States and local governments covered by the Voting Rights Act of 1965 are required to preclear any changes, no matter how minor, in their election system with the U.S. attorney general or the U.S. District Court for the District of Columbia.[17] This preclearance requirement also applies to the redistricting of U.S. House of Representatives districts if the state or part of it is subject to the preclearance requirement. In 1977, the U.S. Supreme Court in effect upheld a 1974 racial gerrymander by the New York state legislature, whose redistricting plan provided for dividing a Brooklyn assembly district whose residents were principally Hasidic Jews in order to ensure a black candidate would be elected in a new assembly district.[18] The U.S. attorney general would not approve the state legislature's redistricting plan unless the Hasidic district was divided, and 1974 was an election year that made implementation of a plan critical.

The SMD plan has been implemented in a number of state and local governments covered by the act either to obtain the approval of the U.S. attorney general or the District Court for the District of Columbia for implementation of a change(s) in election systems or by court order to promote the prospect of the election of black candidates and, since the act's 1975 amendment, Hispanic candidates to office.[19]

Rory A. Austin studied the impact of three electoral systems in six cities— one SMD city in the North and one in the South, one at-large city in the North and one in the South, and one mixed system (SMD and at-large) in the North and one in the South. He reported in 1998 "[a]t-large elections allow factors other than race, most importantly partisanship, to affect minority office holding," and "the drawing of electoral lines along racial or ethic boundaries will increase the importance of race in politics."[20]

The SMD requirement, of course, can be repealed by a simple act of Congress. A repeal, nevertheless, will not produce automatically more representatives of underrepresented groups since state legislatures must decide whether to abandon the SMD system and adopt a specific replacement system. Furthermore, the SMD system will continue to be used in states entitled to only one representative unless the number of House members is increased substantially.

"Run-off" Election

This second ballot modification of the plurality SMD system is designed to ensure the winner of the election is selected by a majority vote should three or more candidates seek the same office. A second election is held if no candidate received a majority of the votes cast in the regular election, and voting typically is restricted to the two candidates who received the largest number of votes. This modification is used in a number of cities in the United States in general elections and also in New York City for primary elections if no candidate for mayor, public advocate, or comptroller receives 40 percent of the votes cast.[21]

Second ballots also were used in the Fifth French Republic prior to 1986 to select deputies for the National Assembly and in New Zealand parliamentary elections between 1908 and 1911.

The second ballot suffers from two disadvantages. First, the "runoff" election is a special election in which the turnout of voters is considerably less than the turnout in the general election, thereby possibly resulting in the election of a candidate who received fewer votes in the general election than the number received by one or more candidates excluded from the "runoff" election.

Second, a number of voters may not cast ballots in the regular election for their favorite candidates for fear they will be excluded from the "runoff" election and hence cast ballots for less acceptable candidates who might be included in the second election.

Experience reveals the "runoff" election modification of the plurality SMD system is not beneficial in most instances for "minority" candidates and may have the effect of injecting emotional ethnic or racial concerns into the election.

The Alternative Vote

If Congress does not repeal the requirement, a strong case can be made the plurality SMD system should be modified by adoption of a type of preferential voting, known as the alternative vote, used to elect members of the lower house of most Australian states and since 1918 the Australian House of Representatives. Under this system, an elector expresses preferences for candidates by writing numbers before candidates' names, with "1" indicating first preference, "2" indicating second preference, and so forth. This system eliminates the need for a primary election and a "runoff" election to select the most preferred candidate. These two types of elections typically have a low voter turnout.

Under the standard form of majority preferential ballot counting, a candidate receiving more than one-half of the votes cast is elected. If no candidate receives a majority of the votes, the candidate with the fewest number "1" votes is declared defeated and his or her ballots are distributed to the second choices marked on them. The next procedural step is the counting of the number "1" and "2" ballots received by each candidate to determine whether a candidate received a majority of the ballots. If no candidate is elected on this count, the process continues with the declaration of the defeat of the candidate with the smallest number of votes and redistribution of the candidate's ballots to the voters' second or third choices.[22]

The supplementary vote system (SVS) is a simplified version of the alternative vote and will be employed to elect on May 4, 2000, the mayor of Greater London (city of London and 32 boroughs).[23] SVS appears similar to the second ballot system, but only one ballot is employed, and voters mark their first and second preferences of candidates on the ballot by an X for each of two candidates instead of using numbers. A voter is not required to mark a second preference. If no candidate receives a majority of the votes, all but the two top vote receivers are eliminated, and the second preferences on the ballots of defeated candidates are cast for the two top candidates provided their names are the second choice on the ballots. The winner is the candidate who receives the most votes.

Preferential voting may not affect significantly the number of "minority" and women candidates elected to the House. This electoral system has one major purpose—ensuring the candidate elected has the support of the majority of the voters—and is not designed to promote the election of "minority" or women candidates. Australia has more experience with the alternative vote than any other nation and, according to J. F. H. Wright, "the results . . . have been the same as they would have been with the first-past-the-post method, one candidate having received a majority of first-preference votes. . . . Unfortunately, the basic fact remains that, as only one candidate can be elected in a single-member district, only one group of voters can be really satisfied."[24]

Approval Voting

Although not employed to elect government officers in any nation, this system would allow SMD voters to indicate on the ballot all approved candidates. Each vote received by a candidate counts equally, and the candidate receiving the most approval votes is elected.[25]

This system bears some similarity to the alternative vote, and its proponents claim approval voting has two major advantages. First, the system allegedly is easier for the electorate to understand, compared to the alternative vote, since no rankings are involved in marking the ballot, and no ballots are transferred to other candidates. Second, the lack of preferential marking of the ballot does not lead to voter perceptions certain candidates are elected with low preferences.

The relative crudity of this system accounts for the advantages cited by its supporters. Depriving a voter of the authority to indicate preferences for all candidates does not translate into all candidates being approved equally. Approval voting may discourage candidates from taking stands on important issues for fear of antagonizing some voters and will not promote the election of additional "minority" and women candidates to office.

A multi-member district system generally is preferable to the SMD system in promoting election of candidates of underrepresented groups. However, it is important to note there are several different types of multi-member district systems, and they differ in terms of the representativeness of members of the legislative body. A multi-member district system can be combined with an SMD system, as in a number of U.S. cities. With respect to the House, this combined system could be employed only in states entitled to a large number of representatives.

The plurality, multi-member district system may not prove to be beneficial to a "minority" group whose members are geographically concentrated unless they constitute a significant percentage of the district's population. Four multi-member district systems, however, merit serious consideration as a replacement for the SMD system: cumulative voting, limited voting, party list proportional representation (LIST-PR), and single-transferable vote proportional representation (STV-PR).

Cumulative Voting

Under the plurality, multi-vote, at-large election system, a voter may cast a number of votes equal to the number of seats to be filled. This system has one obvious disadvantage: each vote given to a candidate other than the most preferred candidate may lead to the defeat of this candidate. A second disadvantage is the system's encouragement of "bullet" or "single-shot" voting under which the voter casts a ballot for only one candidate.

Cumulative voting is designed to cure these defects by allowing each voter to cast all votes for a single candidate or give two or more votes to several candidates, depending on the number of candidates to be elected. This system also has the advantage of preserving long-established, multi-member electoral districts.

Relatively easy to understand, cumulative voting makes gerrymandering difficult because of the relatively large geographical size of districts and has special relevance to states and local governments covered by the Voting Rights Act. Courts in approving electoral systems to eliminate past discrimination under the act have demonstrated a preference for single-member districts with a 65 percent majority black or Hispanic population. Such "affirmative racial gerrymandering" has disturbed many citizens and is unnecessary under cumulative voting in multi-member districts. Furthermore, disputes between black and Hispanic voters in certain cities over SMD boundary lines are avoided by use of cumulative voting.

Experience with this preferential system reveals it is a semi-proportional one allowing the largest minority political group or party to elect one or more of its members to a legislative body. The system was used to elect members of the Illinois House of Representatives in three member districts for 110 years until 1980 and usually resulted in the majority party's winning two seats and the minority party's winning one seat.[26] Illinois adopted the system because the Democratic Party dominated the northern half of the state, and its candidates won most of the seats. Similarly, Republicans dominated the southern section of Illinois. The system has been used in Alamogordo, New Mexico, and in Chilton County and three towns in Alabama since 1988.[27]

In Illinois, each elector could give three votes to a candidate, assign two votes to one candidate and one vote to a second candidate, allot one and one-half votes to each of two candidates, or assign one vote to each of three candidates. This system did not ensure a group or a party would be represented directly in accordance with its voting strength because a group or party was unable to require its members to follow instructions, and split-ticket voting reduced the proportionality of the representation produced. In addition, Illinois experience revealed a major party may be overly optimistic in calculating its strength and nominate three candidates who split the party's vote and allow the minority party to elect two representatives.

Limited Voting

The SMD system may be described as a type of limited voting system since each elector is limited to casting a ballot for only one candidate seeking election to a multi-seat body.[28] The term, however, is used to describe a system (also known as the single-nontransferable vote) under which voters can cast votes for more than one candidate but fewer votes than the number of legislative seats to be filled. In a multi-member, limited voting system, the elector might be allowed to cast six votes for different candidates in a district where nine candidates will be elected. In Japan, however, three-, four-, and five-member districts are utilized, and each elector may vote for only one candidate.[29]

The origin of limited voting dates to the period immediately following the Civil War, when one major party would dominate completely the election of candidates in a number of single-member districts, and the other major party would dominate other districts. If an elector is restricted to voting for six candidates in a nine-member district, the majority party typically would elect six candidates, and the minority party would elect three candidates. It should be noted limited voting has been utilized in political party primary elections in cities, including New York City, in the past to ensure the majority party would not elect all members of a council.

This semi-proportional system will produce direct representation for members of the largest group or political party, with the number of its candidates elected dependent on the district magnitude (number of seats to be filled), number of candidates an elector may cast ballots for, and group or party discipline.

Limited voting does not permit each voter to express preferences among the candidates, and a voter may contribute to the defeat of his or her favorite candidate by giving a vote to a second or other choice. Hence, "bullet" or "single-shot" voting is encouraged. This system is an inadequate one for guaranteeing "minority" representation and neither ensures each group or party will be represented on the basis of ballots cast for its candidates nor makes it impossible for a "minority" group or party to elect a majority of its candidates if the votes cast are divided among several slates of strong candidates.

This system also is open to another weakness: the majority party may direct a number of its supporters to cast ballots for a certain "minority" group or party candidates and thereby encourage all "minority" group or party candidates to seek the favor of the largest party. In addition, the majority party can promote the formation of two slates of candidates to divide the opposition vote.

LIST-PR

There are two proportional representation (PR) systems—the party list (List-PR) system, predicated on the existence of political parties, and the single-transferable vote (STV-PR) system. Only the latter has been employed in the United States. List-PR is the most common form in the world. Sixty-six (31%) of 211 nations, as of May 1997, utilized the List-PR system, including 15 (42%) of the 42 established democracies.[30]

The electoral district employed may be a nation—Israel, Namibia, Netherlands, and Slovakia—or a series of regional districts, as in Greece, where voters in each district elect five members, or a series of local area districts or a combination of the three geographical types of districts.

Seats in the legislative body are awarded to each political party in accordance with its proportion of the total votes cast. Typically, a party is entitled to seats only if its total votes meet a specified threshold of the total number of votes cast, such as 1.5 percent in Israel and 5.0 percent in Germany. If several small parties fail to reach, but come close to, a 5 percent threshold, for example, the number of seats allocated to the major parties would be inflated, thereby introducing a degree of disproportionate representation.

One List-PR variant (closed list), utilized in Israel, is a simple one, with each political party preparing a list of candidates for submission to the voters, who vote only for a political party. After the total number of valid ballots is determined, each party is allocated a number of seats in the concerned legislative house in direct proportion to the party's proportion of the total ballots cast. The candidates on a party's list are elected in the order in which their names appear on the list. In a 200-seat house, a party receiving 10 percent of the total votes cast would be allocated 20 seats, and the first 20 candidates on the list will be declared elected.

This variant does not allow voters to express preferences for individual candidates or to determine the candidates to appear on the ballot or the order of their appearance. In fact, party leaders determine the names and order of candidates on the ballot. In consequence, List-PR can encourage a faction to break away from a party and organize a new party to present a list of candidates to the voters.

The second variant is the open list system, utilized in Belgium and Italy, which permits voters to indicate their preferences from one or more political parties (a completely open list), and a third variant—used to elect the Brazilian House of Representatives, state assemblies, and local government councils—is a partially open one allowing the voters to change the order in which candidates appear on a party's list.[31]

A fourth variant allows a voter to cast a ballot either for a party list of candidates or for an individual candidate on the list, with the vote for an individual candidate also counted as a vote for the party list. In effect, this variant makes it possible for a candidate to be placed in a higher position on the ballot that may prove beneficial to the candidate when the party is allocated its seats. The open list, while appearing more democratic than the fixed list variant, may result in a number of voters' casting ballots for candidates who are not high enough on the list to be elected and hence are denied the opportunity to help determine the candidates to be allocated seats. This variant also generates a long national ballot that may confuse many voters, produce problems in ballot counting, and result in intraparty competition to the detriment of the party.

List-PR emphasizes the important roles of political parties in a democratic nation, simplifies the act of voting for electors, affords constituents a number of legislators to contact for assistance, and encourages parties to place "minority," regional, and women candidates on their election lists.

George H. Hallett, Jr., explained in 1984 that List-PR does "not offer proportionality on any other basis than that of political party," and an ethnic group desiring to elect some of its members to public offices has to "form a party for the purpose, or act dividedly within some of the parties."[32] He added:

Perhaps the most serious defect of the party list systems is that most of them require complete adherence to one party. There is no facility for splitting party votes. The voter has to pretend, in voting, that all of the candidates of the party he chooses are better than all other candidates.[33]

The Mixed Member Proportional System

List-PR can be combined with the SMD system to establish a mixed member proportional system (MMP), also known as the additional member system, which is designed to produce proportional representation for political parties and provide constituents with a representative elected in a single-member district.

New Zealand recently adopted the MMP system, and the Federal Republic of Germany has utilized the system since 1949 for national and land (state) elections and currently has 328 list seats and 328 single-member district seats in the *Bundestag*.[34] In a German national election, each voter has two votes. One vote is cast for a single constituency candidate, and the other vote is cast for a party's list of candidates. A party receiving a minimum of 5 percent of the list vote or winning three constituency seats is allocated list candidates. A candidate in a constituency also may be a candidate on a party's list. It is important to note that different versions of the MMP system are utilized in the various German Länder (states).

The Royal Commission on the Electoral System in New Zealand in its 1986 report commented favorably on the MMP system and recommended its adoption.[35] The commission noted the system "retains single-member constituencies, yet overcomes the disproportionality between parties that is inherent in plurality voting" and also improves the prospects for the election of minority candidates.[36]

This system, nevertheless, has been criticized as "fundamentally unsound" by Robert A Newland, a former chairman of the Electoral Reform Society of Great Britain and Ireland, in the following terms:

Half or more of the places are filled in single-place constituencies with their restricted choice of electors, and denial of representation to up to half or more of those who vote.

The remaining places, up to half of those in the parliament or council, are filled either from ordered lists without choice of candidates, or by other candidates not elected in the constituencies. Such additional members have no constituency or territorial responsibilities. They are not representatives, but are only party make-weights whose function is merely to fabricate party proportionality.[37]

Furthermore, a political party with a few geographical pockets of strength could win seats to which it would not be entitled based on the votes its list received. The New Zealand Royal Commission also reported "[t]here is a remote possibility that deliberate manipulation of the system could occur whereby 2 parties used their combined vote to gain a disproportionate share of seats."[38]

STV-PR

This system, also known as the "Hare" system, has been used to elect members of the Tasmanian House of Assembly since the 1909 election, all national and local government legislators in the Republic of Ireland since 1921, members of the Maltese parliament since 1921, members of the Northern Ireland parliament from 1919 to 1929 and 1973 to date, local legislators in Northern Ireland since 1973, members of the Australian Senate since 1949 and upper houses of several Australian states, members of the Cambridge, Massachusetts, City Council and school committee since 1941, and members of the 32 New York City community school boards since 1971.

STV-PR is a preferential voting system in which each voter expresses a preference for candidates by placing a number next to the names of candidates, with "1" indicating first preference, "2" indicating second preference, and so forth. Each voter can assign preferences on a political party basis or on personal grounds, and no votes are wasted since a ballot is transferred to the next choice if the first preference candidate already has been elected or defeated. In other words, STV-PR encourages voters to give a number "1" vote to their most favored candidate regardless of his or her chance of winning since the ballot will be transferred to the second preference if the first preference candidate is defeated.

The winning candidates are determined by a quota—total number of valid ballots cast divided by the number of representatives to be elected plus one. Assuming 1 million valid ballots were cast to elect nine representatives in a district, the quota would be

$$\frac{1,000,000}{9 + 1} + 1 = 100,001$$

This formula automatically produces the smallest number of votes cast that ensures a candidate's election regardless of how the number of votes cast is distributed among candidates.

Whereas marking the ballot is easy for the voter to understand, the counting of ballots requires a more detailed explanation. As soon as the quota is determined, ballots can be processed by computer and sorted by first choices, with all candidates receiving number "1" votes equal to or greater than the quota declared elected. Surplus ballots received by a winning candidate are transferred to the remaining candidates according to indicated second preferences. If no candidate is elected following this step, the candidate with the fewest number "1" votes is declared defeated, and his or her ballots are transferred to the remaining candidates according to the next preference written on each ballot. Should the second preference already be elected, the ballot is distributed to the third choice. A new count of ballots takes place, and candidates with a total of first and other preferences exceeding the quota are declared elected.

Surplus ballots are distributed by one of two methods. The first method does not allow any candidate to receive additional ballots once he or she has reached the quota, and surplus ballots are distributed in accordance with the next preference indicated. The second method involves a reexamination of the number "1" votes received by a candidate exceeding the quota to determine the distribution of number "2" preferences, and the surplus ballots are distributed proportionally in accordance with the second preferences.

The principal advantage of STV-PR is that it ensures majority rule while guaranteeing minority representation and avoiding the constraints of List-PR (see Chapter 12 in this volume). This electoral system recognizes there are numerous factional divisions in society, and the system makes it impossible for any political party or faction with a slight electoral plurality or majority to elect all members of a legislative body. John Stuart Mill was a strong advocate of STV-PR and noted in 1861 "it secures representation" for "every minority in the whole nation, consisting of a sufficiently large number to be, on principles of equal justice, entitled to a representative."[39]

Since STV-PR is based on constituency voting, the system is not designed to ensure that each party will elect a number of candidates in precise proportion to its share of the nationwide total votes cast. District magnitude (number of seats per district) will influence the proportionality of the results, with smaller parties faring better in districts of large magnitude. Irish and Tasmanian experience reveals the two largest parties receive a slightly higher percentage of seats than their respective percentage of number "1" votes warrants.

In contrast to the SMD system, a geographically dispersed "minority" of critical size will be able to elect a candidate under STV-PR since the constituency is based on interest and not on residence. The strength of a "minority" group is not dissipated if it gives most of its number "1" votes to one of its candidates or scatters its votes among several of its candidates.

While a "minority" group will be represented fully under this system, the group cannot benefit from a split among opposition groups, as under limited voting and cumulative voting, and elect a majority of the House members in the district. Although STV-PR often is advocated because it provides direct representation for minority parties or groups, the system also enables the majority party or group to gain seats—in contrast to the SMD system—if the majority party or group members are concentrated in a few geographical areas.

In addition to providing "minorities" and women with more direct representation, STV-PR has several other advantages. Under a plurality system, a popular name at the head of a party column can carry weak or unqualified candidates into office. This result cannot happen under STV-PR. Consequently, the services of an able U.S. House member will not necessarily be lost if his or her party fails to win a plurality or majority for STV-PR will enable this candidate to win reelection.

This electoral system with a large district magnitude makes gerrymandering impossible and reduces the possibility of election fraud since ballots are counted centrally by computers or expert tellers under close supervision. The election of House members by SMD and plurality voting tempts unscrupulous individuals to purchase votes or influence the counting of ballots in districts where an election race is a close one. Startling irregularities in the count of STV-PR ballots are unknown.

STV-PR can promote cooperation among members representing a House district. George H. Hallett, Jr., pointed out that "instead of trying to beat a particular person, with the temptation to belittle his ability and blacken his character, each candidate is trying to win a group of supporters for himself out of the whole field. . . . His best course is to make a vigorous statement of what he stands for, without gratuitous attack on anyone else."[40] In their analysis of the use of STV-PR in New York City elections, Belle Zeller and Hugh A. Bone concluded it "forced higher caliber candidates on both the majority and minority political organizations."[41]

Opponents of STV-PR maintain it promotes civic disunity and strife by fostering splinter groups and emphasizing ethnic, racial, and religious politics in contrast with a "good" electoral system that plays down divisive prejudices. An electoral system shutting out "minority" groups, however, does not play down divisive prejudices but does aggravate alienation. There also is no evidence that voting along ethnic, racial, and religious lines is more common under STV-PR than under other electoral systems.

The major argument advanced in opposition to STV-PR is that it is a fantastically complicated system understood by relatively few persons. Proponents explain the mechanics of voting are simple, the system works, and the method of counting ballots does not have to be understood completely by every citizen.

Hallett dismissed the charge STV-PR is a complicated system by use of analogies.

> The comparative complexity of the Hare system count is a matter of trifling concern to the intelligent voter. He does not have to count the ballots any more than he has to make his own watch or repair his own car. The watch is more complicated than the sun dial and the car than the stage coach, but they give better results.[42]

QUOTAS FOR UNDERREPRESENTED GROUPS

Formal and informal quotas have been established in several nations for members of groups that otherwise could lack descriptive representation in the national legislature. New Zealand has reserved four seats in its parliament for Maori, who total approximately 20 percent of the population and have the choice of voting in the single-member Maori districts or other districts.[43] To date, only Maori men have been elected.

The 1946 Constitution of the Republic of China reserves seats in the National Assembly (which amends the constitution and elects the president and vice president) and the legislative *Yuan* (which enacts statutes) for members of occupational groups, "overseas Chinese," and racial minority groups. Bih-Er Chou and Janet Clark noted that while "the reserved-seat system ensures that women have some representation in each legislative body, the electoral system alone has not been the cause of women's participation in the political system. Cultural changes resulting from economic development also contributed to women's role in Taiwan's political system."[44]

An informal quota system for women was utilized in Argentina by the Peronist movement subsequent to congressional enactment of a 1947 statute extending the voting franchise to women under which approximately one-third of the party's nominations would be reserved for women.[45]

The Argentine Congress in 1991 enacted a statute continuing the List-PR system but adding a quota system for presidential electors, national deputies, and Federal District Senate electors by stipulating each party's list of candidates must contain at least 30 percent women candidates "in proportions with the possibilities of being elected."[46] In the 1992 election to choose 54 electors who would select a Federal District senator, all party lists met the quota of women, and nineteen (35%) women were elected.[47]

ENLARGEMENT OF THE HOUSE

The first House of Representatives, which met in 1789, contained districts with approximately 30,000 inhabitants in each, and, after the first national census of population, each district had approximately 33,000 inhabitants in 1793. Today, the number of citizens per district is approximately 743,600.

The House grew rapidly in size from 65 members in 1789, to 103 in 1791, to 213 in 1820 and reached 435 in 1910. There was no reapportionment of seats following the 1920 census of population, and the size of the House was not changed after the 1930 census because of the belief it was too large to handle its responsibilities efficiently and expeditiously. Writing in 1935, Professor Charles A. Beard concluded the House was an "already unwieldy assembly."[48]

The House of Representatives is relatively small compared to the lower house of many national legislative bodies and the unicameral German parliament (*Bundestag*), which has 656 members.[49] The United Kingdom's House of Commons, after which the House of Representatives was modeled, has 659 members. It is apparent that enlargement of the House would provide more opportunities for the election of candidates of underrepresented groups, depending, after the first election, on whether the SMD system continues to be employed (see Chapter 12 in this volume).

Although the larger house in other national legislatures generally functions adequately, it is important to note these legislatures are part of a parliamentary system under which most powers are confined to the executive (cabinet), and the roles of the backbenchers are to vote as their respective party leaders direct and to provide constituent services.

The current size of the House of Representatives precludes genuine debate and requires intricate procedural rules and reliance on committees, which may not be representative of the House, throughout the legislative process. It generally is agreed the quality of debate speeches is not high and possibly is attributable in part to the strict time limitations imposed on each member desiring to speak. Increasing the size of the House would necessitate even more stringent time limits on debates and speeches by individual members (see Chapter 16 in this Volume).

A legislative body the size of the current U.S. House elected by the SMD system is not predestined to have a low turnover rate of members. The 400-member New Hampshire House of Representatives has had a two-year turnover rate exceeding 40.0 percent on five occasions since 1951–1952, although the turnover rate decreased in more recent years from 36.5 percent in 1993–1994 to 24.0 percent in 1997–1998.[50] The turnover in the New Hampshire House membership generally is promoted by the salary established by the state constitution adopted in 1784: $250 per biennium for the presiding officer of each house and $200 per biennium for other members.[51]

TERM LIMITS

The incumbent House member seeking reelection is reinforced by the SMD system and associated fund-raising advantages that make it very difficult for a challenger under normal political circumstances to win the election, with the possible exception of a marginal seat in a district. As a result, it is highly doubtful a sharp increase in the number of members of underrepresented groups elected to the House will occur in the foreseeable future without a change in the electoral system or the imposition of term limits.

Congress has had experience with term limits. The Articles of Confederation and Perpetual Union (1781–1789) provided for annual elections and limited members of the unicameral Congress to no more than three years of service during a six-year period.[52] It also should be noted that ten of the thirteen states held annual elections at the time of the constitutional convention of 1787, which debated a one-, two-, or three-year term for representatives.[53] Advocates of a one-year term stressed keeping representatives responsive to constituents, and proponents of a three-year term placed emphasis on the need for members of Congress to become familiar with the legislative process and their duties. President George Washington established an extraconstitutional term limit for the presidency by refusing to seek a third term, and the precedent was followed until 1940, when President Franklin D. Roosevelt successfully won a third term. Growing resentment of an unlimited number of terms for the president led to adoption of the 22nd Amendment to the U.S. Constitution, limiting a president to two terms.

Term limits apply to state legislators in nineteen states and were adopted by referenda in eighteen states and by a statute in Utah (see Chapter 14 in this volume).[54] Courts in Massachusetts and Washington invalidated term-limit statutes on the ground such limits can be imposed only by a constitutional amendment.

The U.S. Court of Appeals for the Ninth Circuit in 1997, by a two-to-one vote, invalidated California Proposition 140 of 1990, which established term limits for state legislators on the ground it failed to provide adequate notice to voters the proposition would establish a lifetime term limit.[55] The Court of Appeals for the Ninth Circuit, sitting *en banc*, reversed the decision in 1997.[56] The U.S. Supreme Court in 1998 refused to hear an appeal from the decision of the U.S. Court of Appeals for the Ninth Circuit.[57]

Term limits work with respect to promoting turnover in legislative membership. A 100 percent turnover has occurred in California since term limits were adopted by the initiative proposition 140 in 1990, and the 1993 Maine term-limit initiative proposition produced a 99 percent turnover.[58]

Critics of such limits cite a 1997 survey—by the Council of State Governments of legislators, their staff, and government relations professionals—revealing the belief the influence of staff and lobbyists in the legislative process has increased, and the work of appropriations committees has been compromised.[59] Approximately two-thirds of the persons surveyed reported legislators facing the maximum term limit in the next election are less accountable to constituents.[60]

A number of states and cities have had considerable experience with tenure restrictions, as illustrated by a single, four-year limit for the governor in Virginia and a two-term limit for the Atlanta, Georgia, mayor. Term limits are associated directly with the population size of municipalities. A survey of 4,413 municipalities, published in 1998, revealed larger cities tend to have mayoral term limits, with such limits in 55.6 percent of units in the 500,00 and over population group, compared with only 28.0 percent of the units in the 100,000–249,999 group.[61] Hence, it is apparent there is relatively strong support for the concept of term limits in the United States.

Henry Flores in 1998 argued a "high degree of racial polarization combined with a small pool of potential city council candidates makes term limitations a candidate for inclusion as a dilutive mechanism under section 5 of the VRA" (Voting Rights Act).[62] Flores is convinced term limits are a barrier to the election of members of a racial minority to public office and reported the Texas cities included in his study that had been sued under the Voting Rights Act had instituted term limits that appear to be a strategy "to prevent Hispanics from holding office for too long a term."[63]

Several congressional critics have advocated term limits and refute the arguments such limits would make it impossible for capable members to gain sufficient experience to be effective lawmakers, deprive voters of their democratic right to elect the most competent candidates, and enhance the influence of lobbyists and bureaucrats in the legislative process. James L. Payne explained "the argument about experiences does not . . . apply to all jobs," and voters are not in a position to judge the competence of members in analyzing problems and drafting bills.[64] Payne added " 'ability' is not a single-one-dimensional variable. It has two distinct components: the skills, drives, and personality needed to succeed in mass popularity contests; and the skills, interests, and character needed to craft sound legislation. Longevity in Congress implies only the first ability."[65]

Relative to the democratic right of the elector to cast a ballot for any candidate, one must note the U.S. Constitution does not guarantee this right and, on the contrary, does not permit the election of a candidate to the House of Representatives prior to his or her 25th birthday or to the Senate prior to his or her 30th birthday.[66] Although electors do not vote directly for a presidential candidate, such a candidate is ineligible for the office until he or she has reached the age of 35.[67]

Payne rejected the contention term limits will increase the influence of lobbyists and bureaucrats on spending decisions over the relatively inexperienced legislators because it is based on the assumption "congressmen currently hear both sides of spending questions, that the self-interested claims of administrators and special-interest lobbyists are counterbalanced by the arguments of critics of spending programs."[68] He is convinced there is no such counterbalance, and long-tenured congressmen favor the expansion of federal government programs.

Thomas E. Mann of the Brookings Institution in 1992 maintained such "limits are the wrong medicine for what ails the congressional election system" and attributed the election success of House incumbents to the lack of "credible challengers."[69] Mann specifically was referring to relatively unknown candidates who lacked adequate campaign funds. He explained "[t]here is no compelling reason to insist on 100 percent turnover in Congress every twelve years when fifty to seventy-five percent of the members of the House and Senate are routinely replaced every decade.''[70] Mann anticipated most elections would not be competitive under term limits because challengers would wait for an open seat prior to filing nomination papers.

Other arguments against term limits include (1) a possible shift in congressional-presidential balance of power, with the president exercising more influence over the average House member, who would be relatively inexperienced as a national legislator, (2) unhealthy staff influence over members, and (3) growth in the influence of lobbyists.

Voters in 21 states employed the initiative to limit terms of members of Congress, and the Utah state legislature enacted a term-limit statute applicable to the state's congressional delegation. These limits are little more than advisory since the U.S. Constitution does not establish such limits or authorize states to impose them. The U.S. Supreme Court in 1995, by a five-to-four vote, invalidated section 3 of amendment 73 to the Arkansas Constitution, which limited representatives from Arkansas to the U.S. House of Representatives and Senate to three terms and two terms, respectively.[71]

House Resolution 73, providing for a twelve-year constitutional term limit for U.S. representatives and senators, was defeated in 1995 in the House by a vote of 227 to 204, 61 votes short of the required two-thirds vote to propose a constitutional amendment.[72] House members may be more sympathetic to term limits if their term of office was increased to four or six years. The United States is the only nation with a national house that serves a fixed term of office as short as two years. The brevity of the term necessitates continual campaigning for reelection and associated fund-raising activities. On the other hand, the short term compels members to render to voters a biennial accounting that should make the members more responsive to the wishes of the electorate.

Although a constitutional term-limit amendment has slim prospects of being adopted, there is no constitutional barrier to a state legislature's enacting a statute containing a "moral obligation" provision authorizing candidates for the U.S. House of Representatives to file a preprimary pledge to serve only a specified maximum number of terms. The Arizona state legislature in 1973 enacted a similar statute containing a clause for a "moral obligation" resignation by authorizing candidates for the U.S. House and Senate to file a preprimary pledge to resign their seats should they lose a recall election.[73]

TWO RADICAL ALTERNATIVES

The reforms examined earlier may be termed moderate ones, yet strong opposition to them suggests *in extremis* proposals for change do not merit analysis. Such proposals, however, may generate public thinking on representation problems in the United States and support for modifications that may prove to be more popular in the distant future.

The parliamentary system versus the presidential system was a widely debated topic in the late 19th century and the first half of the 20th century. The current national governmental system could be replaced by a unicameral or bicameral parliament elected by LIST-PR, or STV-PR, cumulative voting, or limited voting. Such a system would permit election of a larger House but would lack separation of executive and legislative powers and its occasional gridlocks.

A second radical alternative would be election of House members by STV-PR and employment of the corporate principle to elect members of the Senate. This alternative is utilized by the Republic of Ireland, where members of *Dáil Éireann*, the lower house of the *Oireachtas* (parliament), are chosen by STV-PR, and 49 of the 60 members of the *Seanad Éireann* are elected by the corporate principle.[74] The *Taoiseach* (prime minister) appoints 11 members, 3 members are elected by the National University of Ireland, 3 members are elected by the University of Dublin (Trinity College), and 43 members are elected from five panels of candidates, established by statute, who have knowledge and practical experience relative to (1) national language and culture, literature, art, and education, (2) agriculture and fisheries, (3) labor, (4) industry and commerce, and (5) public administration and social services, including voluntary social activities.[75]

Candidates for election to *Dáil Éireann* may nominate themselves or may be nominated by a registered voter of the pertinent corporate constituency. Candidates for election to the *Seanad* on a given panel may be nominated by four members of the *Oireachtas* or, alternatively, by a registered nominating organization such as the Association of Secondary Teachers, Ireland, for the cultural and educational panel. Panel members are elected by the newly chosen *Dáil Éireann*, members of the outgoing *Seanad Éireann*, and members of county boroughs (consolidated city-county) and county councils.

The Irish electoral system is designed to ensure each political party elects candidates in proportion to the popular vote for its candidates, and all corporate interests are represented directly in a nation that is relatively homogeneous in social characteristics. Perhaps it is time to place less representational emphasis on ethnicity and race and more emphasis on ensuring all corporate interests have direct representation in the House.

CONCLUSIONS

The question has arisen on sundry occasions whether the House of Representatives is sufficiently representative. This question is becoming more central and critical because of the increasing societal diversity and the general decline in the turnout of voters at the polls. The SMD electoral system is responsible, in part, for what appears to be growing citizen apathy relative to their exercise of the franchise, because casting a vote for a losing candidate in such an election deprives the elector of the opportunity to make a direct contribution to the election of any candidate to the House, and the existence of a high percentage of incumbent safe seats encourages voters of the minority party to boycott the polls.

This chapter examines in detail four relatively moderate possible reforms—electoral system change, quotas for underrepresented groups, enlargement of the House, and term limits—and two radical reforms to increase the representative character of the House and emphasizes the positive correlation that exists between the electoral system employed and the responsiveness of the House to the views of all citizens. The changed socioeconomic composition of the nation's population makes it imperative to replace a system favoring middle-class, white males with a more representative one strengthening participatory democracy by encouraging all citizens to become better informed on national issues and voters to participate in elections.

Of the electoral systems designed to provide representation for "minorities" and women, STV-PR is the preferable one, but opposition to it is so strong and emotional that it probably will not be adopted in the foreseeable future.

Should this system be adopted, the legislative process may become increasingly difficult, because more compromises will be necessary in order to reconcile the conflicting interests of the various groups of citizens represented by House members. On the other hand, the quality of legislation should improve when the needs and views of all citizens are represented directly in the House. Major decisions still will be made by members of the majority party, but the composition of the members will not be identical on as many issues as when members were elected by the SMD system.

The president may experience greater problems in winning House support for his or her programs and may have to make concessions to groups ignored in the past. If the president's policies have broad appeal, he or she may fare better with a more representative House than with one overrepresenting white, middle-class men. Mayor Fiorello H. LaGuardia of New York City wrote in 1940 that the City Council elected by STV-PR had "been annoying and exasperating" but added: "Is not every executive subjected to criticism, or even if you please, to be harassed by the legislative body? I am glad that I am living under a system of government that permits an executive to be criticized, even if that criticism extends to the point of unjustifiable abuse."[76]

In sum, the House of Representatives electoral system should promote political integration and encourage all citizens to respect the views of others and consider the good of society as well as their personal interests.

NOTES

1. See *The Federalist Papers* (New York: New American Library, 1961); Ralph Ketcham, ed., *The Anti-Federalist Papers and the Constitutional Convention Debates* (New York: New American Library, 1986).

2. Ketcham, *The Anti-Federalist Papers*, p. 313.

3. Ibid., p. 342.

4. *The Federalist Papers*, p. 214.

5. Richard S. Childs, *The Short Ballot: A Movement to Simplify Politics* (New York: National Short Ballot Organization, 1916), p. 4.

6. Richard S. Childs, *The First Fifty Years of the Council-Manager Form of Municipal Government* (New York: National Municipal League, 1965).

7. Heinz Eulau, "Changing Views on Representation," in Heinz Eulau and John C. Walke, *The Politics of Representation: Continuities in Theory and Research* (Beverly Hills, CA: Sage, 1978), p. 49.

8. Ibid., p. 51.

9. Joseph F. Zimmerman, "Fair Representation for Minorities and Women," in Wilma Rule and Joseph F. Zimmerman, eds., *United States Electoral Systems: Their Impact on Women and Minorities* (Westport, CT: Greenwood Press, 1992), pp. 9–11.

10. Douglas J. Amy, *Real Choices/New Voices* (New York: Columbia University Press, 1993), p. 22.

11. *Electing the People's House: 1988* (Washington, DC: Center for Voting and Democracy, 1998), p. 2.

12. *Reapportionment Act of 1842*, 5 Stat. 491.

13. *Reapportionment Act of 1911*, 37 Stat. 14.

14. *Reapportionment Act of 1929*, 46 Stat. 21.

15. *Wood v. Broom*, 287 U.S. 1 at 6, 53 S.Ct. 1 at 2 (1932).

16. 81 Stat. 581, 2 USC § 2c (1997). This requirement was added as a rider to a private relief act.

17. *Voting Rights Act of 1965*, 79 Stat. 437, 42 U.S.C. § 1973.

18. *United Jewish Organizations of Williamsburg, Incorporated v. Carey*, 430 U.S. 144 at 156 and 159–60 (1977).

19. *Voting Rights Act Amendments of 1975*, 89 Stat. 438, 42 U.S.C. § 1973.

20. Rory A. Austin, "Measuring the Effects of Local Electoral Structures," paper presented at the annual meeting of the American Political Science Association, Boston, September 5, 1998, p. 33.

21. *New York Election Law*, § 6–162.

22. The argument has been advanced the alternative vote may result in the exclusion of the most preferred candidate. To ensure this electoral system does not produce this result, Condorcet pairwise counting or the Borda points system can be employed. For details, consult Robert A. Newland, *Comparative Electoral Systems* (London: Electoral Reform Society of Great Britain and Ireland, 1982), pp. 15–21.

23. *A Mayor and Assembly for London: The Government's Proposals for Modernising the Governance of London* (London: Department of the Environment, Transport & the Regions, 1998), p. 32.

24. J. F. H. Wright, *Mirror of the Nation's Mind: Australia's Electoral Experiements* (Sydney: Hale & Iremonger, 1980), p. 136.

25. Steven J. Brams and Peter C. Fishburn, *Approval Voting* (Boston: Birkhäuser, 1983).

26. George S. Blair, *Cumulative Voting: An Effective Electoral Device in Illinois Politics* (Urbana: University of Illinois Press, 1960).

27. Edward Still, "Cumulative Voting and Limited Voting in Alabama," in Rule and Zimmerman, eds., *United States Electoral Systems*, pp. 184–90.

28. Ibid., pp. 190–96.

29. Theodore McNelly, " 'Women Power' in Japan's 1989 Upper House Election,"

in Wilma Rule and Joseph F. Zimmerman, eds., *Electoral Systems in Comparative Perspective: Their Impact on Women and Minorities* (Westport, CT: Greenwood Press, 1994), pp. 150–59.

30. Andrew Reynolds and Ben Reilly, eds., *The International IDEA Handbook of Electoral System Design*, 2nd ed. (Stockholm: International Institute for Democracy and Electoral Assistance, 1997), p. 20.

31. Fanny Tabak, "Women and Politics in Brazil: Legislative Elections," in Rule and Zimmerman, eds., *Electoral Systems in Comparative Perspective*, pp. 202–9.

32. George H. Hallett, Jr., "Proportional Representation with the Single Transferable Vote: A Basic Requirement for Legislative Elections," in Arend Lijphart and Bernard Grofman, eds., *Choosing an Electoral System: Issues and Alternatives* (New York: Praeger, 1984), p. 116.

33. Ibid.

34. Consult Beate Hoecker, "The German Electoral System: A Barrier to Women?" in Rule and Zimmerman, eds., *Electoral Systems in Comparative Perspective*, pp. 65–77.

35. *Towards a Better Democracy: Report of the Royal Commission on the Electoral System* (Wellington, New Zealand, 1986), p. 64.

36. Ibid., p. 37.

37. Robert A. Newland, *Comparative Electoral Systems* (London: The Electoral Reform Society of Great Britain and Ireland, 1982), p. 59.

38. *Towards a Better Democracy*, p. 45.

39. John Stuart Mill, *Utilitarianism, Liberty, and Representative Government* (New York: E. P. Dutton, 1951), p. 354.

40. George H. Hallett, Jr., *Proportional Representation: The Key to Democracy* (New York: National Municipal League, 1940), pp. 72–73.

41. Belle Zeller and Hugh A. Bone, "The Repeal of P.R. in New York City: Ten Years in Retrospect," *The American Political Science Review*, December 1948, p. 1137.

42. Hallett, *Proportional Representation*, p. 57.

43. Joan Rydon, "Representation of Women and Ethnic Minorities in the Parliaments of Australia and New Zealand," in Rule and Zimmerman, *Electoral Systems in Comparative Perspective*, p. 230.

44. Bih-Er Chou and Janet Clark, "Electoral Systems and Women's Representation in Taiwan: The Impact of the Reserved-Seat System," in Rule and Zimmerman, *Electoral Systems in Comparative Perspective*, p. 168.

45. *Argentine Statute 13010 of 1947*.

46. *Argentine Statute 24012 of 1991*.

47. N. Guillermo Molinelli, "Argentina: The (No) *Ceteris Paribus Case*," in Rule and Zimmerman, *Electoral Systems in Comparative Perspective*, pp. 201–2.

48. Charles A. Beard, *American Government and Politics* (New York: Macmillan, 1935), p. 86.

49. The *Bundesverfassungsgericht* (constitutional court) opined the *Bundesrat* is not the upper house of parliament.

50. Data provided by New Hampshire deputy secretary of state Robert Ambrose, July 8, 1998.

51. *Constitution of the State of New Hampshire*, Part Second, Article 15.

52. *Articles of Confederation and Perpetual Union*, Article 5.

53. "Origins of Term Limits," *Congressional Digest*, April 1995, p. 99.

54. "Who's Next?" *State Government News*, December 1997, p. 16. See also "Term Limits for Members of Congress: Background and Contemporary Issues, 1990–1996," *CRS Report for Congress* (Washington, DC: Congressional Research Service, 1997).

55. *Bates v. Jones*, 127 F.3d 839 (9th Cir. 1997).

56. *Bates v. Jones*, 131 F.3d 843 (9th Cir. 1997).

57. *Bates v. Jones*, 118 S.Ct. 1302 (1998).

58. "Term Limits and Turnover," *Commonwealth*, Spring 1998, p. 23.

59. Drew Leatherby, "The Truth about Term Limits," *State Government News*, December 1997, pp. 14–16.

60. Ibid., p. 17.

61. Tari Renner and Victor S. DeSantis, "Municipal Form of Government: Issues and Trends," *The Municipal Year Book 1998* (Washington, DC: International City/County Management Association, 1998), p. 38.

62. Henry Flores, "Term Limits and the Voting Rights Act: The Case of San Antonio, Texas," paper presented at the 1998 annual meeting of the American Political Science Association, Boston, September 5, 1998, pp. 9–10.

63. Ibid., pp. 17–18.

64. James L. Payne, "Limiting Government by Limiting Congressional Terms," *Public Interest*, Spring 1991, pp. 107–8.

65. Ibid., p. 110.

66. *U.S. Constitution* Article 1, §§ 2–3.

67. Ibid., Article 2, § 1.

68. Payne, "Limiting Government," p. 115.

69. Thomas E. Mann, "The Wrong Medicine: Term Limits Won't Cure What Ails Congressional Elections," *The Brookings Review*, Spring 1992, pp. 24–25.

70. Ibid., p. 25.

71. *U.S. Term Limits, Incorporated v. Thornton*, 115 S.Ct. 1842 (1995).

72. "House Rejects Term Limits; GOP Blames Democrats," *CQ Weekly Report*, April 1995, p. 918.

73. *Arizona Laws of 1973*, Chapter 159; *Arizona Revised Statutes*, §§ 19–221, 19–222.

74. *Bunreacht Na hÉireann* (Constitution of Ireland), Article 16 (5)–17 (1, 4–7).

75. Ibid., Article 18 (3–7).

76. "Mayor LaGuardia on P.R.," *National Municipal Review*, April 1940, p. 275.

Chapter 16

If It Ain't Broke Bad, Don't
Fix It a Lot

C. Lawrence Evans and Walter J. Oleszek

The House of Representatives is one of the most dynamic of governmental institutions. Formally and informally, the House regularly revises its rules, procedures, practices, and structures to adapt and adjust to, among other things, membership and workload changes. Absent its capacities for reform, the House would soon find itself unable to meet the diverse challenges of the day. Generally, the House's reorganization imperative is driven by the constant influx of new lawmakers who bring fresh perspectives on how the House should work; typically, they want to make changes in the status quo.

House reform also is triggered by a wide variety of other forces. For instance, when the House is dissatisfied with some aspect of its structure or procedures, a critical mass may unite to establish a select reorganization panel to address the problems. Times of transition and turbulence often produce legislative reform movements whose members may seek to modernize the House or to redistribute internal power from those who have it to those who want it. Public anger at the institution—the House ''bank'' scandal of the early 1990s is an example—also provokes introspective reviews of institutional operations. Party leaders, too, may take the lead in procedural and organizational transformations.

Change and reform, in short, are common phenomena on Capitol Hill. Worth noting is the difference between the two terms. Reform is a ''plan to do things differently, often so as to embody change; change is the result of new developments.''[1] The electoral earthquake of November 1994 certainly produced a ''change'' in the majority composition of the House. This new development also triggered action on a purposeful plan to ''reform'' the structures (committee, subcommittee, and committee staff reductions, for instance) and procedures (e.g., more authority lodged in the Speakership) of the House. Although reform can be a ''tricky'' word, as former president and House GOP leader Gerald Ford once said, our commonsense understanding is that congressional reform means that things will improve and get better.[2]

In this chapter, our bottom line is that legislative reforms should at least try to fix something in House operations that is plainly broken. Several "semi-radical" reforms seem to address imaginary problems with unnecessary solutions. To us, "semi-radical" reforms include those intended to transform the basic structure, membership, or procedures of the contemporary House. These reforms include such ideas as instituting proportional representation (PR) for the House, enlarging its size from 435 to 650, or increasing the term of representatives from two to four years.[3] Accordingly, we first examine several "semi-radical" ideas and then outline our reform objectives for the contemporary House.

PROPORTIONAL REPRESENTATION FOR HOUSE ELECTIONS

Compared to the "winner-take-all" electoral system employed for House elections—where the candidate winning the most votes represents a distinct geographic area—PR is used by many European democracies. Under some PR versions, candidates run on party slates in multi-member districts; a party that receives a certain percentage of the popular vote receives the same percentage of seats in the legislature (see Chapter 15 in this volume). Other parties that receive a certain threshold vote elect the remaining officeholders on a proportionate basis. The argument for PR is that it more accurately reflects voter preferences. Under the winner-take-all system, a plurality winner may attract the most votes but not represent the real majoritarian preference. In a three-way race, for example, a conservative may end up the winner with less than 50 percent of the vote because most of the electorate split their ballots between two liberal candidates. On the other hand, PR for House elections is likely to undermine America's traditional two-party system by encouraging the formation of numerous splinter parties. In a 650-seat House, for instance, California would be entitled to 78 seats based on 1990 census figures; so many targets of opportunity would provide incentives for splinter groups to vie for some of those seats.

Some champions of this reform argue for PR on the theory House members do not represent the diversity of their constituencies very well. In fact, the reverse argument is more accurate: House members are often too responsive to constituency sentiments. Most lawmakers travel every weekend to their districts; the House's work is compressed into a Tuesday–Thursday time frame to accommodate their weekend visits; many personal staff aides work full-time in districts to maintain a constant constituency-service presence; when in Washington, lawmakers beam daily messages to the home folks; faxes, polls, and e-mails from constituents bombard Capitol Hill offices. Today's lawmakers appear to be at risk of becoming almost full-time ombudsmen for their constituents. PR would further encourage this tendency and, thus, divert members' attention away from their lawmaking and oversight responsibilities.

FOUR-YEAR TERMS FOR HOUSE MEMBERS

The idea of extending the terms of House members from two to four years is an old one. In 1966 President Lyndon B. Johnson recommended a four-year term in his State of the Union message. The arguments for extending House terms are well known: longer terms would enable lawmakers to spend more time on the job addressing complex issues; representatives must currently focus inordinate attention on the campaign "money chase"; off-year elections, with their relatively low levels of turnout, are unrepresentative of the country's sentiments; concurrent, four-year terms for House members and the president would strengthen legislative-executive party unity.[4]

These are all interesting notions, but they are not as compelling as those for maintaining the two-year term for representatives. The Framers of the U.S. Constitution deliberately chose the compromise (between one-year and three-year terms) of two-year terms to foster, as James Madison said, "an immediate dependence on, and an intimate sympathy with the people."[5] Why should voters have to wait four years to oust a lawmaker who they believe is not doing a good job? Second, the issue of campaigning can be addressed without constitutional tinkering with the electoral term of House members. Third, mid-term elections provide attentive voters an opportunity to express a judgment on what the Congress and the president have accomplished—or not accomplished. Mid-term elections provide an important electoral "safety valve" for our diverse society. Finally, four-year House terms concurrent with the president's might alter our "checks and balances" system by making representatives somewhat more susceptible to both his or her blandishments and "coattails." In sum, why fundamentally change an electoral arrangement that has stood the test of time?

INCREASING THE SIZE OF THE HOUSE

The U.S. Constitution provides for the minimum and the maximum size of the House. It can be as small as 50 members (one per state) or as large as about 8,300 (one member per 30,000 persons, using 1990 census figures). Today, the size *statutorily* is fixed at 435, but some suggest that House membership should be increased to 650 lawmakers. The argument for a larger House is that it would ease the constituency burdens of lawmakers by changing the population ratio per member, provide greater opportunities for the underrepresented to win House seats, and facilitate closer ties between the representatives and the represented. Periodically, proposals are made in the House to increase its membership; sometimes measures are introduced to reduce its size.

Our contention is that a 650-seat House would produce far more negative than positive consequences. First, members hardly know each other. As House

Democratic leader Richard Gephardt (D-MO) once said: "Members are islands. They're very busy, and they don't often have the time to get to know one another."[6] Contemplate what it might be like with 650 lawmakers interacting as "strangers" in a partisan environment where the incentives are to go for the political jugular. Second, the job of coalition-building would certainly be more difficult as party and other leaders strove to make the compromises and adjustments needed to enact legislation. Delays and stalemates would multiply with a 650-member chamber, even though the "majority rule" principle undergirds House operations. Finally, there is a host of practical issues—providing more space and staff for the new lawmakers, reconfiguring the House chamber, increasing the number of committees and/or committee sizes, and revising House rules to accommodate the membership increase. Maybe 435 is not the right size for today's House, but 650 seems too large.

REFORM OBJECTIVES FOR IMPROVING THE HOUSE

There are many reforms that would improve the organization and operations of the House. Five reorganization categories are listed briefly, in no special order. Whether adopted singly or in combination, each recommendation, in our view, has merit in its own right. These ideas are illustrative of the types of reforms that appear to us to be practical, focused on the realistic concerns of lawmakers, and, under the right conditions, capable of adoption.[7]

Strengthen Deliberation

Scholars recently have identified a significant drop-off in the quality of deliberation in the House. Increasingly, "the House floor is a processor of bills rather than an arena of deliberation."[8] The decline of deliberation stems from at least three factors: lack of timely information during floor debate, lack of member time to attend debates, and lack of institutional structures to encourage debate. To address the first, we propose that the House consider revising its rules to permit lawmakers to use personal laptop computers on the floor so they can instantly access policy-specific information and analysis. Broader and more informed participation in floor debate might increase as rank-and-file members employ their laptop computers to acquire data and analysis previously available only to committee members. Use of such computers would be governed by rules and regulations promulgated by the House Oversight Committee.

Second, to alleviate at least some time pressures, the current ban on proxy voting in committee and subcommittee could be restricted to the reporting stage. The prohibition on proxy voting, intended to increase committee attendance and participation, has not worked in practice. Instead, members now sprint back and forth from committees to the floor (or between committees marking up measures concurrently) to cast their votes with minimal opportunity to participate in debates. Third, the House should undertake a major reexamination of ways to enhance deliberation through means such as wider use of Oxford Union-style debates, which were used on a trial basis in the 103rd Congress. Improvements in scheduling the House's business also could strengthen deliberation, especially if the current "Tuesday-Thursday" workweek is expanded to allow members longer and more concentrated time periods in which to debate the issues of the day. A four-day workweek with alternating two-day and four-day weekends is an option that merits consideration by the party leadership.

Promote Civility

The House today is a meaner-spirited institution than it has been for several decades. The lack of civility makes negotiation far more difficult and causes more time to be spent on unproductive personal and partisan attacks rather than on constructive lawmaking and debate. Part of the incivility results from trends in the broader society as well as other changes, such as heightened partisanship.[9] The rise of incivility in the House even led to a March 1997 Civility Retreat in Hershey, Pennsylvania, where lawmakers were encouraged to get to know each other and to relate to one another as colleagues instead of partisan adversaries or enemies. Much more needs to be done to promote civility on Capitol Hill, including stricter enforcement of the rules against unparliamentary language.[10] For example, we suggest that if the Speaker rules that a lawmaker has used unparliamentary language during debate, he or she would lose the right to speak on the floor not just for the remainder of that day (the current practice) but for several consecutive days or for a legislative week.

Adjustments to the Committee System

Because committees are the "workshops" of the House, where many of the most important decisions are made, it is essential that they be as representative and efficient as possible. At present, important policy areas are divided across several committees, making comprehensive approaches difficult; further, committees sometimes fail to represent a sufficiently wide range of interests. To address these shortcomings, the House should restructure its committees so that both broad and competing substantive areas (e.g., energy and environment) are incorporated as completely as practicable within the jurisdictional mandate of a single committee. Unrepresentative committees filled with advocates for specific interests are unlikely to serve the broader deliberative and policy interests of the House. As the 1973–1974 Bolling Committee (named for the late representative Richard Bolling (D-MO) phrased it: "Committees should be able to attract a broadly representative membership and embrace a variety of viewpoints on the questions within their jurisdiction."[11]

Reduction in Workload

Today, each lawmaker represents almost 600,000 constituents, compared to a little more than 400,000 in the 1960s. Moreover, demands from constituents have increased, and the complexity of policy has become far greater. Yet, the House has not systematically examined how it might reduce some of its current workload since enactment of the Legislative Reorganization Act of 1946, which delegated certain of Congress' responsibilities (the settlement of private claims against the government, for instance) to other federal entities. Given increases in the complexity of the House's workload, it may be time for another major review of whether some matters could be handled by other public or private entities. We suggest, for instance, that the House revisit the idea of establishing a congressional ombudsman to assist representatives in handling their burgeoning constituent service (or "casework").

Public Understanding of the House

Today, scores of individuals can watch gavel-to-gavel floor coverage of House (and Senate) proceedings over C-SPAN; they also can tune in to many televised committee hearings. Despite being in the "electronic gallery," a large percentage of the public fails to understand or appreciate how Congress works. As two scholars point out, people have a "patently unrealistic" view of the legislative process.[12] In short, the challenge of explaining Congress to the public remains an unfinished assignment. We have two proposals for promoting public understanding. First, during "dead time" (votes, quorum calls, etc.), C-SPAN might, on a regular basis, explain to viewers what is happening on the floor. Parliamentary language is often arcane and ornate, and interpretive explanations would likely be informative to the viewing public. Second, the House's rule book is written for parliamentarians and not the general layperson. A readable, widely distributed (over the Internet, for instance), and easy-to-use manual should be developed (and kept updated) to accompany the formal rule book. This manual—perhaps with an accompanying videotape of floor illustrations—would explain the basic operating procedures and practices of the House.

In conclusion, the House is not some "creaky institution" that cannot reform itself either incrementally or comprehensively. Institutionally minded lawmakers—probably fewer today than in previous years—regularly strive to put "the House in order." Where we differ with some analysts is on the kind of reforms that will ostensibly enhance the House's governing capacities. We tilt toward revisions that track the House's long-standing reform tradition. We are unsupportive of reforms that, while appealing in their broad sweep, are unlikely to work in the real world of Capitol Hill politics and policy making. In matters of House reform, said Representative John Dingell (D-MI), the great and wise counsel of the shade tree mechanic needs to be observed: "If it ain't broke, don't fix it."[13]

NOTES

This chapter is a revised version of an article that appeared in *PS: Political Science and Politics*, vol. 31, no. 1, March 1998, pp. 24–28. The authors thank Ron Rapoport for his helpful review of this article.

1. Charles O. Jones, "Radical Change in Makeup of Congress Will Occur Regardless of Reform Efforts," *Roll Call*, August 8, 1994, p. 8.

2. Mary McInnis, ed., *We Propose: A Modern Congress* (New York: McGraw-Hill, 1966), p. xii.

3. A "radical" reform would be replacing our congressional-presidential system with parliamentary government.

4. There are other election options with different implications besides concurrent four-year terms, such as in the off-years or split between the two, as with the Senate.

5. Paul L. Ford, ed., *The Federalist: A Commentary on the Constitution of the United States* (New York: Henry Holt, 1898), p. 350.

6. Dave Doubrava, "House Democrats Huddle over Plans," *Washington Times*, March 1, 1985, p. A4.

7. To be sure, many other reform issues merit review, such as ethics, budgeting, oversight, party leadership, or congressional campaign costs.

8. George E. Connor and Bruce I. Oppenheimer, "Deliberation: An Untimed Value in a Time Game," in Lawrence C. Dodd and Bruce I. Oppenheimer, eds., *Congress Reconsidered*, 5th ed. (Washington, DC: CQ Press, 1993), p. 318.

9. Eric Uslaner, *The Decline of Comity in Congress* (Ann Arbor: University of Michigan Press, 1993).

10. Kathleen Hall Jamieson, *Civility in the House of Representatives: A Background Report* (Philadelphia: Annenberg Public Policy Center, University of Pennsylvania, 1997).

11. U.S. Congress. House of Representatives. 1974. *Committee Reform Amendments of 1974*, 93rd Cong., 2d sess., H. Rept. 916, pt. II, p. 19.

12. John R. Hibbing and Elizabeth Theiss-Morse, *Congress as Public Enemy: Public Attitudes toward American Political Institutions* (New York: Cambridge University Press, 1995), p. 147. For further information about congressional reforms, see Thomas E. Mann and Norman J. Ornstein, *Renewing Congress: A Second Report* (Washington, DC: American Enterprise Institute and the Brookings Institution, 1993).

13. U.S. Congress, Joint Committee on the Organization of Congress, *Committee Structure*, 103rd Cong., 1st sess., April 29, 1993, p. 186.

Chapter 17

Political Reform Is Political

Daniel H. Lowenstein

One advantage of asking a group of political scientists rather than law professors to address issues of congressional and electoral reform is that, as the chapters in this volume show, there are few, if any, calls for the judiciary to solve all our problems. Still, the courts have influenced major parts of the electoral system that is criticized and defended in this volume, and it is widely supposed the courts play a major role in the defense of political liberty and representational equality.

Space does not permit even a summary of the ways in which judicial intervention has helped shape the contemporary House of Representatives.[1] Instead, I describe and criticize one of the central theoretical justifications for aggressive judicial review of political procedures. That justification is based on the assumption "process" questions are distinct from "substantive" political issues—such as taxation, welfare, and environmental protection—based on conflicting interests and therefore inherently are contestable. In contrast, political procedural questions, such as campaign finance and electoral system design, are imagined to be subject to impartial resolution based on principles of fairness and equality. I argue disputes over political processes are as inherently "political" as disputes over substantive issues.

In a volume devoted to reforming House elections and procedures, some attention to judicial review and its justifications is worthwhile for the sake of completeness. In addition, I show criticism of the theoretical justification for judicial review has more bearing on some of the other chapters than at first might seem likely. I argue much of the debate over electoral reform suffers from the same faulty premise underlying some of the justifications for judicial review—namely, the fairness and impartiality of political procedures can be assessed apolitically.

JUDICIAL REVIEW OF POLITICS

During the first third of the 20th century, U.S. courts frequently struck down economic regulations they regarded as unreasonable abridgments of personal freedom. In *Lochner v. New York*, the case that lent its name to this era of jurisprudence, Justice Oliver Wendell Holmes famously dissented. The Constitution, he wrote, "is not intended to embody a particular economic theory."[2]

In the late 1930s and early 1940s the Supreme Court abruptly withdrew from its project of overseeing most economic regulations. Although this shift can be attributed to the appointment of liberal justices to the Court by President Franklin D. Roosevelt, it was accompanied by a powerful criticism of *Lochner*-era judicial interventionism, built on the foundation of Holmes' *Lochner* dissent.

Even the most conservative judges in the *Lochner* era acknowledged economic activity could be regulated if it caused harm to others. Whether economic activity—for example, paying or accepting a wage below the level a legislature has declared to be the minimum—imposes costs on others usually turns on complex empirical questions that probably have no definitive answers but that legislatures and administrative agencies can cope with more effectively than courts. More fundamentally, the conceptual question of what counts as a harm—do I harm you by insisting you not smoke in a public place we both are occupying, or do you harm me by insisting on smoking?—is often more intractable than the empirical questions.

These considerations suggest—and the difficulty of finding consistent patterns in judicial decisions confirms—the deciding element was often the particular political, social, or economic outlook of a judge deciding a case, even when that outlook was by no means consensual in the society as a whole. The shift away from judicial review of economic regulation reflected agreement with Holmes' statement in his *Lochner* dissent the U.S. Constitution "is made for people of fundamentally differing views."[3] Those who are dissatisfied with current policies or who believe their rights are infringed may organize and seek to change the policies through the ordinary political process.

Carolene Products

The Court did not get out of the business of judicial review altogether. In *United States v. Carolene Products*, Chief Justice Harlan F. Stone wrote the famous footnote 4, setting forth three situations in which the Court might continue to seriously scrutinize statutes despite the empirical and conceptual difficulties that critics of the *Lochner* era had emphasized.[4]

The least controversial of these applied to cases arising under relatively specific provisions of the Constitution. No difficult empirical or conceptual problems would prevent the Court from striking down a statute extending House terms to four years. Overturning a specific constitutional provision requires a constitutional amendment.

A second category of cases, which has played an especially prominent role in subsequent constitutional history, consisted of challenges to government practices that adversely affect "discrete and insular minorities." Prejudice against these groups may disadvantage them in political competition, creating a greater than usual need for judicial intervention into substantive policy areas in their behalf.

The remaining category is the one most pertinent for present purposes. Justice Stone left open the possibility that "legislation which restricts those political processes which can ordinarily be expected to bring about repeal of undesirable legislation [would] be subjected to more exacting judicial scrutiny."[5]

Carolene Products has been an influential—though far from dominant—element in the constitutional structure that has developed in the second half of the twentieth century.[6] The logic of its "political processes" plank is clear and, at first blush, appealing. Judicial deference to the political branches on substantive matters is based largely on the assumption the processes controlling them are indeed democratic, open, and impartial. If that assumption is false, the judiciary would be deferring to policies lacking in legitimacy. Thus, substantive judicial deference is not only compatible with but seems to require judicial activism in ensuring a democratic, open, and impartial political process.

Alas, there is a fly in the *Carolene* ointment. Most of the arguments leveled against judicial review of economic regulation in the *Lochner* era have equal force when applied to judicial review of political processes. Tinkering with electoral and legislative procedures is no less subject to empirical imponderables than tinkering with the economy. What constitutes a democratic or impartial political procedure is just as conceptually contestable as what constitutes an externality in the economic realm. Why, following Holmes, is not the U.S. Constitution "made for people of fundamentally differing views" about democratic theory and practice? If those who are aggrieved by an economic regulation ordinarily are consigned to the political arena to seek relief, why should not the same be true for those who disagree with some aspect of the political process?

Entrenchment

Ay, there is the rub, *Carolene Products* fans will respond (especially if they happen also to be fans of *Hamlet*). To be forced to seek relief from the very political process that by hypothesis is unfair is itself unfair. Would-be reformers will be confronted at every turn by "entrenchment" and "partisan lockups."[7]

The entrenchment hypothesis underlying the political process prong of *Carolene Products* is subject to numerous objections. Most obviously, it overlooks the pervasiveness of political reform in American history. The secret ballot; direct primary; direct election of senators; extension of the franchise to women and, later, to blacks in the South and to young people; adoption of the initiative in approximately half the states; almost universal adoption of campaign finance regulation ranging from disclosure to limits to public financing; and legislative term limits in many states—these are only a few of the electoral reforms brought about by political means.[8] Only one electoral reform for which the judiciary is primarily responsible—adoption in the early 1960s of the one-person, one-vote rule—is of comparable significance.[9]

The ability of participants in the political system to bring about change and reform without the aid of the judiciary is even more apparent if we turn from House elections to the internal workings of the House. As C. Lawrence Evans and Walter J. Oleszek wrote:

Absent its capacities for reform, the House would soon find itself unable to meet the diverse challenges of the day. Generally, the House's reorganization imperative is driven by the constant influx of new lawmakers who bring fresh perspectives on how the House should work; typically, they want to make changes in the status quo.[10]

Only once—when it declared unconstitutional the House's refusal to seat Adam Clayton Powell after the 1966 election—has the Supreme Court ventured into the internal affairs of Congress.[11]

Contrary to the predictions of the entrenchment hypothesis, reform is the rule, rather than the exception, in U.S. political history. Proponents of the entrenchment hypothesis overlook the diverse paths to political change that routinely make it possible either to overcome or to bypass seeming blockages to reform. Consider, for example, one of the favorite hobbyhorses of the entrenchment scholars, the question of partisan gerrymandering.[12] Gerrymandering, we are told, is "entrenchment, pure and simple," a device for controlling elections "without regard to the will of the voters"[13]:

Such scholars rarely note that gerrymandering, in Justice O'Connor's words, is a self-limiting enterprise. . . . In order to gerrymander, the legislative majority must weaken some of its safe seats, thus exposing its own incumbents to greater risks of defeat—risks they may refuse to accept past a certain point.[14]

Researchers have found partisan gerrymanders sometimes—not always—succeed in producing moderate partisan gains, albeit generally short-lived.[15] To the extent partisan gerrymandering produces gains for one party in some states' House delegations, they will be offset at least partially by gains for the opposing party in other states. Despite fears of "incumbent gerrymandering," redistricting does not seem to be a significant factor in the high reelection rate of House incumbents.[16]

When compared with the facts, the characterization of gerrymandering as "entrenchment" has little connection with reality. The traditional redistricting process, consisting of hard-nosed political competition and negotiation, tends to create an intensely partisan atmosphere in state legislatures at the beginning of each decade, can have major effects on the electoral prospects of individual politicians, and, by creating the possibility of a modest partisan advantage or disadvantage, provides an incentive for partisan electoral activity in election years ending in "8" and, especially, in "0." These are probably the only systemic effects of redistricting. To me they seem benign. Others may reasonably differ, but in any event, the presence of gerrymandering in our system does not create a major impediment to those who would reform either political processes or substantive policies.

The greatest bugaboo for recent entrenchment theorists is the endurance of the two-party system. Supposedly, the Republicans and Democrats conspire to disadvantage third parties, resulting in stifling of diverse views on issues.[17] In fact, the Republicans and Democrats compete vigorously against each other and almost never feel the need to compete against third parties. When the major parties concern themselves with third parties, it is almost always to use them competitively against the other major party.

The two-party system does not exclude political interests or viewpoints from consideration. Rather, it provides the vehicle through which new or shifting interests and viewpoints can be brought forward. One reason, widely recognized, is that the two parties tend not to occupy narrow spaces on the political spectrum but make as broad an appeal as possible. Another reason is that, as Mark Rush noted, direct primaries permit candidates with new approaches to compete for electoral victory.[18] No party leaders or party platform can block candidates from testing new ideas.

So it goes throughout the American political system. That system is open and entrepreneurial, with innumerable paths to procedural as well as substantive change. Certainly, there are also barriers to procedural reform—why shouldn't there be?—but these barriers never are insurmountable to a movement with broad, deep, and enduring support. The federal system is one important assurance that this is the case. Reforms that cannot be enacted initially at the national level often can be put into effect in the 24 states—allowing statutes and/or constitutional amendments to be adopted by the initiative. Campaign finance and term limits are areas in which reformers, frustrated by the difficulty of obtaining national legislation, have had considerable success in states, especially by making use of the initiative process.

Campaign Finance

It is true, as Clyde Wilcox and Wesley Joe remind us, there is widespread public sentiment for improved campaign finance regulation.[19] The same sentiment is probably widespread among scholars, though the improvement favored by some is deregulation.

The status quo originates from the Federal Election Campaign Act Amendments of 1974 (FECA) as modified by the Supreme Court in *Buckley v. Valeo* (1976) and by Congress in amendments enacted in 1979 to allow parties to raise and spend "soft money" for party-building and grassroots campaign activity. That legislative system served the country well for two decades in presidential elections and less well, though not disastrously, in congressional elections. Wilcox and Joe hardly exaggerated when they wrote the system crumbled in 1996. The immediate cause was widespread use of the loophole known as "issue advocacy" as a means of evading not only spending and contribution limits but also disclosure requirements. The underlying reason may have been that inflation of campaign costs caused the limits in the system to become too restrictive.

The reason reformers have been unable since the 1970s to obtain national legislation is not that there is insufficient support for change but that there is no agreement on the direction that change should take or even on the problems that campaign finance reform should solve.[20] In my view, there are three problems with our existing system serious enough to warrant legislative reform. First, although claims about a Congress that is bought and paid for are wildly extravagant, the pressure to raise large amounts of campaign funds from interest groups puts legislators and candidates into conflicts of interest that ought to be obviated if possible. Second, there are too many House districts in which competitive races are possible but do not occur because the challengers do not raise sufficient funds. Third, the system imposes too many unnecessary restrictions and regulations.[21]

Of course, others would add a host of problems to the list. Some believe campaign finance regulation should promote equality by preventing interests with money from using it to affect elections. Others think liberty should be promoted by removing some or all of the restrictions that presently exist. There are those who think campaign finance regulation should create greater opportunity for third parties and independent candidates. Others (including myself) would prefer reforms strengthening the two-party system. Many would like campaign finance regulation to improve the content or format of campaign messages or shorten the time of campaigns or otherwise affect the ways in which campaigns are conducted.

In short, the problem of campaign finance is an extremely complex one. The failure to solve it reflects its intractability and the many divergent views on how elections should work, not some lack of responsiveness in the legislative system.

Term Limits

Compared to campaign finance regulations, legislative term limits are simple. Other than the number of years to which legislators should be limited, the details are relatively insignificant. Supporters may point to term limits as a classic example of a reform favored by a strong majority of the public but successfully resisted by entrenched politicians who place the prolongation of their personal careers over the public interest.

But if the mechanism of term limits is simple, the consequences are not. They are likely to be far-reaching and not entirely predictable. In the ten years or so that legislative term limits have been on the national agenda, they have been adopted in nearly one-half the states—usually, where the initiative process is available—and in numerous local governments (see Chapter 14 in this volume). The term-limits movement has been led primarily by Republicans and may have lost much of its steam in 1994, when the Republicans ended the Democrats' long hegemony in the House of Representatives.[22] If the system of checks and balances means anything, it means far-reaching changes should not be made at the national level on untried proposals that may well reflect an attempt at short-term, political gain rather than a solution to a long-term, systemic problem. At present, the jury is still very much out on whether term limits work well, and active support for them will prove enduring. The fact that they have not yet been adopted nationally is no sign the system blocks needed reforms.

Political Struggles

I have attempted to show the faultiness of the premise underlying both the political process prong of *Carolene Products* and entrenchment theory—defects, real or imagined, in our democratic procedures are especially resistant to reform. Successful and unsuccessful struggles for political reform are neither disinterested debates over political principle nor battles between special interests on one side fighting to preserve their privileges against the disinterested forces of good government on the other side.

Political reform contests are political struggles, not much different in kind from the political struggles that take place on "substantive" issues. Even this brief survey has shown the controversies typically place Republicans and Democrats on opposite sides for mixed reasons of self-interest and ideology, while an immense variety of other groups with similarly mixed motives pitches in.[23]

This view does not deny questions of political procedure can be and should be debated in terms of efficacy, fairness, and other considerations relating to the public interest. Nor does it deny we have common ground on many aspects of our political process.[24] Political reform conflicts occur among us because we differ in many ways, including our particular conceptions of basic principles such as freedom of speech; our senses of how politics work and therefore our guesses as to the consequences of either changing or not changing the political ground rules; our substantive political goals, which may cause us to favor rules we think will be conducive to those goals; and our immediate political situations, which may be benefited or harmed by a particular proposal.

To say that a controversy is political is not to say that it is nothing more than a competition of raw power among opposing (self-) interests. One may concede political reform conflicts, like controversies on substantive issues, include genuine public interest elements. But like substantive conflicts, political reform struggles are inescapably and rightly political.

I emphasize I am not making an argument against judicial review on political procedural issues. My claim is simply the *Carolene Products* rationale for such judicial review is weak. It implicitly rests on mistaken premises, namely, that the barriers to political reforms are generally greater than the barriers to substantive reforms, and political procedural issues are less inherently political and therefore more amenable to disinterested judicial resolution than substantive issues.

THEORY AND POLITICAL REFORM

The notion reform of political procedures is less political than substantive reform turns up in contexts other than the debate on judicial review. Indeed, it underlies some of the contributions to this volume, and it is just as erroneous in one context as in the other.

In a very fine book, Hibbing and Theiss-Morse argued the American public tends to believe in democratic government in the abstract but to have unrealistic expectations for how it should operate and to find distasteful the public debate, negotiation, and compromise that most students of government believe to be intrinsic to democracy (see Chapter 11 in this volume).[25] In a 1998 essay, Hibbing and Theiss-Morse made two points:

"[B]ecause the people want them" is not a good justification for adopting procedural reforms and 2) actual enactment of the reforms craved by the people will not necessarily leave us with a system that is more liked even by the people who asked for the reforms in the first place.[26]

It is with the first of these points that I wish to take issue.

As noted, the question of whether popular wishes should be translated directly into governmental policy is the question raised by Edmund Burke, who called for representatives to act as trustees of the public rather than as delegates.[27] Hibbing and Theiss-Morse take no general position on the Burkean debate in their essay, and neither do I. Their position is that even if the delegate approach is correct for matters of substantive policy, it is unsound for matters of political procedure. My position is that for purposes of the Burkean debate, matters of procedure are not much different from matters of substance.

The main argument they give is that procedural rules ought to be "sticky." Otherwise, continual changes dictated at least in part by the desire of some to get short-term tactical advantages would tend to destabilize and delegitimate the system. There is considerable truth in this argument, but I would qualify it in at least two ways.

First, neither the fact nor the desirability of stickiness is much greater on political procedures than on substance. A sound economy undoubtedly depends, to a considerable degree though by no means absolutely, on the predictability of regulations. Hibbing and Theiss-Morse give welfare reform as an example of a substantive policy that should arguably be subject to change in accord with popular opinion. Yet, the congressional welfare reform legislation of 1996 was the first such major change in decades. Most areas of substantive regulation—antitrust, drug regulation, and labor law are typical examples—receive fundamental revisions only at long intervals.

Admittedly, there is typically a great deal of tinkering that goes on almost continuously in substantive areas, whereas federal election law has not changed significantly since the 1979 amendments to FECA. But what is overlooked is that most election regulation and administration occur at the state level, where continuous tinkering occurs about to the same extent as with substantive areas of law. If we consider the other major area of procedure most relevant to the present volume, House rules and procedure, they also receive continuous tinkering. As we have seen, Evans and Oleszek regard such tinkering as essential if the House is to perform its functions.[28]

The second qualification of Hibbing and Theiss-Morse's argument is that the question of how often major changes are or should be made is not the same question as the extent to which public opinion should be considered in making changes. Public opinion often is described as highly volatile, in which case it might be expected to drive more frequent change than a Burkean representative system. Whether or not public opinion is more volatile than opinions on political procedures held by political elites—and it is the elites, after all, who are most likely to seek change for purposes of short-term advantage—occasions on which public opinion is mobilized around particular procedural proposals are not especially common.[29]

Probably Hibbing and Theiss-Morse's view that procedural questions are especially unfit for control by public opinion is influenced by their other main point—popularly favored reforms are apt to result in public opinion being even more dissatisfied. Again, there is much truth in their argument. The voters of my state this decade have approved initiatives for legislative term limits, ''blanket'' political primaries, and very tight restrictions on campaign contributions and spending. I regard it as highly improbable that any of these measures will enhance public confidence in California government. It is an illusion to imagine popular beliefs about how the system should work can be bypassed permanently. Those of us who are skeptical of the ''populist'' reforms now in vogue must set out to convince the public.

Whereas Hibbing and Theiss-Morse examine procedural change in general, Joseph F. Zimmerman, Wilma Rule, and Arend Lijphart put forth specific proposals.[30] Even more than the *Carolene Products* jurisprudence criticized earlier, their essays appear to assume basic political procedure questions are amenable to disinterested, technical evaluation—in short, that such questions are apolitical. Rush has done an excellent job of showing that arguments such as those of Zimmerman, Rule, and Lijphart consider only a narrow range of the considerations relevant to the proposals they put forth.[31] Therefore, I address these authors' style of argumentation.

In a revealing passage in this volume, Lijphart writes: ''That PR provides more *accurate* representation than majoritarian election methods is not controversial.''[32] My deskside dictionary defines ''accurate'' as follows:

1: free from error esp. as the result of care . . . 2: conforming to truth or to a standard . . . 3: able to give an accurate result.[33]

''Accuracy'' of representation therefore would refer most naturally to whether votes are tabulated and results declared correctly in terms of whatever electoral system is in force. Though creative methods of tabulation sometimes have been used in places like Texas and Illinois, Lijphart is criticizing the single-member district (SMD) system generally, not dishonest election officials. The only imaginable way that his statement can be given meaning is to apply the second dictionary definition of "accurate" and assume a particular standard, namely, the one favored by proponents of proportional representation. But the question of whether that standard is the correct one is precisely the point at issue.[34]

What this inaccurate use of "accurate" reveals is the tendency to think of questions of political procedure as neutral, technical questions. The question becomes not whether, taking everything into account, a system that has been used almost universally in American democracy for two centuries should be abandoned. That is a political question. Rather, the question becomes whether proportional representation (PR) will yield more "accurate" results. That sounds like a technical, perhaps a mathematical question, the kind of question a professor who has unquestioned expertise on the technical aspects of electoral systems but who admits to "[n]ot being an expert on the details and intricacies" of House politics can answer better than the rest of us.

If the standard of accuracy for electoral systems is to permit a geographically defined area to be represented by the individual preferred by the greatest number of voters of the area, the SMD system is more "accurate" than a proportional system. If the standard of accuracy is that any political party able to attract more than some threshold percentage of votes should be awarded seats proportionate to the number of votes received, the proportional system is more accurate. The question is which system is better, not which system is more accurate.

Rule and Zimmerman wrote that in proportional systems, in contrast with the SMD system, "every vote counts toward a party's representation in parliament."[35] But it depends on what you mean by "counts."

If a vote counts only if the outcome would have been different if the vote had not been cast or had been cast differently, then under either a proportional or an SMD system, votes will count only when they make or break ties. The only difference is the definition of a "tie" is straightforward in an SMD system and slightly more complex in the proportional system. Assuming a large population such as that of the United States, the probability of any one vote making or breaking a tie under either system is so close to infinitesimal that it may be disregarded. Thus, under neither system does a vote count if "count" means being decisive.

Another plausible definition of what it means for a vote to count is that it is counted and weighted toward the result the same as all other votes.[36] By this definition, all votes count in both systems.

For Rule and Zimmerman's statement to be accepted, one must understand the word "counts" in an unusual way. What they mean for a vote to count is that it be cast for a party that is awarded at least one seat from the district in which the vote was cast. In other contexts, that is not the way we talk about things "counting." In football, for example, if a team scores a touchdown in the first quarter but is eventually outscored by the other team, we do not say the first team's touchdown did not count; we say the touchdown counted, but the team lost the game. According to Rule and Zimmerman, the only way that each score in a sporting event could be counted would be to give up the concept one team won and the other lost, but to award, say, 0.6 of the championship to one team in the Super Bowl and 0.4 to the other.

No one could be against making all votes "count," and if that were the only issue, we could safely leave the solution to technically competent people like Rule and Zimmerman. However, the issue is not making votes count but whether we should change the electoral system. That is a political question.

Rule and Zimmerman rely on a "model," which they claim "perpetuates the unrepresentativeness of the House."[37] Their complete statement of this "model" is as follows:

high rates of incumbent reelection, large contributions to incumbents' campaigns, non-competitiveness of political parties in most districts, low voter turnout in elections, and low diversity in representation.[38]

This potpourri of slogans taken from contemporary reform debates illustrates their proposal to overturn an electoral system that is two centuries old is driven precisely by the sort of short-term considerations that Hibbing and Theiss-Morse caution us against. Nor are these considerations simply neutral, "good govern-ment" concerns. For example, more than anything else, Rule and Zimmerman seem to be concerned about the lack of "diversity" that allegedly results in "egregious underrepresentation" for groups that do not have a proportionate number of group members sitting in the House.[39] But the only groups they are concerned about are women, blacks, and Hispanics. They do not inquire whether other ethnic groups, such as persons of Slavic origin, or religious groups, such as evangelical Christians, or economic groups, such as small business owners, are over- or underrepresented, "egregiously" or otherwise (see Chapter 15 in this volume). If they were simply concerned about equal representation, these and other groups would be of equal importance. They also would hesitate before using the term "representation" to refer to only one form of representation—descriptive—when they are presumably aware of the extensive theoretical and empirical literature on competing forms of representation.[40] They would ac-knowledge research suggesting descriptively "proportional" representation may not even be in the substantive interests of the very groups for which they profess solicitude.[41]

In short, Rule and Zimmerman's proposals are driven by a political agenda. Certainly, there are familiar reasons for giving special solicitude to women, blacks, and Hispanics, and there are familiar reasons for supposing that increas-ing their descriptive representation in Congress may be an appropriate way to express that solicitude. How much weight should be given to those reasons is not my concern. Even less am I suggesting there is anything wrong with Rule and Zimmerman's proposing procedural changes so that, in their estimation, the chances of reaching certain political results they favor will be enhanced. What is wrong is for PR proponents to suggest that their proposed change is merely a technical device to eliminate "egregious underrepresentation."

Lijphart repeatedly stresses that his proposals are already in use in other countries and that, in some instances, the United States stands virtually alone. He is correct that, in a sense, this information rebuts a possible contention that his proposals are immoderately radical.[42] Indeed, although I am opposed to most of his proposals, I would not be inclined to call them radical at all—not, at least, if "radical" means what happened after the French and Russian Revolutions or even the U.S. Civil War. But abandoning single-member districts would be a drastic change within the little world of American law, and none the less so because we would be moving to a system that is familiar in other countries.

As an affirmative reason for adopting PR, the fact it is widely used elsewhere is no reason at all unless it can be shown the other countries are better governed or, at least, careful consideration of their experience shows we would be better governed if we adopted their system. Hibbing and Theiss-Morse suggest we take the long view. Doing so, I find it suggestive that nearly every country that uses PR has, one or more times in this century, had to be rescued from atrocious tyranny by the countries that now use or until very recently used single-member districts.

I also find it suggestive that after a slump in the 1970s and early 1980s, the U.S. economy has led the world for nearly the past two decades. Many things— for example, reduced crime rates and reduced illegitimacy rates—have been going well in the United State this decade.[43] Perhaps things would have gone even better if we had been using proportional representation all these years.[44] But until Lijphart demonstrates there is good reason to believe so, his argument that proportional systems are used in other countries will have no force.

To show, as I have attempted to show here, debates over political procedures are incorrigibly, intractably, and, some would add, gloriously *political* debates is not, of course, to argue there is anything improper about those debates, any more than to show judicial review of political procedures involves political considerations is an argument against judicial review.

The contemporary PR movement is confined to some academics, some lawyers, and a handful of activists. The power of ideas should not be underestimated, and it is possible this movement ultimately will succeed, perhaps with assistance from judges. I hope not, but I do not suppose that PR, if it comes, will bring down the republic. For most people, there won't even be much of a bump in the road, though there will surely be some confusion and, for politically active people, a host of unpredictable consequences.

Slogans—make every vote "count"; decide elections "accurately"—undoubtedly have political sway, and it would be folly to suggest they be abandoned. But academics writing in publications addressed to academics should hold themselves to a high standard. If they really believe, contrary to what I have argued, that systemic changes such as PR are apolitical and should be decided on technical, apolitical grounds, they should defend that position rather than assume it. To be sure, even political conflicts have technical aspects, and many of the writers in this volume, including those I have criticized most sharply, have made important contributions to our knowledge of those technical questions. But the technical questions are not the ultimate questions. If these writers presume to recommend major systemic changes to their fellow citizens, they should address the complex and manifestly political dimensions of the debates they are entering.

NOTES

1. Two recent anthologies contain ample commentary on the judicial role in many of the areas examined in the present volume. See Mark E. Rush, ed., *Voting Rights and Redistricting in the United States* (Westport, CT: Greenwood Press, 1998); Frederick G. Slabach, ed., *The Constitution and Campaign Finance Reform* (Durham, NC: Carolina Academic Press, 1998). For extensive references to the political science and legal literature, see Daniel H. Lowenstein, *Election Law: Cases and Materials* (Durham, NC: Carolina Academic Press, 1995).

2. *Lochner v. New York*, 198 U.S. 45 (1905).

3. Ibid. at 76.

4. *United States v. Carolene Products Company*, 304 U.S. 144 (1938).

5. Ibid. at 152 n. 4.

6. See John Hart Ely, *Democracy and Distrust: A Theory of Judicial Review* (Cambridge, MA: Harvard University Press, 1980).

7. Michael J. Klarman, "Majoritarian Judicial Review: The Entrenchment Problem," *Georgetown Law Journal*, February 1997, pp. 491–553; and Samuel Issacharoff and Richard H. Pildes, "Politics as Markets: Partisan Lockups of the Democratic Process," *Stanford Law Review*, February 1998, pp. 643–717.

8. By referring to these major changes as "reforms," I do not imply I necessarily regard all of them as changes for the better.

9. *Baker v. Carr*, 369 U.S. 186 (1962); *Wesberry v. Sanders*, 376 U.S. 1 (1964); *Reynolds v. Sims*, 377 U.S. 533 (1964). Admittedly, the Supreme Court played a significant role in the extension of the franchise to blacks in the South through its *White Primary Cases*. See Steven F. Lawson, *Black Ballots: Voting Rights in the South, 1944–1969* (New York: Columbia University Press, 1976). However, the decisive step was the enactment of the Voting Rights Act of 1965.

Most of the electoral reforms referred to in the text affect House elections. The direct election of senators and the adoption of the initiative are obvious exceptions.

10. C. Lawrence Evans and Walter J. Oleszek, "If It Ain't Broke Bad, Don't Fix It a Lot," *PS: Political Science and Politics*, March 1998, pp. 24–28; David W. Rohde, *Parties and Leaders in the Postreform House* (Chicago: University of Chicago Press, 1991); and Barbara Sinclair, *Unorthodox Lawmaking: New Legislative Processes in the U.S. Congress* (Washington, DC: CQ Press, 1997) are among the many excellent commentaries on change in the House in recent decades.

11. *Powell v. McCormack*, 395 U.S. 486 (1969).

12. Two of the essays in a 1998 symposium—Joseph F. Zimmerman and Wilma Rule, in "A More Representative United States House of Representatives?" and Mark E. Rush, in "Making the House More Representative: Hidden Costs and Unintended Consequences"—refer to gerrymandering in passing, but the issue is not a significant theme. See *PS: Political Science and Politics*, March 1998, pp. 5–10 and 21–24. The reason is probably that most of the contributors are Democrats. For the last couple of decades, Republicans have led the charge against gerrymandering, primarily because of their dissatisfaction with the districting plans enacted by Democrats in California for the 1980s. See, for example, Lee Atwater, "Altered States: Redistricting Law and Politics in the 1990s," *Journal of Law & Politics*, vol. 6, 1990, pp. 661–72. California, because of the large size of its House delegation, occupies center stage in redistricting debates. But the issue has been relatively quiet for the past few years because Republican governor Pete Wilson, elected in 1990, was able to veto plans enacted by the Democratic legislature, with the result redistricting was done by the Republican-dominated California Supreme Court. The election of Democrat Gray Davis as governor of California in 1998 and the probability of continued Democratic control of the California state legislature through the 2000 election suggest the volume on gerrymandering is likely to be turned up shortly.

13. Klarman, "Majoritarian Judicial Review," p. 534; and Atwater, "Altered States," p. 664.

14. *Davis v. Bandemer*, 478 U.S. 109 (1986) (concurring opinion).

15. Peverill Squire, "The Partisan Consequences of Congressional Redistricting," *American Politics Quarterly*, vol. 23, 1995, pp. 229–40.

16. Gary C. Jacobson, *The Electoral Origins of Divided Government: Competition in U.S. House Elections, 1946–1988* (Boulder, CO: Westview Press, 1990); Albert D. Cover, "One Good Term Deserves Another: The Advantage of Incumbency in Congressional Elections," *American Journal of Political Science*, vol. 21, 1977, pp. 523–41; and John A. Ferejohn, "On the Decline of Competition in Congressional Elections," *The American Political Science Review*, vol. 71, 1977, pp. 166–76.

17. See Klarman, "Majoritarian Judicial Review"; and Issacharoff and Pildes, "Politics as Markets."

18. Rush, "Making the House More Representative," p. 23.

19. Clyde Wilcox and Wesley Joe, "Dead Law: The Federal Election Finance Regulations, 1974–1996," *PS: Political Science and Politics*, pp. 14–17.

20. See Daniel Hays Lowenstein, "On Campaign Finance Reform: The Root of All Evil Is Deeply Rooted," *Hofstra Law Review*, vol. 18, 1989, pp. 301–67.

21. These problems could best be solved by providing funds to the party leadership in each chamber for them to distribute to party candidates as they see fit. Private funds could be raised with a minimum of regulation up to a point that would supplement the public funding and provide some opportunities for candidates who receive little or nothing from the party leadership. Beyond that point, contribution limits would be restrictive enough to minimize the conflicts of interest created by interest group contributions. For details of such a plan, see Lowenstein, "On Campaign Finance Reform."

22. See Nelson W. Polsby, "Some Arguments against Congressional Term Limitations," *Harvard Journal of Law and Public Policy*, vol. 16, 1992, pp. 101–7.

23. The major parties are not invariably opposed to each other on political process issues. Both major parties and third parties have joined in challenging the blanket primary adopted by initiative in California in 1996. See *California Democratic Party v. Jones*, 984 F.Supp. 1288 (E.D.Cal. 1997).

24. Pluralist theorists generally argued a common conception of the public good was necessary for the pluralist system of government to work. See Frank Sorauf, "The Public Interest Reconsidered," *Journal of Politics*, vol. 19, 1957, pp. 616–39; Anthony Downs, "The Public Interest: Its Meaning in a Democracy," *Social Research*, vol. 29, 1962, pp. 1–36; David B. Truman, *The Governmental Process*, 2nd ed. (New York: Alfred A. Knopf, 1971), p. 512.

25. John R. Hibbing and Elizabeth Theiss-Morse, *Congress as Public Enemy: Public Attitudes toward American Political Institutions* (Cambridge: Cambridge University Press, 1995).

26. John R. Hibbing and Elizabeth Theiss-Morse, "Too Much of a Good Thing: More Representative Is Not Necessarily Better," *PS: Political Science and Politics*, March 1998, pp. 28–31.

27. Edmund Burke, "Speech to the Electors of Bristol," in Lowenstein, *Election Law*, pp. 8–9.

28. Evans and Oleszek, "If It Ain't Broke Bad."

29. It is true that initiatives affecting the political process are common. But the process by which initiatives qualify for the ballot usually favors measures proposed by organized groups, not proposals favored by unorganized majorities. See Daniel Hays Lowenstein and Robert M. Stern, "The First Amendment and Paid Initiative Petition Circulators: A Dissenting View and a Proposal," *Hastings Constitutional Law Quarterly*, vol. 17, 1989, pp. 175–224.

30. Zimmerman and Rule, "A More Representative U.S. House"; Arend Lijphart, "Reforming the House: Three Moderately Radical Proposals," *PS: Political Science and Politics*, March 1998, pp. 10–13.

31. Rush, "Making the House More Representative."

32. Lijphart, "Reforming the House," p. 10 (emphasis added).

33. *Webster's Ninth New Collegiate Dictionary* (Springfield, MA: Merriam-Webster, 1988).

34. Despite his criticism of majoritarian methods of representation, accuracy is not a quality on which Lijphart appears to place much value in his essay. He wrote that "increasing the membership of the House by about 50 percent entails a decrease in the population size of the average congressional district by about 50 percent." On reflection, I think Lijphart would agree the decrease in population would be one-third, not one-half.

35. Zimmerman and Rule, "A More Representative U.S. House," p. 8.

36. Strictly speaking, that is a definition of what it means for a vote to count equally. A vote could count, even if it is weighted less than another vote. Thus, a field goal counts in a football game, though it counts less than a touchdown.

37. Zimmerman and Rule, "A More Representative United States House," p. 5.

38. Ibid.

39. Ibid.

40. Hannah Fenichel Pitkin, *The Concept of Representation* (Berkeley: University of California Press, 1967).

41. Charles Cameron, David Epstein and Sharyn O'Halloran, "Do Majority-Minority Districts Maximize Substantive Black Representation in Congress?," *The American Political Science Review*, vol. 90, 1996, pp. 794–812.

42. Lijphart, "Reforming the House," p. 10.

43. Gregg Easterbrook, "America the O.K.," *The New Republic*, January 4 and 11, 1999, pp. 19–25.

44. To suggest otherwise would be to fall into the fallacy skewered by W. S. Gilbert in *Iolanthe*:

> When Wellington thrashed Bonaparte,
>   As every child can tell,
> The House of Peers, throughout the war,
> Did nothing in particular,
>   And did it very well:
> Yet Britain set the world ablaze
> In good King George's glorious days!

William Schwenk Gilbert and Arthur Seymour Sullivan, "Iolanthe," in *The Complete Plays of Gilbert and Sullivan* (New York: W. W. Norton, 1976).

I acknowledge the possibility the contribution of the SMD system to America's long-term and recent successes may be equivalent to the contribution of the House of Peers to the Napoleonic Wars.

Part V

Prospects for Reform

Chapter 18

The Outlook for Reform

Joseph F. Zimmerman and Wilma Rule

Reform has been a watchword of Americans since the period prior to the Revolutionary War, when the failure of the British government to enact reforms desired by the colonists precipitated the war.[1] The Continental Congress representing the states in 1777 submitted the Articles of Confederation and Perpetual Union to the states, but the thirteenth state did not ratify the proposed fundamental document until 1781. Unsatisfactory experience with the articles led the unicameral Congress to call a constitutional convention to meet in Philadelphia in 1787. The delegates were reformers and drafted a new constitution converting the confederation into a federation. Subsequent U.S. and state constitutional reforms have made the national and state governments more representative bodies, but much remains to be accomplished.

Many changes to meet present-day reform objectives can be accomplished without resorting to amendment of the U.S. Constitution. Electoral changes and campaign finance practices can be reformed by a vote of Congress (refer to Chapters 6 and 15 in this volume). Term limits would require a constitutional amendment, as would concurrent election of the president-vice president and members of the House (see Chapters 12 and 14 in this volume). Yet the amendment route has been taken successfully 27 times, and several amendments have made national political institutions more democratic. Consider the guarantee of individual civil and political liberties (1st through 10th Amendments, 1791); slavery abolished (13th Amendment, 1865); guarantee of due process of law, equal protection of the laws, and privileges and immunities (14th Amendment, 1868); voting rights for blacks (15th Amendment, 1870); voting rights for women (19th Amendment, 1920); presidential two-term limit (22nd Amendment, 1951); and enfranchisement of 18-year-old citizens (26th Amendment, 1971).

Certain constitutional reforms proceeded at a snail's pace—70 years of meetings, parades, testimonies, and ratification by state legislatures amid predictions of dire outcomes preceded ratification of the 19th Amendment. By contrast, other constitutional reforms have come quickly; the Bill of Rights was ratified within two years of its proposal, and the 26th Amendment was ratified during the Vietnam War. In retrospect, it appears most successful democratic amendments were correlated with volatile societal contexts such as wars and civil unrest and with reform movements questioning political institutions and procedures.

DISILLUSIONMENT, DESPAIR, AND DEMOCRACY

James Madison, a principal architect of the U.S. Constitution, urged in *The Federalist Number 57* that "the most effectual precautions" be taken to keep elected leaders in pursuit of the common good of society.[2] By the late 20th century, however, there were a falling off of the vote for candidates for the House, an extremely high incumbency rate, and a question of political legitimacy. The House initiated no major actions to reform itself, and many citizens are disillusioned by and despair of the gap between the ideal of representation and the degree of its fulfillment in the House.

There clearly is a democratic deficit since numerous ordinary citizens view the House as light-years away from them and their everyday concerns and regard their representatives as instruments of special interests who make their election possible by large campaign contributions (see Chapter 11 in this volume). Fortunately, some citizens, in common with earlier reformers, began to work to make the U.S. House, state legislatures, and local governing bodies more representative.

Populist, Progressive, and Other Democratic Reformers

The democratic ideal of political equality has galvanized many citizens into seeking reforms. Property and taxpaying requirements for exercising the suffrage were eliminated in the early 19th century (see Chapter 2 in this volume). Subsequently, Populists and Progressives campaigned against corrupt state and local legislative bodies. Populists concluded many state legislatures were pseudorepresentative assemblies that enacted statutes favoring major railroads, trusts, and other special interests. A similar charge is echoed in today's criticism of the U.S. House.

Populists called for new or amended state constitutions designed to maximize citizen participation in public policy making and cancel the political influence of economic interests termed "the invisible government."[3] Their major reform proposals included voter empowerment in the form of the initiative, referendum, and recall. As is well known, the Progressive movement developed as the Populist movement was declining and sought to promote the adoption of the three participatory devices to encourage members of state and local legislative bodies to be more responsive to the wishes of their constituents. Although faced with strenuous opposition, Progressives experienced considerable success in achieving their goals over the decades. Currently, 23 states have constitutional provisions for the initiative and the protest referendum, the *Utah Code* authorizes the initiative and the protest referendum, and the recall is authorized by the constitution in 16 states. Furthermore, these citizen control devices are available to voters in several thousand general-purpose local governments.

Another late 19th-century popular movement—the Municipal Reform movement—focused its attention on corruption, particularly in large cities, and sought electoral and structural changes to improve the ethical behavior and representativeness of local governing bodies.[4] These reformers, through determined efforts, also achieved numerous successes over many decades in spite of the opposition of entrenched interests.

A MORE REPRESENTATIVE HOUSE

Political scientist Robert A. Dahl outlined a process whereby unrepresented groups are included in, for example, a national legislature. His paradigm may be utilized for understanding the course of representation reform in the U.S. House. In phase 1, the consent of "subordinates" is sought by the dominant group to reduce resistance and lower the costs of enforcing inequalities.[5] In this way some practices based on equality for "superordinates" are extended to outsiders demanding inclusion. Thus, a highly exclusive elite begins to be more inclusive. In the second phase, the elite may find that enforcing its domination is costly and decides to include more outsiders. Hence, the latter become insiders, representation is broadened, and the institution is transformed.[6]

Turning to the House, one can apply this process of reform to the adoption of the franchise for nonpropertied citizens, women, and minorities by 1920. These groups also gained the *de facto* right to be represented in the House. A few more of these groups were elected, and the House became a little more diverse. In this initial phase, although some 40 years later, the House responded to the turbulence connected with the Civil Rights movement and enacted the Voting Rights Act of 1965 (VRA) and its amendments in 1970, 1975, and 1982. This act made voting rights a reality for many African Americans, and the 1982 amendments made it clear they had the right to choose representatives of their choice. The act has resulted in the doubling of African-American, Latino, and women representation in the House in the period 1983 to 1996.[7] Hence, a largely exclusive House became more inclusive in slow, incremental steps.

But transformation of the House is, at most, only half-done, as increasing each underrepresented group's representation/population ratio, accelerating turnover of House members, improving competitiveness of the two major political parties, and other goals remain. Enactment of a bill introduced by Representative Cynthia McKinney of Georgia in 1997 could help remedy the current situation.[8]

The bill would allow the use of a semi-proportional or proportional representation (PR) election system in place of the current single-member district (SMD) plurality system, which has contributed to the unrepresentativeness of the House. It is a mistake, however, to attribute underrepresentation of certain minority groups and women solely to the SMD system. Other societal, political, and personal factors are at work, including educational and professional opportunities, experience in elective office, political party encouragement and support, and adequate campaign funding.

Another possibility for moving more quickly to phase 2 of the transformation process might be initiated by Democratic or Republican funding sources that have experienced or fear losses of seats of friendly members in the House. This trend is under way in California, where the Republican Party, after suffering severe elections defeats since 1986, announced its intent to recruit aggressively and financially support only women and minorities in future primary elections. In consequence, many more outsiders could be included eventually and become insiders, and the House's representational composition could reflect, demographically, the citizenry at large.

The preceding method of inclusion operated early in the 20th century. Ethnic and religious groups and women were slated for state offices on a political party's "balanced"/broadly representative ticket. Now that House campaigns are financed nationally and statewide, voluntary quotas for nomination of underrepresented group members may lie ahead for the major political parties (for quotas in the Labour Party of the United Kingdom, see Chapter 13 in this volume).

However, third parties and other politically minority views and increased membership turnover still would need to be included in a truly representative House. Allowing use of a PR or semi-PR electoral system or a mixed PR-SMD system, as in New Zealand and Scotland (see Chapters 12 and 13 in this volume), is a viable solution for expeditiously improving political equality in the House provided campaign finance regulation also is reformed. Countries with this or a similar electoral system have lower incumbency rates and higher turnover of membership, and citizens have a much higher regard for their national legislatures (see Chapter 10 in this volume).

Prospects for Electoral Reform

The alternative vote (AV) appears to have the best possibility for adoption by Congress, as it does not change the SMD majority characteristics of the electoral system and has the advantage of obviating the need for a primary election while ensuring the winner of the election will be the most favored candidate. The supplementary vote system (SVS), a modified AV system, probably would be favored by majority party candidates since each voter is limited to expressing only two preferences instead of several as with AV (see Chapter

15 in this volume). AV and SVS produce majority legislatures with few minority representatives

Cumulative voting (CV) has been implemented on a number of occasions in recent years by court orders or by local governments seeking to settle a VRA suit. This electoral system has two major advantages—facilitation of the election of members of underrepresented groups and inhibition of gerrymandering. The replacement of the SMD system—which encourages minorities to segregate themselves to increase their voting strength—by a multi-member one necessitated by CV probably will ensure Congress will give the system little or no consideration. Limited voting also is a semi-proportional representation system employing multi-member districts and is not apt to receive serious consideration by Congress for the same reasons as CV. Furthermore, those systems are semiproportional and do not measure up well to PR in terms of broad and accurate representation.

The two PR systems—list and single-transferable vote (STV)—offer the most extensive change. List-PR is used in many European nations, while STV is used rarely and has fewer prospects for adoption than list-PR. A mixed system using list-PR and single-member districts, as in Germany and Scotland, has somewhat higher prospects because it is a compromise.

Proposals for House electoral change immediately encounter the exceptionally strong opposition of a most important group—the incumbents. PR or a mixed-PR system is not in the interest of most representatives. Furthermore, the special interests contributing large sums to the campaign committees of House incumbents also may fear the election of less sympathetic members. In addition, opposition to reform in the scholarly community hinders prospects for electoral change (see Chapters 16 and 17 in this volume). In turn, incumbents may utilize scholarly arguments to support their contention no need exists for changing the electoral system.

Other Reforms

Prospects for enlarging the House and campaign finance reform may improve if a reform-minded member is elected Speaker. Opposition to these reforms is not as strong as opposition to more major reforms. While initiation of these reforms is to be applauded, they will do little to broaden representation in the House.

The sharp population growth in the United States in recent decades suggests a modest increase in the size of the House is a possibility in the next two decades (see Chapter 12 in this volume). This goal can be achieved by a simple act of Congress. Major arguments, nevertheless, will be employed against the proposal with emphasis placed on the unwieldy nature of the current House (see Chapter 16 in this volume). Note should be made of Madison's statement in *The Federalist Number 55* that "no political question is less susceptible of a precise solution than that which relates to the number most convenient for a representative legislature.''[9]

It is extremely unlikely the House would approve a resolution proposing a constitutional amendment establishing term limits for its members. Voter employment of the initiative to establish term limits for members of 21 state legislatures is evidence there is strong public sentiment for such limits. A private organization, U.S. Term Limits, may continue to capitalize on this sentiment and obtain term-limit pledges from candidates for House seats. Moreover, the organization has achieved a degree of success in obtaining pledges from 45 House members (10%) to serve a maximum of three terms.[10] In addition, there is no constitutional roadblock to a state constitutional or statutory provision authorizing candidates for House seats to file a preprimary ''moral obligation'' pledge to serve a stated maximum number of terms if elected (see Chapter 7 in this volume).

Chapter 6 in this volume presents persuasive evidence federal regulation of campaign finance is inadequate and promotes disproportionately high representation for certain groups and disproportionately low representation for other groups. Proposed enactment by Congress of amendments to the corrupt practices act to curb ''soft'' money and to limit strictly ''hard'' money contributions has encountered what appears to be an insurmountable opposition. Opponents of strict campaign finance statutes may propose instead that public financing be provided to candidates who agree to limit their total campaign expenditures.

CONCLUSIONS

It is difficult to quarrel with the conclusion in Chapter 12 in this volume that ''the House does not perform its representative function very well.'' Similarly, there is some evidence the secular decline in voter participation in House elections is attributable in part to a legislative body lacking adequate demographic representation and the public's perception members are indebted to special interests that contribute large amounts of campaign funds.

Will the 21st century witness a House that is more representative of the U.S. population, and will substantial inequalities in campaign finance for candidates be corrected? Several of our proposed reforms are visionary in nature and are designed to focus public and scholarly attention on the ideal of representation and its fulfillment in the House. Out of the interactions of reformers, their followers, legislators, and other elected officers, changes will be made in the 21st century, as they were made in the previous century, to expand political equality and democracy.

NOTES

1. Gordon Wood, *The Creation of the American Republic, 1776–1787* (Chapel Hill: University of North Carolina Press, 1969), pp. 173–75.

2. James Madison, *The Federalist Papers* (New York: New American Library, 1961), pp. 350–51.

3. Consult Joseph F. Zimmerman, *The Recall: Tribunal of the People* (Westport, CT: Praeger, 1997); Joseph F. Zimmerman, *The Initiative: Citizen Law-Making* (Westport, CT: Praeger, 1999).

4. Richard S. Childs, *The First Fifty Years of the Council-Manager Plan of Municipal Government* (New York: National Municipal League, 1965).

5. Robert A. Dahl, "Equality versus Inequality," *PS: Political Science and Politics*, December 1996, p. 645.

6. Ibid.

7. U.S. Bureau of the Census, *Statistical Abstract of the United States* (Washington, DC: U.S. Government Printing Office, 1998), p. 289.

8. "The Voter's Choice Act" (H.R. 3068 of 1997).

9. Madison, *The Federalist Papers*, p. 341.

10. Francis X. Clines, "Keeping Politicians True to Their Inner Selves," *New York Times*, March 15, 1999, p. A14.

Select Bibliography

Abramowitz, Alan I. "Incumbency, Campaign Spending, and the Decline of Competition in U.S. House Elections." *The Journal of Politics*, February 1991, pp. 34–57.

Amy, Douglas J. *Real Choices/New Voices: The Case for Proportional Representation in the United States*. New York: Columbia University Press, 1993.

Bacon, Donald C., Robert H. Davidson, and Morton Keller, eds. *The Encyclopedia of the United States Congress*. New York: Simon & Schuster, 1995.

Baker, Gordon. "Whatever Happened to the Reapportionment Revolution in the United States?" In Bernard Grofman and Arend Lijphart, eds., *Electoral Laws and Their Political Consequences*. New York: Agathon Press, 1986.

Bauer, Monica and John R. Hibbing. "Which Incumbents Lose in House Elections: A Response to Jacobson's 'The Marginals Never Vanished.'" *The American Journal of Political Science*, March 1989, pp. 262–72.

Bickford, Charlene B. and Kenneth R. Bowling. *Birth of the Nation*. Madison, WI: Madison House, 1989.

Biersack, Robert, Paul S. Herrnson, and Clyde Wilcox. "Seeds for Success: Early Money in Congressional Elections." *Legislative Studies Quarterly*, vol. 18, 1994. pp. 535–52.

Blair, George S. *Cumulative Voting: An Effective Electoral Device in Illinois Politics*. Urbana: University of Illinois Press, 1960.

Boeckel, Richard. *Voting and Non-Voting in Elections*. Washington, DC: Editorial Research Reports, 1928.

Bositis, David, ed. *Redistricting and Minority Representation*. Washington, DC: Joint Center for Political and Economic Studies, 1998.

Bowen, Catherine D. *Miracle at Philadelphia*. Boston: Little, Brown, 1966.

Boyd, Julian, ed. *The Jefferson Papers*. Princeton, NJ: Princeton University Press, 1952.

Brown, Alice. "Deepening Democracy: Women and the Scottish Parliament." *Regional and Federal Studies*, Spring 1998, pp. 103–19.

————. "Women and Politics in Scotland." *Parliamentary Affairs*, January 1996, pp. 26–40.

Bullock, Charles S. III. "Winners and Losers in the Latest Round of Redistricting." *Emory Law Journal*, vol. 44, 1995, pp. 943–77.

Burrell, Barbara. *A Woman's Place Is in the House: Campaigning for Congress in the Feminist Era*. Ann Arbor: University of Michigan Press, 1994.

Cain, Bruce, John Ferejohn, and Morris Fiorina. *The Personal Vote: Constituency Service and Electoral Independence*. Cambridge, MA: Harvard University Press, 1987.

Campbell, James. *Cheap Seats: The Democratic Party's Advantage in U.S. House Elections*. Columbus: Ohio State University Press, 1996.

Canon, David T. *Race, Redistricting, and Representation*. Chicago: University of Chicago Press, 1999.

Caress, Stanley M. "The Impact of Term Limits on Legislative Behavior: An Examination of a Transditional Legislature." *PS: Political Science and Politics*, vol. 29, December 1996, pp. 671–77.

Carroll, Susan J. *Women as Candidates in American Politics*. 2nd ed. Bloomington: Indiana University Press, 1994.

Collie, Melissa P. "Incumbency, Electoral Safety, and Turnover in the House of Representatives, 1952–1976." *The American Political Science Review*, vol. 75, March 1981, pp. 119–31.

Cook, Elizabeth A. "Voter Reaction to Women Candidates." In Sue Thomas and Clyde Wilcox, eds., *Women and Elective Office: Past, Present, and Future*. New York: Oxford University Press, 1998.

Cover, Albert D. "One Good Term Deserves Another: The Advantage of Incumbency in Congressional Elections." *American Journal of Political Science*, vol. 21, 1977, pp. 523–41.

Dahl, Robert A. "Equality versus Inequality." *PS: Political Science and Politics*, December 1996, pp. 639–48.

————. *Democracy and Its Critics*. New Haven, CT: Yale University Press, 1989.

Darcy, Robert, Susan Welch, and Janet Clark. *Women, Elections, and Representation*. 2nd ed. Lincoln: University of Nebraska Press, 1994.

Davidson, Roger H. and Walter J. Oleszek. *Congress and Its Members*. Washington, DC: CQ Press, 1998.

Democracies Still in the Making. Geneva: Inter-Parliamentary Union, 1997.

Downs, Anthony. "The Public Interest: Its Meaning in a Democracy." *Social Research*, vol. 29, 1962, pp. 1–36.

Dwyre, Diana. "Spinning Straw into Gold: Soft Money and U.S. House Elections." *Legislative Studies Quarterly*, vol. 21, 1996, pp. 409–24.

Eismeier, Theodore J. and Philip H. Pollock III. *Business, Money, and the Rise of Corporate PACs*. Westport, CT: Quorum Books, 1988.

Electing the People's House. Washington, DC: Center for Voting and Democracy, 1998.

Epstein, David and Sharyn O'Halloran. "A Social Science Approach to Race, Redistricting, and Representation." *The American Political Science Review*, vol. 93, March 1999, pp. 187–91.

Erikson, Robert S. and Robert Thomas R. Palfery. "Campaign Spending and Incumbency: An Alternative Simultaneous Equations Approach." *Journal of Politics*, May 1998, pp. 355–73.

The Federalist Papers. New York: New American Library, 1961.

Fenno, Richard F. *Home Style: House Members in Their Districts.* Glenview, IL: Scott, Foresman, 1978.

Ford, Paul L., ed. *The Federalist: A Commentary on the Constitution of the United States.* New York: Henry Holt, 1898.

Franklin, Mark N. "Electoral Engineering and Cross-National Turnout Differences: What Role for Compulsory Voting?" *British Journal of Politics*, vol. 29, 1999, pp. 205–16.

Gaddie, Ronald K. "Research Note: Congressional Seat Swings: Revisiting Exposure in House Elections." *Political Research Quarterly*, September 1997, pp. 699–710.

Grier, Kevin and Michael C. Munger. "Comparing Interest Group PAC Contributions to House and Senate Incumbents, 1980–1986." *The Journal of Politics*, August 1993, pp. 615–44.

Grofman, Bernard, Lisa Handley, and Richard G. Neimi. *Minority Representation and the Quest for Voting Equality.* New York: Cambridge University Press, 1992.

Guinier, Lani. *The Tyranny of the Majority.* New York: Free Press, 1994.

Hallett, George H., Jr. *Proportional Representation: The Key to Democracy.* New York: National Municipal League, 1940.

Herrnson, Paul S. *Congressional Elections: Campaigning at Home and in Washington.* 2nd ed. Washington, DC: CQ Press, 1997.

Hibbing, John R. and Elizabeth Theiss-Morse. *Congress as Public Enemy: Public Attitudes toward American Political Institutions.* Cambridge: Cambridge University Press, 1995.

Jacobson, Gary C. *The Electoral Origins of Divided Government: Competition in U.S. House Elections, 1946–1988.* Boulder, CO: Westview Press, 1990.

Karlan, Pamela. "The Right to Vote: Some Pessimism about Formalism." *Texas Law Review*, June 1993, pp. 1705–40.

Katz, Richard S. "Malapportionment and Gerrymandering in Other Countries and Alternative Electoral Systems." In Mark E. Rush, ed., *Voting Rights and Redistricting in the United States.* Westport, CT: Greenwood Press, 1998.

Ketcham, Ralph, ed. *The Antifederalist Papers and the Constitutional Convention Debates.* New York: New American Library, 1986.

Kyomica, Will. *Multicultural Citizenship: A Liberal Theory of Minority Rights.* New York: Oxford University Press, 1995.

Lakeman, Enid. *Power to Elect: The Case for Proportional Representation.* London: Heinemann, 1982.

Lijphart, Arend. *Patterns of Democracy.* New Haven, CT: Yale University Press, 1999.

———. "Unequal Participation: Democracy's Unresolved Dilemma." *The American Political Science Review*, vol. 91, March 1997, pp. 1–14.

———. *Electoral Systems and Party Systems: A Study of Twenty-seven Democracies, 1945–1990.* New Haven, CT: Yale University Press, 1994.

Lowenstein, Daniel H., ed. *Election Law: Cases and Materials.* Durham, NC: Carolina Academic Press, 1995.

Mann, Thomas E. and Norman J. Ornstein. *Renewing Congress: A Second Report.* Washington, DC: American Enterprise Institute and the Brookings Institution, 1993.

Matland, Richard and Deborah D. Brown. "District Magnitude's Effects on Female Representation in U.S. State Legislatures." *Legislative Studies Quarterly*, vol. 17, November 1992, pp. 469–92.

Monopoly Politics. Washington, DC: Center for Voting and Democracy, 1997.

Newland, Robert A. *Comparative Electoral Systems*. London: The Electoral Reform Society of Great Britain and Ireland, 1982.

Nieman, Donald G. *Promises to Keep: African-Americans and the Constitutional Order, 1776 to the Present*. New York: Oxford University Press, 1991.

Norris, Pippa and Joni Lovenduski. *Political Recruitment: Gender, Race, and Class in the British Parliament*. Cambridge: Cambridge University Press, 1994.

Parker, Glenn R. *Congress and the Rent Seeking Society*. Ann Arbor: University of Michigan Press, 1995.

Pitkin, Hannah F. *The Concept of Representation*. Berkeley: University of California Press, 1967.

Polsby, Nelson W. "Some Arguments against Congressional Term Limitations." *Harvard Journal of Law and Public Policy*, vol. 16, 1983, pp. 101–7.

Reed, Robert W. and D. Eric Shansberg. "The House under Term Limits: What Would It Look Like?" *Social Science Quarterly*, vol. 76, 1995, pp. 698–719.

Reynolds, Andrew, and Ben Reilly, eds. *The International IDEA Handbook of Electoral System Design*. 2nd ed. Stockholm: International Institute for Democracy and Electoral Assistance, 1997.

Rule, Wilma. "Women, Representation and Political Rights." In Mark E. Rush, ed., *Voting Rights and Redistricting in the United States*. Westport, CT: Greenwood Press, 1998, pp. 177–93.

———. "Parliaments of, by, and for the People: Except for Women?" In Wilma Rule and Joseph F. Zimmerman, eds., *Electoral Systems in Comparative Perspective: Their Impact on Women and Minorities*. Westport, CT: Greenwood Press, 1994, pp. 15–30.

———. "Electoral Systems, Contextual Factors, and Women's Opportunity for Election to Parliament in Twenty-three Democracies." *Western Political Quarterly*, September 1987, pp. 477–98.

Rule, Wilma and Joseph F. Zimmerman, eds. *United States Electoral Systems: Their Impact on Women and Minorities*. Westport, CT: Greenwood Press, 1992.

Rush, Mark E., ed. *Voting Rights and Redistricting in the United States*. Westport, CT: Greenwood Press, 1998.

———. "In Search of a Coherent Theory of Voting Rights: The Supreme Court's Vision of Fair and Effective Representation." *The Review of Politics*, Summer 1994, pp. 504–23.

Shugart, Matthew S. "Minorities Represented and Unrepresented." In Wilma Rule and Joseph F. Zimmerman, eds., *Electoral Systems in Comparative Perspective: Their Impact on Women and Minorities*. Westport, CT: Greenwood Press, 1994, pp. 31–41.

Slabach, Frederick G., ed. *The Constitution and Campaign Finance Reform*. Durham, NC: Carolina Academic Press, 1998.

Sorauf, Frank. "The Public Interest Reconsidered." *Journal of Politics*, vol. 19, 1957, pp. 616–39.

Squire, Peverill. "The Partisan Consequences of Congressional Redistricting." *American Politics Quarterly*, vol. 23, 1995, pp. 229–40.

Still, Edward. "Cumulative Voting and Limited Voting in Alabama." In Wilma Rule and Joseph F. Zimmerman, eds., *United States Electoral Systems: Their Impact on Women and Minorities*. Westport, CT: Greenwood Press, 1992, pp. 183–96.

Swain, Carol M. *Black Faces, Black Interests: The Representation of African-Americans in Congress*. Cambridge, MA: Harvard University Press, 1995.

Task Force on Campaign Reform. *Campaign Reform, Insights, and Evidence*. Princeton, NJ: Woodrow Wilson School of Public and International Affairs, 1998.

Taylor, Charles. *Multiculturalism and the Politics of "Recognition."* Princeton, NJ: Princeton University Press, 1992.

Thompson, Joel A. and Gary Moncrief. "The Implications of Term Limits for Women and Minorities: Some Evidence from the States." *Social Science Quarterly*, vol. 74, 1993, pp. 300–309.

Timpone, Richard J. "Structure, Behavior, and Voter Turnout in the United States." *The American Political Science Review*, vol. 92, March 1998, pp. 145–58.

Towards a Better Democracy: Report of the Royal Commission on the Electoral System. Wellington, New Zealand, 1986.

U.S. Department of Commerce. *Statistical Abstract of the United States*. Washington, DC: U.S. Government Printing Office, 1996, 1997, 1998.

van der Eijk, Cees, Mark Franklin, and Michael Marsh. "What Voters Teach Us about Europe-Wide Elections: What Europe-Wide Elections Teach Us about Voters." *Electoral Studies*, vol. 15, 1996, pp. 149–66.

Verba, Sidney, Kay Schlozman, and Henry Brady. *Voice and Equality: Civic Voluntarism in American Politics*. Cambridge, MA: Harvard University Press, 1995.

West, Daniel M. and Burdett A. Loomis. *The Sound of Money*. New York: W. W. Norton, 1998.

Whitby, Kenny. *The Color of Representation*. Ann Arbor: University of Michigan Press, 1999.

Wilcox, Clyde. *The Latest American Revolution?* New York: St. Martin's Press, 1995.

———. "I Owe It All to Me: Candidates' Investments in Their Own Campaign."*American Politics Quarterly*, vol. 16, 1988, pp. 266–79.

Wolfinger, Raymond E. and Steven Rosenstone. *Who Votes?* New Haven, CT: Yale University Press, 1980.

Wood, Gordon. *The Creation of the American Republic, 1776–1787*. Chapel Hill: University of North Carolina Press, 1969.

Wright, J. H. *Mirror of the Nation's Mind: Australia's Electoral Experiments*. Sydney: Hale & Iremonger, 1980.

Wright, John R. "PACs, Contributions, and Roll Calls: An Organizational Perspective." *The American Political Science Review*, vol. 80, 1985, pp. 400–414.

Young, Iris M. *Justice and the Politics of Difference*. Princeton, NJ: Princeton University Press, 1990.

Zeller, Belle and Hugh A. Bone. "The Repeal of P.R. in New York City: Ten Years in Retrospect." *The American Political Science Review*, vol. 38, December 1948, pp. 1127–48.

Zimmerman, Joseph F. *The Initiative: Citizen Law-Making*. Westport, CT: Praeger, 2000.

———. *The Recall: Tribunal of the People*. Westport, CT: Praeger, 1997.

———. "Fair Representation for Minorities and Women." In Wilma Rule and Joseph F. Zimmerman, eds., *United States Electoral Systems: Their Impact on Women and Minorities*. Westport, CT: Greenwood Press, 1992, pp. 3–11.

———. "The Federal Voting Rights Act and Alternative Election Systems." *William & Mary Law Review*, vol. 19, Summer 1978, pp. 621–60.

SELECT LEGAL CASES

Anderson v. Celebrezze, 460 U.S. 780 (1981)

Baker v. Carr, 369 U.S. 186 (1962)

Bates v. Jones, 118 S.Ct. 1302 (1998)

Buckley v. Valeo, 424 U.S. 1 (1976)

Burns v. Fortson, 410 U.S. 686 (1973)

Bush v. Vera, 116 S.Ct. 1941 (1997)

Carrington v. Rash, 380 U.S. 89 (1965)

Colorado Republican Federal Campaign Finance Committee v. Federal Election Commission, 116 S.Ct. 2309 (1996)

Davis v. Bandemer, 478 U.S. 109 (1986)

Dunn v. Blumstein, 405 U.S. 330 (1972)

Evans v. Cornman, 398 U.S. 419 (1970)

Holder v. Hall, 512 U.S. 874 (1994)

Kramer v. Union Free School District, 395 U.S. 621 (1969)

Lassiter v. Northampton County Board of Elections, 238 U.S. 347 (1959)

Lochner v. New York, 198 U.S. 45 (1905)

Mahan v. Howell. 410 U.S. 315 (1973)

Marston v. Lewis, 410 U.S. 679 (1973)

Miller v. Johnson, 515 U.S. 900 (1995)

Minor v. Happersett, 88 U.S. 162 (1975)

Mobile v. Bolden, 466 U.S. 55 (1980)

Morse v. Republican Party of Virginia, 116 S.Ct. 1187 (1996)

Oregon v. Mitchell, 400 U.S. 112 (1970)

Powell v. McCormack, 395 U.S. 486 (1969)

Reynolds v. Sims, 377 U.S. 533 (1964)

Shaw v. Reno, 509 U.S. 630 (1993)

Symm v. U.S., 439 U.S. 1105 (1979)

Thornburg v. Gingles, 478 U.S. 30 (1986)

Timmons et al. v. Twin Cities Area New Party, 117 S.Ct. 1364 (1997)

United Jewish Organizations of Williamsburg v. Carey, 430 U.S. 144 (1977)

United States v. Carolene Products Company, 304 U.S. 144 (1938)

United States Term Limits, Incorporated v. Thornton, 514 U.S. 779 (1995)

Vera v. Bush, 517 U.S. 952 (1996)

Westberry v. Sanders, 376 U.S. 1 (1964)

Williams v. Rhodes, 393 U.S. 23 (1968)

Wood v. Broom, 287 U.S. 1 (1932)

Wright v. Rockefeller, 376 U.S. 52 (1964)

Index

About the Contributors

GAYLE BINION is Professor of Political Science and Law & Society at the University of California, Santa Barbara. Her research focuses on the role of the judiciary in the definition and protection of civil rights and liberties. Articles by Professor Binion have been published in a wide range of social science journals and law reviews.

ALICE BROWN is Professor of Politics at the University of Edinburgh, Co-Director of the University's Governance of Scotland Forum, and Vice-Convener of the Unit for the Study of Government in Scotland. Her research interests cover Scottish politics, women and politics, equal opportunities, and economic policy. Her publications, with others, include *The Scottish Electorate* (1999) and *Politics and Society in Scotland* (1998). She is a member of the cross-party Consultative Steering Group established by the secretary of state for Scotland to draw up the standing orders and procedures for the new Scottish parliament.

BARBARA BURRELL is head of the survey design and analysis section of the University of Wisconsin's Survey Research Laboratory. She is the author of *Public Opinion, the First Ladyship, and Hillary Rodham Clinton* (1997) and *A Woman's Place Is in the House: Campaigning for Congress in the Feminist Era* (1994).

STANLEY M. CARESS is the Southeastern Regional Director for the Center for Future Democracy, a nonprofit research organization. He has published several articles on the ramifications of legislative term limits and is an Associate Professor of Political Science at the State University of West Georgia.

C. LAWRENCE EVANS is Associate Professor of Political Science at the College of William and Mary. He is author of *Leadership in Committee: A Comparative Analysis of Leadership Behavior in the U.S. Senate* (1991) and co-author of *Congress under Fire: Reform Politics and the Republican Majority* (1997).

DIANA EVANS is Professor of Political Science at Trinity College in Hartford, Connecticut. Her research interests include the strategic uses of pork barrel politics in congressional policy making, interest groups and congressional committees, and the role of PAC contributions in the policy-making process.

MARK FRANKLIN is the John R. Reitemeyer Professor of Political Science at Trinity College in Hartford, Connecticut. He is the author or co-author of seven books, including *Choosing Europe?* (1996), *Electoral Change* (1992), and *The Decline of Class Voting in Britain* (1985); and over 60 articles in various scholarly journals.

RONALD KEITH GADDIE is Associate Professor of Political Science at the University of Oklahoma. He is co-author of five books, including *The Economic Realities of Political Reform: Elections and the U.S. Senate* (1995) and journal articles on congressional elections.

JOHN R. HIBBING is Professor of Political Science at the University of Nebraska–Lincoln. He has served as department chair and as editor of the *Legislative Studies Quarterly* and has published articles on Congress, elections, comparative legislatures, and, most recently, public attitudes toward government.

WESLEY JOE is a doctoral candidate in the Department of Government at Georgetown University, where he studies the influences of deliberation processes and associated procedural justice judgments on the legitimacy accorded environmental policy conflict outcomes. He has also co-authored works on U.S. elections and campaign finance reform.

AREND LIJPHART is Research Professor of Political Science at the University of California, San Diego and past president of the American Political Science Association. He has written many books, articles, and book chapters on divided societies, democratic institutions, and electoral systems. His most recent book is the 36-nation study *Patterns of Democracy* (1999).

DANIEL H. LOWENSTEIN has been Professor of Law at UCLA since 1979. He is the editor of *Election Law* (1995), the first textbook on that subject published in the twentieth century. He has written numerous articles on campaign finance, redistricting, initiatives, bribery, and other subjects.

LESLI E. McCOLLUM is a Ph.D. candidate and fellow in the Carl Albert Center for Congressional Studies at the University of Oklahoma. She won (with Ronald Keith Gaddie) the 1999 Pi Sigma Alpha Best Paper Award at the Southwestern Political Science Association for research on the incumbency advantage.

WALTER J. OLESZEK is a Senior Specialist in the legislative process at the Congressional Research Service and an adjunct faculty member at the American University. He is author of *Congressional Procedures and the Policy Process*, 4th ed. (1995) and co-author of *Congress and Its Members*, 6th ed. (1998).

WILMA RULE is Adjunct Professor of Political Science at the University of Nevada, Reno. She is co-editor with Joseph F. Zimmerman of *U.S. Electoral Systems: Their Impact on Women and Minorities* (1992) and *Electoral Systems in Comparative Perspective: Their Impact on Women and Minorities* (1994), and with Norma Noonan of *Russian Women in Politics and Society* (1996).

MARK E. RUSH is Associate Professor of Politics at Washington and Lee University and Chair of the Representation and Electoral Systems Section of the American Political Science Association. He is author of *Does Redistricting Make a Difference?* (1993), editor of *Voting Rights and Redistricting in the United States* (Greenwood, 1998), and co-author of *Electoral Reform and Minority Rights* (with Richard L. Engstrom, forthcoming).

CAROL M. SWAIN is Professor of Politics and Professor of Law at Vanderbilt University and Director of the Vanderbilt Center for the Study of Democracy and the Law. She is the author of *Black Faces, Black Interests: The Representation of African Americans* and editor of *Race versus Class: The New Affirmative Action Debate*, as well as articles and essays on affirmative action, representation, and voting rights. Her book-in-progress is titled *When Whites and Blacks Agree: Fairness in Opportunities*. Swain is the winner of the 1994 Woodrow Wilson Foundation Award given to "the best book published in the United States during the prior year on government, politics or international affairs." She is also the co-winner of the 1994 V. O. Key Award for the best book published on southern politics and of the 1995 D. B. Hardeman Prize for the best scholarly work on the U.S. Congress. She is a recipient of the National Science Foundation's Young Investigator Award and received grants from the Mellon Foundation, the Ford Foundation, the Sloan Foundation, and the Smith Richardson Foundation.

ELIZABETH THEISS-MORSE is Associate Professor of Political Science at the University of Nebraska–Lincoln. Her specialty is political psychology, and she is the co-author of two books: *With Malice toward Some*, an investigation of tolerance, and *Congress as Public Enemy*, a study of public attitudes toward American political institutions.

CLYDE WILCOX is Professor of Government at Georgetown University. He has published a number of books and articles on campaign finance and on the role of interest groups in politics. His other research interests include gender politics, religion and politics, and social movements.

JOSEPH F. ZIMMERMAN is Professor of Political Science in the Graduate School of Public Affairs of the State University of New York at Albany and author of numerous books and articles. His recent books include *The New England Town Meeting: Democracy in Action* (Praeger, 1999), *The Recall: Tribunal of the People* (Praeger, 1997), *Interstate Relations: The Neglected Dimension of Federalism* (1996), and *State-Local Relations: A Partnership Approach*, 2nd ed. (Praeger, 1995).